Acclaim for Raymond Bonner's

AT THE HAND OF MAN

"A welcome introduction to the new conscience in African wildlife conservation, which recognizes at long, long last the needs and wishes of the African people themselves."
—Peter Matthiessen

"A damning indictment . . . that breaks important ground on a subject that is rarely examined with a critical eye . . . rich in ironic nuggets unearthed by Bonner's painstaking reporting."
—*Philadelphia Inquirer*

"Should be mandatory reading for the next generation of environmentalists . . . Bonner is a superb reporter."
—Bill McKibben, author of *The End of Nature*

"Fascinating . . . . Bonner has produced both a thorough review of conservation history and a persuasive argument for sustainable utilization." —*Los Angeles Times Book Review*

Raymond Bonner

AT THE HAND OF MAN

Raymond Bonner has been a foreign correspondent for the *New York Times* and a staff writer at *The New Yorker*. His earlier books, *Weakness and Deceit: U.S Policy and El Salvador* and *Waltzing with a Dictator: The Marcoses and the Making of American Policy*, won the Robert F. Kennedy, Overseas Press Club and Sidney Hillman Foundation awards. A graduate of MacMurray College and Stanford Law School, Mr. Bonner practiced public interest law for several years before turning to journalism. From 1988 through 1992 he lived in Nairobi. He now lives in Warsaw.

ALSO BY RAYMOND BONNER

Waltzing with a Dictator:
The Marcoses and the Making of American Policy

Weakness and Deceit:
U.S. Policy and El Salvador

AT THE HAND OF MAN

AT THE HAND OF MAN

PERIL

AND

HOPE

FOR

AFRICA'S

WILDLIFE

RAYMOND BONNER

VINTAGE BOOKS

A DIVISION OF RANDOM HOUSE, INC.

NEW YORK

FIRST VINTAGE BOOKS EDITION, OCTOBER 1994

The Library of Congress has cataloged
the Knopf edition as follows:
Bonner, Raymond.
At the hand of man : peril and hope for Africa's
wildlife / by Raymond Bonner. — 1st ed.
p. cm.
Includes bibliographical references and index.
ISBN 0-679-40008-7
1. Wildlife conservation—Africa.   2. Man—
Influence on nature—Africa.   3. Economic
development—Environmental aspects—Africa.
4. Wildlife management—Africa.   I. Title.
QL84.6.A1B66   1993
333.95'16'096—dc20   92-25988   CIP
Vintage ISBN: 0-679-73342-6

Book design by Anthea Lingeman

Manufactured in the United States of America
10 9 8 7 6 5 4 3 2 1

For Alphonce Odoyo and Hanson Otundo
and *their* children's children

And surely your blood of your lives will I require;
at the hand of every beast will I require it;
and at the hand of man; at the hand of every
man's brother will I require the life of man.

GENESIS 9:5

And the fear of you and the dread of you shall be upon
every beast of the earth, and upon every fowl of the air,
upon all that moveth upon the earth, and upon all the fishes
of the sea; into your hand are they delivered.

GENESIS 9:2

CONTENTS

PROLOGUE

||||| A TEN-FOOT-TALL GIRAFFE, still an adolescent, stretched its neck, stuck out its long tongue, grabbed the branch of an acacia, stripped off the thorns and began chewing. The tree did not look like a normal one. Rather than having shaggy branches, the underside of the tree was as flat as a table bottom, from years of being nibbled at by the world's tallest species. I watched for at least twenty minutes, then laughed as the giraffe loped away, rocking from side to side on those long legs, which can carry him at speeds of up to thirty-five miles an hour, fast enough to escape most predators.

I moved off, too, across the open plains of Kenya's Maasai Mara, through herds of wild animals. There were large antelope with bright bluish patches on their flanks—topi, the guide explained. Clusters of smaller, graceful antelope with rufous coats and antlers sprinted by or looked up from eating the short grass to stare back at us. They all looked to me like deer. Later, I would learn to distinguish an impala, with its lyre-shaped horns, from a gazelle, and among the gazelle, a Thomson's and a Grant's—the "Thommy" is smaller and has a black stripe. But this was the first time I had ever seen these wild animals, except in cages in a zoo, and frankly, I was giddy.

The next day we flew north to Kora National Reserve, a harsh five hundred square miles of scrub and umbrella thorns astride the equator, and bounced down on a dirt airstrip. We walked over to a warning nailed crookedly to a tree, hand-lettered on a piece of wood, weathered by the hot sun: "Lions on the road. Buzz camp. Wait until picked up." The camp, a few miles down the dirt road, was a simple compound of eight thatched structures belonging to George Adamson, who, with his late wife, Joy, had created the legend of Elsa, the lion of *Born Free*. Adamson, now beginning his ninth decade, his long beard and shoulder-length hair white, his shirtless torso wrinkled and tan from a life in the African sun, had recently adopted three lion cubs, whose mother had been killed.

After dark, sitting in the quiet, warm air, we listened to lions howling in a symphonic unity; they were prowling only a few feet away, but they were on the other side of a chain-link fence. We were in the zoo. That night my wife and I bedded down on the top of one of Adamson's battered Land Rovers, quite a change for a couple who only weeks earlier had been living in a New York City apartment where the view from the bedroom was a brick wall.

We were not in Africa on a safari holiday, however. We had come because my wife had been sent as the East Africa correspondent for the *New York Times;* I would continue to write for *The New Yorker*, mostly about politics and foreign affairs, I assumed, for that is what I had generally written about. Neither of us had given much thought to writing about wildlife, other than some articles about safaris my wife thought she would write for the *Times* Travel section. Before leaving the United States, we had interviewed State Department officers in the African bureau, African diplomats, and academics who specialized in Africa. But we had not thought to stop by the World Wildlife Fund (WWF),* the world's largest conservation organization, best known by its cuddly panda logo, or the African Wildlife Foundation (AWF), smaller, but for many years the leader in conservation in Africa. That trip to the Mara and Kora, however, during our first month on the continent, was to be the beginning of enchantment with Africa's wildlife, an interest that provided us with great pleasure and as much grist for intellectual and journalistic thought as anything we had previously explored as reporters.

Early on we visited the tiny Central African country of Rwanda, pitching our two-person tent on the edge of Akagera National Park, in the yard of a Belgian biologist who preferred living alone, but allowed an occasional visitor to intrude. Throughout the night, I heard grunting and snorting noises. Pigs, I told my wife. What else did I know, having spent my boyhood in the suburbs and small towns of Minnesota and most of my adult years in San Francisco and New York? In fact, the noise had come from hippopotamuses, and they were only a few hundred yards away. We passed by them the next morning; they were submerged except for their eyes and backs, as we glided in a flat-bottom boat through Akagera's papyrus waterways, one of the largest inland swamps in Africa.

---

*In 1988, the World Wildlife Fund, which has its international headquarters in Switzerland and national organizations throughout the world, changed its name to the World Wide Fund for Nature. The United States and Canada have stayed with the original name—World Wildlife Fund. All these organizations prefer to be identified by the abbreviation WWF.

What would happen if one of these one-ton behemoths, who can remain submerged for four minutes, came up under the boat from one of its dives? The Belgian biologist assured us it wouldn't happen. We were only partially reassured, and at one point, a hippo did survey us suspiciously, submerging and surfacing several times, before lunging out of the water with a bellow. We jumped, frightened, but the experienced guide merely clapped his hands and the hippo disappeared in its own wake.

A couple of days later, still in Rwanda, we went in search of the mountain gorillas, the ones made famous by Dian Fossey. I had done a fair amount of backpacking in the California Sierra Nevada and had once spent several days hiking and camping in the Peruvian Andes to reach Machu Picchu. This hike was as tough as any, and not only because the air had less and less oxygen as we ascended above a mile and a half. We hiked through bamboo forests and then jungle so dense that a guide had to hack away the foliage with a machete to get us through. It was raining. When we grabbed vines to keep from slipping, we ended up with a handful of thistles. I wished at times that I walked on all fours and had thick padding on my feet and hands. But the exertion was worth it. It is an extraordinary encounter, to meet with a gorilla family—in their home. We sat in a thicket only a few feet away from a massive silverback, the patriarch of the family, who weighed several hundred pounds. Infant gorillas frolicked in the trees. When our guide saw that a branch was between my camera lens and the mother of one of the infants, he reached out to move it; the gorilla, apparently not wanting to lose a bit of food, grabbed it from him. I'm convinced that after we left, the gorillas talked about their most recent light-skinned visitors with only two legs.

You can watch *Out of Africa* as often as you wish; you can read all the Hemingway and Isak Dinesen you want. You should read Theodore Roosevelt's *African Game Trails*, the classic account of his safari in 1909, and Winston Churchill's *My African Journey*, about his adventures in East Africa the previous year, in which these men, as outstanding writers as they were politicians, evoke an Africa still in the Pleistocene era. You must read Beryl Markham's *West With the Night*, and Peter Matthiessen's stirring *The Tree Where Man Was Born*. You will learn from the photos and text in Peter Beard's *The End of the Game*, written in 1965, and Bartle Bull's *Safari: A Chronicle of Adventure*, which came twenty years later. But nothing can prepare you for the magnificence of Africa's wildlife and open spaces. Nothing. We once saw a cheetah uncoil its sleek power and sprint down a Thommy. The cheetah may be the fastest animal on earth (seventy miles an hour) but it is certainly not the most courageous—when a hyena approached, the cheetah slunk off, abandoning its prey to the notorious scavenger. In a remote park in Zaire, visited by fewer than a hundred tourists a year, we crawled to within three hundred yards of a rhinoceros. We watched rhino mating on the floor of Ngorongoro Crater in Tanzania, a symmetrical caldera, truly one of the natural wonders of the world. I was entertained by a bull elephant shaking the pods off an acacia tree in Botswana, awoken several times by roaring lions during a night camping in Tanzania, and on another occasion was startled by a full-maned lion walking through our campsite. After all these wondrous encounters, I still exclaimed when I saw zebra, and they are as common in much of Africa as longhorns in Texas.

HOW LONG will it last? How long before the wild animals disappear? They have largely vanished from Europe and the United States. Why not from Africa?

That first time my wife and I visited George Adamson, in August 1988, he had left a scribbled note for us under the windshield of a time-battered Land Rover: "Gone to look for poached elephant." When Adamson first arrived at Kora, in 1971, he would see up to five hundred elephants come to drink from the nearby Tana River. These days, he told us, there were probably fifty elephants wandering in Kora, at most a hundred. In just the previous three weeks, fourteen elephants had been killed in Kora. Adamson had been unable to find the most recent victims of the lust for ivory, and the next day we helped him. We scrambled up a rock outcropping and scanned the horizon with powerful binoculars. (It was near this spot that in August 1989 Adamson and two of his aides were cut down by automatic rifle fire when they happened upon poachers.) We saw nothing from the rocks, so we made our way back to the plane, and with David Allen—an experienced pilot, former warden and hunter and now a safari guide—at the controls, we flew low over the umbrella acacia trees (from above, it looks as if thousands of parachutes have settled on the park). Eventually, we spotted some large black vultures, swooping and gliding against the blue sky, and Allen knew immediately that we had found the dead elephants. We flew over them, took a fix on where they were, then landed, and on foot we worked our way through the thorny bush. Allen shouldered an old shotgun; I was afraid to ask if it was to protect us against the poachers, who might still be in the area, or against a lion or hyena that might be after the elephant carcasses. A horrible stench reached us before we saw them.

The largest elephant lay on her side, her legs splayed. "I reckon she's about twenty-five," Allen said. Blood dripped from where her tusks had been hacked off. A few feet behind her was a youngster, maybe five years old. Its headless body was wedged in a tree, as far as the youngster had been able to stagger in an effort to escape. As I looked at the gruesome scene, images of El Salvador in the early 1980s came to mind. Then I and other journalists had looked for vultures to lead us to bodies, the bodies of students and peasants, the tortured victims of the army and death squads. I wondered if it was right to feel the same revulsion about the brutal killing of an animal as I did for humans, but I did. I was sickened and furious.

Poachers were killing Kenya's elephants at the rate of at least three a day in 1988, and in the West, a movement to ban all ivory trading as the means of stopping the poaching was gaining momentum. "Ban the Bloody Ivory Trade" was one of the slogans. I joined the chorus. The ivory trade had to be stopped, I shouted to myself, and to anyone else who would listen. It was natural for me to take up this cause. I am a liberal, and a former public interest lawyer; I was a vegetarian for a period in the seventies and still eat very little red meat, and I have been opposed to commercial whaling and cutting down forests.

The longer I stayed in Africa, however, the more I realized that the issues weren't so simple. The more Africans I met and talked with, particularly outside the capitals and cities, the more I realized that the way I, a Westerner, looked at wildlife wasn't necessarily the way Africans did.

Western attitudes toward wildlife are fixed by *National Geographic* and David Attenborough documentaries. They depict the wonder and magnificence of the animals. But they provide little if any understanding of the people of Africa. Very few Westerners who come to Africa on safari leave with any feelings for the people, either. They stay in Western-managed hotels, fly between parks, are chauffeured around in minivans. The only contact they have with Africans, other than with those who wait on them, is through the lens of a camera.

When we see an elephant or a rhino, a lion or a leopard, a giraffe or a zebra, or just about any other wild animal, we think "priceless heritage." When an African sees one of these animals, he is more likely to think of a source of meat—in Swahili and many Bantu languages, the word for

"meat" and "wildlife" is the same. We think of the majesty and beauty
of wild animals. An African who has to live with them is likely to think
about the devastation that a rampaging elephant can wreak on his crops
or the death that a lion or a leopard can bring to his children. The
American settlers feared the wilderness and wild animals as they pushed
West—these were to be conquered, not conserved. That is how many
Africans feel today. Try telling a woman who is barely eking out an
existence on a tiny plot that she should preserve the elephants who
trample her crops. And why should a rancher who wants to produce beef
for the commercial market not be allowed to kill the lions that kill his
cattle?

On a safari with friends in Tanzania once, we spotted an elephant
family, twelve cows and their offspring, fifty yards off the road, munching
on trees and shrubs as they ambled along. A long red bus had already
stopped and German tourists were taking photographs. So did my friends
and I; we were thrilled. On the dirt road, Tanzanians were going about
their lives—young boys and girls coming from school; women wrapped
in bright cloths, water gourds and bags of maize balanced on their heads;
a man leading a donkey. When the elephants started to cross the road,
to enter Lake Manyara National Park, the local people ran. I walked over
to two boys, who looked to be about fifteen; they had stopped running
and were now two hundred yards from where a large elephant was
browsing on a baobab tree. What did they think of the elephants, I asked.
"Elephants are bad," one of them answered. Why, I asked. "They kill
me."

AT THE TURN of the century, the population of Africa was
100 million; today it is 450 million. People were once an island in a sea
of wildlife. Now wildlife survives in parks that are islands in an ocean of
people.

Many Westerners are convinced there would be no conflict between
the game and people if only the Africans did something about their
exploding population. Africa's growth rate is too well known to belabor.
But even if it were reduced to what Westerners consider "acceptable"
levels, African populations would continue to grow. As they do, the
competition for land will increase, and the wildlife populations will de-
crease. It's seemingly inexorable. Wildlife disappeared in the United

States and Europe as populations grew, open spaces were settled, agriculture expanded, and economies industrialized.

In just the few years I was in Africa, I witnessed the decline in the game, and felt a sadness. The first time I drove the ninety miles from the Kenyan border to the northern Tanzanian town of Arusha, in September 1988, I saw giraffes and zebra; Thomson's and Grant's gazelle grazed near the road; baboons and monkeys scampered across our path. On the same drive two years later, I saw nothing, not a single animal. "Look at this area," John Bennett, the owner of a small safari company in Arusha, said as we drove past plains rolling east to snow-covered Mount Kilimanjaro. "Two or three years ago, there were so many giraffes on this road, I often had to slow down, even stop." Why have they disappeared? I asked. "More and more settlement. More and more grazing." By Western standards, the area doesn't look very settled—there aren't expanding suburbs of tract homes. But there are signs of new settlements, simple houses made of dirt packed between a latticework of tree branches. "In thirty years," Bennett went on, "there won't be any game in these unprotected areas."

The game is disappearing, but it's not over yet. Just as he has destroyed it, man can save it. We must. We have an obligation to future generations. Our obligation may also be an ethical one—that all creatures have a right to live, animals as well as humans. Or saving the wildlife may be more selfishly founded—we need the biodiversity, the benefits to man from animals. Whatever the reasons, the issue is not whether we should preserve Africa's wildlife. The only issue is how we do so.

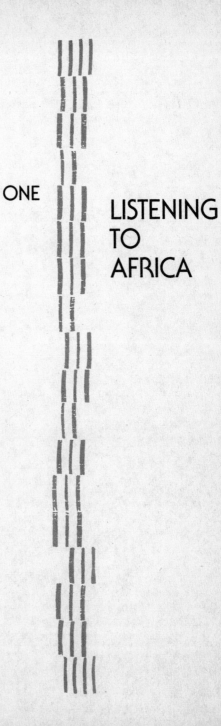

ONE

LISTENING
TO
AFRICA

||||| WE WERE HEADED up the Hoanib River bed, dry nearly all the time, when from the driver's seat of his battered Land Rover, Garth Owen-Smith, a lean and lanky conservationist who has been roaming the Kaokoveld in northwestern Namibia for more than a decade, spotted elephant tracks. He got out and studied the indentations in the sand more closely—there was a herd upriver and one bull was going downstream, he said. He knew it was a bull by the size of the footprints and because it was alone. Elephant society is matriarchal and bulls roam by themselves or in the company of other bulls. Owen-Smith picked up more tracks—two or three days old, he said. Then he found fresh spoor, but even these were barely visible, merely brushes of the soft dirt. It is extraordinary that our largest remaining land animals, which can weigh three hundred pounds at birth and eventually reach six *tons*, make such a slight impression in the earth when they walk. And they move more like a soft breeze than a thundering herd; the crunching of branches as they eat is about the only noise they make. We drove upstream and soon spotted the bull, or at least the top of his wrinkled grey back, above the bushes. We got out of the vehicle for a closer look and Owen-Smith cautioned us to talk very softly. Elephants cannot see much farther than fifty meters, he said, but they can pick up human voices three times farther away than we are able to.

After observing the bull for ten to fifteen minutes, we crossed the river bed and set off on foot in search of the herd. Again Owen-Smith urged us to be alert. We moved slowly through the brush and trees, nervously glancing over our shoulders, unsure of the whereabouts of the herd, fearing it might be behind us. Finally, we spotted some grazing elephants. "They're mean, they're dangerous; if they see us, they might charge; they're not used to humans," Owen-Smith whispered. "I'm worried where the others are." We stayed several hundred yards away, concealing ourselves amid a clump of mustard bushes and mopane trees.

Sensing that something or somebody was around, at one moment the elephants froze and stared in our direction through tiny eyes set in their massive foreheads. Deciding there was no danger, they resumed eating, using their long trunks to pick pods off the ground and toss them into their mouths.

Keeping upwind, we moved over to a rocky ridge and climbed up the steep slate face. Now we could see the elephants more clearly. There were nineteen altogether, including five youngsters; Owen-Smith judged the baby to be about eighteen months—it could not quite walk under its mother and they can usually do that until they are about one year old. The pachyderms tossed sand over their bodies and flapped their ears to keep cool. Owen-Smith explained that they had been going downstream when they caught our scent and had turned back. Now, two or three of the older elephants, in their forties, spread their ears and put their trunks in the air, listening and smelling for danger. Again deciding that it was safe, they moved out in a file. The lead cow was followed by a male of five or six years, then came three adults, with an infant between them. Their trunks dangled to the dirt, curled back slightly at the tip. When they passed the spot where we had been standing, they sniffed at our tracks. Thirty yards farther on, the elephants stopped, making a circle around an acacia tree, facing outward, like pioneers circling the wagons.

"They are afraid of us now because they were really hammered," Owen-Smith said, referring to the poaching spree of the late 1970s and early 1980s. "When I came here in 'eighty-two, when they heard a car they'd panic." The elephants would run to escape the danger. "They would be black with sweat." Many baby elephants died when their mothers were shot. Or sometimes, Owen-Smith explained, the cows would get to a water point, suspect someone was there, panic, and move on, without getting enough water; their offspring could not keep up and eventually died. Owen-Smith remembers what it was like before the poaching. "I walked down this river in 1970, eighty kilometers, with my brother, and we saw eighty-six elephants," he said. A couple of days later, stopping at a spring, a circle of green in the desert, he reminisced again: "I sat here on a moonlight night twenty years ago and saw fifty elephants, and eight rhino; the whole night you could hear lions roaring." When Owen-Smith first arrived in the Kaokoveld, in 1968, there were some 1,200 elephants; by 1982, when he returned after an absence of several years, there were fewer than 300. In the late 1960s, there were between 100 and 150 black rhino; in 1982, there were fewer than 55. The springbok, the most graceful member of the gazelle family, with a coat of light-brown and white streaks, which can run on its spindly legs at more than fifty miles an hour, declined from more than 10,000 to around 1,000; gemsbok and zebra herds suffered similar sickening collapses. The end of the game seemed nigh. "People said forget it, they're gone," Owen-Smith said, recalling the attitude of both the local people and conservationists, particularly about the elephants and rhino.

But in the Kaokoveld today there are more elephants and rhino, as well as springbok and giraffes and zebra and just about every other species, than there were in 1982, when Owen-Smith began talking to the village headmen and together they came up with the idea to involve the local people in conservation.

I HAD COME to be with Garth Owen-Smith, in July 1989, because I was searching for a successful anti-poaching program. Kenya, where I had been living for a year, was an elephant killing field—two or three elephants were being slain daily by poachers. On just one day in March 1989, seventeen elephants were killed in Tsavo National Park. A few days earlier, twenty-four elephants had been killed—probably by the same gang—on Galana Ranch, a privately owned cattle spread abutting Tsavo on the east. In the 1970s, poachers had just about finished off Kenya's rhino, reducing their numbers from 20,000 to a few hundred. The animals had been killed to satisfy the lust for rhino horn, primarily in Asia, where it was ground up and used in medicines—it is thought to be successful in reducing fever—and in Arab countries, where it was carved into dagger handles. Now, it seemed that poachers were threatening to wipe out the elephants to satisfy the greed for ivory.

It was obvious that the Kenyan government was unable to control the poaching. It was not so apparent *why* it was unable to do so. I gained some insight into why on another visit to George Adamson and Kora National Reserve, this time in April 1989. During one conversation, Adamson said that the area warden was so strapped for money and equipment that he, Adamson, supplied gas for the warden's vehicles and had told the garage in Garissa, a small frontier town fifty miles east of the reserve, to charge him for all repairs; a recent bill had been for $350. Not far from Adamson's place, thirty rangers from the Kenyan wildlife department made their camp on a bend in the Tana River, which flows east from the slopes of Mount Kenya, then turns south for the Indian Ocean four hundred miles away. The camp was set among acacia, towering palm, and yellow-flower cassia trees; fish eagles and sand grouse flew about; crocodiles slithered into the Tana's reddish-brown water. Behind strands of barbed wire, the rangers lived in eighteen-sided galvanized tin huts, which became ovens in the brutal equatorial sun; the men had placed palm fronds on the metal roofs in a vain effort to mitigate the heat.

The rangers had no uniforms, and their mufti was tattered and soiled. One of the men, who had been a ranger for ten years, was paid 1,500 Kenyan shillings a month, roughly the equivalent of $75. Their mission, simply stated, was to stop poaching; they hoped their presence would discourage poachers, but the reality was that they often engaged in shootouts with the poachers. The rangers were armed with old bolt-action rifles—"shoot-and-wait" rifles, the men jokingly called them. But it was no joke. While the ranger pulls the bolt and waits until the next round is in the chamber before firing, the poacher is squeezing off rounds from his AK-47. "When you have to decide between your life and saving the elephant tusk, you choose your life," one of the men said. They were responsible for patrolling 400 square miles. There were a dozen or so camels in the compound, their saddles piled in one of the huts, and these were what the rangers had patrolled on—until they realized that sitting so high made them easy targets for the poachers. The unit had only one vehicle, an old military truck. It was parked on inclined logs—it had no battery, so each time rangers wanted to use it they had to jump-start it. It could not be used at night because it had no headlights.

This camp provided one explanation of why Kenya was being defeated by poaching—a lack of resources. Not far away, another camp, which belonged to a military unit, offered more revelations. Hidden among the flat-topped acacia and camphora trees, which the elephants love to eat, this camp consisted of seven large military field tents; one of the larger ones was the dormitory, collapsible cots neatly aligned down each side; another served as the mess. The entrance to the camp was guarded by a soldier alertly brandishing a G-3 automatic rifle.

"There are no more poachers around here," the camp commander said confidently. A muscular man, a veteran of eighteen years with Kenya's police and paramilitary forces, he was wearing solid green utility trousers, combat boots and a floppy green jungle hat; he was willing to reveal only his first name—Julius. "We got rid of the illegal grazers," he answered when I asked him how the poachers had been eliminated from the area.

While people are prohibited from going into a national park (except as tourists), they may make minimal use of a reserve, such as Kora. After a drought there in 1984 had made life even more difficult and precarious for the pastoralists living in the area, most of whom were Somali, the Kenyan government allowed them to graze their cattle and goats inside Kora. Soon there were some 500 to 600 Somali families in the reserve, accompanied by upwards of 50,000 goats, sheep, camels and cows. With the herdsmen came the poachers; the herdsmen's presence made it easier for the poachers to operate and more difficult for the rangers to catch them—the rangers could not determine whether the tracks they were following belonged to a poacher or a grazer. So, the herdsmen were forcibly moved out. "I don't think these people will dream of coming back to Kora again," Julius said. Flying over Kora's vast stretch of flat-top thorn trees in a single-engine plane, I understood why when we spotted what had been a Somali settlement—the livestock corral, made of a circle of thorn branches; water holes; and conical huts fashioned from mud and sticks. It was actually only the remains of the huts, for they had been smashed and burned by Julius's men. He pointed out several other settlements that his men had destroyed. Adamson approved of Julius's actions, and described him as one of the best anti-poaching people who had ever worked in Kora. In fact, it would have been hard to find any European or American conservationist in Kenya who did not agree with what Julius had done.

His paramilitary unit had been sent to Kora as part of the Kenyan government's attempt to stop the poaching with military means. Destroying villages was only one of the tactics. In September 1988, after American and European newspaper stories about poaching, accompanied by gruesome pictures of dead elephants, began to do serious damage to Kenya's image as the place to come to see wildlife, Kenya's president, Daniel arap Moi, ordered that poachers be shot on sight. Before the end of the year, eleven suspected poachers were dead. When Richard Leakey took over as director of Kenya's wildlife department, in April 1989, he boasted to reporters: "Soon the press will not be asking permission to film dead elephants but only to film dead poachers." Thirty suspected poachers were killed in the next four months—no game rangers died—and the "enemy's" body count continued to rise, one poacher killed on the average of every four days during Leakey's first year. The African Wildlife Foundation (AWF), the Washington, D.C.–based conservation organization that had been founded to provide leadership training for Africans, applauded the shoot-to-kill approach. "President Daniel arap Moi has committed himself wholeheartedly to preservation of Kenya's wild game, even going so far as implementing the policy of having rangers shoot poachers on sight," the AWF president, Paul Schindler, wrote to the organization's members.

Kenya was not alone in waging war against poachers. Just about every other African country, including Zimbabwe, which also had a shoot-to-kill policy, joined the battle. Most of the poaching in Zimbabwe was of rhino in the Zambezi Valley—300 were killed in 1986 and 1987—which borders on Zambia, and most of the poachers were Zambians, who were paid a few hundred dollars for their work. One senior Zimbabwean game ranger boasted to me that he had personally killed seventeen poachers. "We're fighting it actually as a war," said the white ranger, who seemed to relish this war as much as the one he had fought in the seventies as an officer in the white Rhodesian army, fighting against black independence. Altogether, 145 poachers were killed in Zimbabwe between 1984 and 1991, and 83 were arrested; during the same period, four rangers were killed. "Zimbabwe anti-poaching operations are no place for the faint of heart!" an American government official once commented after a visit to Zimbabwe. The World Wide Fund for Nature (WWF) provided Zimbabwe with the funds to buy a helicopter for its anti-poaching war; deploying the helicopter, Zimbabwean soldiers killed more than fifty suspected poachers.

I was uncomfortable with the militaristic response to poaching, particularly the shoot-to-kill policy. The disparity between the number of poachers killed and the number of rangers dying seemed to belie the claim by many Western conservationists and African officials that all the poachers were "war-hardened, war-conditioned and ruthless," as one conservationist put it in 1989, summing up the prevailing attitude. Some were, but by no means all. Leakey told the U.S. State Department in May 1989 that the number of "hard-core poachers" was probably one hundred or fewer and that almost all of them "are known to us." That relatively low number was not something Leakey or anybody else talked much about—the public was left with the impression that there were hundreds, if not thousands, of poachers. If there were fewer than a hundred, that would hardly seem to have justified an expensive and brutal war. And it probably wasn't the "hard core" but the less well trained and well armed, the average rural peasant, who was being killed. I was also troubled by the concept of killing someone because he was trying to kill an elephant. I understood that elephants and ivory are a valuable resource, as much an asset to a country as money in the bank. But are bank robbers shot on sight? The British *Guardian* once suggested, "If a two-and-a-half-ton rhino can be stunned and immobilized by darts shot from a gun, then this same tactic could be adopted as a last resort against poachers who are insisting on resisting arrest." The idea seems rather absurd upon first reading, but upon reflection, maybe it has some merit, or at least raises serious questions about a shoot-to-kill policy.

Anyway, whatever the ethical qualms are, the war against poaching was simply not working. Like Kenya, governments in Tanzania, in Zambia, in Zimbabwe, in just about every affected country, asked for—and received—more rifles, bullets, helicopters, vehicles and equipment to conduct their war. Poaching escalated. And so, I kept asking conservationists, "Where is there an anti-poaching program that is working?" Most of them believed their own work was the most important, but someone told me about Garth Owen-Smith in Namibia.

OWEN-SMITH'S views on how to combat poaching differ radically from the prevailing ones. "In my book it's immoral to be shooting poachers," he says. "Somebody should do a profile of the guys who have been shot. He's an average normal guy, a poor farmer who is trying to feed his family." In Namibia's Kaokoveld, poachers have been caught and punished by a court. But not one has been shot. "And I hope we never do," Owen-Smith said. "I'd rather lose a few rhino or elephant than the support of the local people." And it is that support that is critical to wildlife conservation in the Kaokoveld. At the core of the program are local people who volunteer to work as auxiliary game guards, supplementing the work of the government rangers, who are too few in number to patrol the vast area.

Making contact with Owen-Smith was not easy. He does not live in the city or hang out at conferences, like most Western conservationists working in Africa. His home, set among a patch of ebony trees in an expanse of rocky terrain, is nothing but a silver trailer—like one of those that American vacationers pulled behind their cars in the 1950s—and an attached reed structure that is not much larger. The trailer is parked far from everywhere, at a place that seems appropriately called "Wereldsend" (Afrikaans for "World's End"). He has no telephone, and once a month he goes to Swakopmund, a coastal town three hundred dusty road miles away, to fetch his mail. The Kaokoveld, which is divided administratively into the provinces of Kaokoland and Damaraland, has not changed much since the Germans began staking out colonial claims during the scramble for Africa toward the end of the last century. More than twenty-three thousand square miles—three times the size of Massachusetts, twice as big as Belgium—the Kaokoveld has barely a hundred thousand human inhabitants and no paved roads.

Owen-Smith thought he wanted to be a forester. But when the twenty-four-year-old South African was posted to the Kaokoveld in 1968, as an agricultural supervisor responsible for conservation, he was changed. "When I saw my first desert, that was me, gone," he says. Understandably. The Kaokoveld encompasses the northern reaches of the Namib Desert, one of our planet's oldest, and the region's arid and semi-arid beauty is raw, silent and overpowering. Pyramidal mountains, little circular knobs on their peaks, turn reddish purple in the early evening. Basalt mesas are draped with waves of sand. On some mornings, coastal fog from the Atlantic Ocean moves across the Skeleton Coast—where ships and men have perished—and slips over the sand dunes, wandering twenty to thirty miles inland. The Kaokoveld is home to the *Welwitschia mirabilis*, a squat plant with leathery-looking leaves that can live for 2,000 years and which is thought to have existed before the Cenozoic era, 70 million years ago. The sandy plains are also dotted with *Euphorbia virosa* plants, their dark green, spiny leaves stretching upward eight to ten feet, like giant porcupine quills. The euphorbia's milky white sap burns the skin of humans and other animals, and local hunters say that the kudu in the area have lost their chin whiskers from eating the plants. But rhino "eat it like ice cream," Owen-Smith remarked, as he drove past a euphorbia that had been matted by the weight of a rhino resting in it.

In the 1970s, Owen-Smith was in and out of South-West Africa and the Kaokoveld, the departures not really of his choice. First, the South African authorities transferred him because he was too outspoken about the poaching. He tried university, which he did not take to—"I stuck it out not even a full six months," he says—and spent a year traveling throughout Australia. Then it was back to the Kaokoveld, this time to study how the Himba and Herero use the indigenous plants. The two groups, semi-nomadic pastoralists who make up the majority of inhabitants of the Kaokoveld, were probably once part of the same tribe. They speak Herero, an unwritten language, have long intermarried and are most distinguishable, at least to the outsider, by their dress. Herero women adopted their attire from the German settlers—long, bright dresses, which are tight at the waist and then billow out over several petticoats; perched on their heads are *ekori*, which look like large pincushions, or a teapot warmer set sideways. The dresses seem particularly inappropriate for the desert, but Herero women laughingly say that because it takes so much material to make a single dress—about twelve meters—a man can only afford one wife. Himba women still wear only pleated, calfskin skirts, coat their bodies with ochre, and adorn their wrists and ankles with copper and silver bands. It is only in the last twenty years that the Himba have begun using cash and sending their children to school, but now change is coming, and the current adult generation of Himba is probably the last that will live and dress in the traditional way.

Owen-Smith reluctantly said good-bye to the Kaokoveld again just as he was about to become a father, when his then wife did not think the isolated region was the perfect place for a baby. He went home to the Natal in South Africa, where he helped set up the first environmental program for black South Africans. But the lure of sparsely populated neighboring land continued to pull at him, and in 1979, he returned to South-West Africa, this time, it has turned out, for good. After several jobs with the Directorate of Nature Conservation, including a stint as a warden in Etosha National Park, which borders the Kaokoveld on the east, he finally made it back to the Kaokoveld in 1982. He was sickened by what poaching had done to the wildlife, and was determined to effect changes.

"When we got here in 'eighty-two, it was really bad," Owen-Smith recalled, squatting by an early-morning fire in a riverbed where we had camped the night before; he was wearing a torn and patched khaki jacket that was too short for his arms and blue jeans that stopped well above the tops of his ankle-high, kudu-skin desert boots. The situation was bad because poaching had gone almost unchecked since the mid-1970s, following a heavy influx of whites into the area; they were sent by the South African government, which acquired South-West Africa from the Germans after World War I, under a League of Nations mandate. Everybody was poaching—policemen, soldiers, civil servants, even South African cabinet ministers. Then the area was hit by one of the worst droughts in recent memory, which lasted from 1979 to 1982.

The Himba and the Herero, who had been among the wealthiest pastoralists in southern Africa, lost at least 80 percent of their stock during the drought—130,000 cattle and tens of thousands of goats. They became dependent on international relief. And they began hunting more. Himba and Herero men had traditionally hunted to feed their families, but this was controlled, not by law but by their own mores and needs, and no species were threatened with extinction because of it. A Himba headman, Venomeho Tjingire, whose hair was wrapped in cloth and who was wearing a calfskin apron, explained how he had hunted gemsbok and springbok with his dogs. They would chase an animal until finally cornering it; then Venomeho (surnames are not commonly used among the Himba) would make the instantaneous kill with his spear. Like many men, Venomeho enjoyed hunting, but he did not do it primarily for sport. He was wearing sandals made from tire rubber, but twenty years ago he would have fashioned them from giraffe skins or rhino hides, and those were better, he said, because they were not so heavy. During the drought, wildlife was also the only source of meat for men like Venomeho, and now they had .303 rifles to hunt with. These had been given to them by the South African government as part of its war against SWAPO (the South-West Africa People's Organization) which was fighting for independence. (In 1990, South-West Africa became independent Namibia.) And since the Himba and Herero saw the white man shooting all the game, why shouldn't they. The results were devastating.

"There was a sense of hopelessness that anything could be done," Owen-Smith said, recalling the days in 1982 when he spent hours patiently discussing the situation with the headmen, listening to what they had to say, what they wanted to do. "There was no hope we'd stop the poaching on our own," Owen-Smith said, "only if we got the support of the local people." Out of the discussions came the community game guard program.

One of the headmen upon whom Owen-Smith relied most was Joshua Kangombe, who lives at Warmquelle (Warm Springs). It is a Herero village of small, rectangular-shaped dung-and-wattle huts, a few with tin roofs. When I arrived, as the huge ball of sun was dropping into the trees, a woman was working the pedal of a black Singer sewing machine, and when she rose to enter her house, it seemed impossible that she could fit through the opening because her dress and headgear were so large. Children were laughing and playing in the dirt, not far from the rusting shells of old trucks; a green pickup listed to the right, resting on its wheelbase. Chairs were brought out and Joshua sat in a low-slung one, canvas stretched over the metal frame. He was wearing a black brimmed hat, a black button-up sweater, and cordovan wingtips without laces; while we talked, he puffed on a pipe.

"I got the idea out of the Bible," Joshua began his explanation of the genesis of the community game guard program. "When God punished the world in the time of Noah, all these wild animals were protected and put on Noah's Ark. And it was written that no animals should be destroyed and that you should protect wildlife in the same way you do your domestic animals. When we realized here that our wildlife was being destroyed, we realized we had to do something.

"In the old days—and I'm talking about the long-ago days—there were rules and a family would shoot one animal a month for food. It was not like recent times when everyone was just shooting everything, everywhere. In this modern world, we saw that there was no protection for wildlife.

"When we saw this, we decided to work out this plan, so that it would be possible that a family could shoot some animals to eat. That way we could take a little game and the game would still be plentiful. And just as we could see wild animals mean something to this land, we also understand that wild animals have a value to us because tourists could come from America to see our animals and this would bring money to us. It is also true that when there is no wildlife left in the land the rain does not come. It was for all these reasons that I was the first man with Garth Owen-Smith to try to find a way to protect wildlife, and stop the hunting. The idea we got spread over the whole land and everyone in this land came to think our way. This is how it happened." He dipped into a string-tied pouch of Black and White tobacco and filled his pipe.

I asked him to explain the connection between rain and wildlife, which I had heard other Herero and Himba refer to.

"Because wild animals are God's animals, if He looks down and sees the animals under the trees without food, He will send rain."

What did he mean by "the old days," I asked.

"It was a long, long time ago, and there were no whites here then," he said. "This story about how the Herero lived with the wildlife has been told to our children over and over again. That is how we know it."

Joshua talked for an hour, and none of the other men gathered about said anything—the headman is not interrupted. But when he finished, a wiry young man who was wearing slacks and a yellow T-shirt with green sleeves, handed out by a political party, spoke up. "It looks to us young people that wildlife is just for white people. We see whites driving around in cars, looking at wildlife and looking after the wildlife," he began. "We also care about wildlife, but the question is why don't black people also get jobs in conservation." The man's name was Jaspar Kasaona, he was twenty-nine years old, and had been a teacher in Windhoek, the capital, but had given that up "because I love wildlife and I would like to make a career in wildlife," he said. He spoke with animation, his hands constantly in motion. "The whites tell us that wildlife is for everyone. But we don't see enough jobs going to black people. It is only whites who seem to have the contracts. Blacks are the workers." He was referring to the contracts given to tour companies for camping sites and to operate generally in the areas.

Owen-Smith agreed with Kasaona. "Conservation is still largely a whitey thing," he remarked at one point. "We're trying to change it here, but we've still got a long way to go." It might be expected that whites would be the major actors in conservation in South African–ruled South-West Africa. But the story is the same throughout the continent. In Kenya, for example, whites hold the senior positions in the conservation organizations, and whites or Asians own and operate most of the safari companies and camps; Africans are secretaries, cooks and drivers.

Owen-Smith cares about Africans, is not condescending toward them, and knows the value of listening to them, which sets him distinctly apart from nearly all other Western conservationists in Africa. Thus, it is the headman, not Owen-Smith, who selects the men from the community who will be the auxiliary guards. "He knows his guys, and his pride is at stake," Owen-Smith said, explaining why he relied on their decisions. It has not always been easy. One of the men Joshua wanted to appoint as a game guard had been a poacher himself. He was not a casual poacher who had killed a zebra to feed his family, but someone who had killed at least eleven elephants and three rhino—he was paid by a Windhoek businessman—and had been convicted twice. Owen-Smith was shocked by the suggestion that he be a game guard. Joshua argued that because the man had been a poacher, he knew how poachers operated. Owen-Smith accepted the headman's decision, though he was very nervous about it for six months. But now, he says, "I trust him one hundred percent. He's turned out to be a damn good auxiliary."

One of the first auxiliary guards Joshua appointed was Sakeus Kasaono, who lives just outside the small town of Sesfontein—the name comes from the six springs in the area. The Germans had a military fort here in the early part of this century and some of the palm trees they planted are still growing; today, there are also a primary school and a few stucco houses with windows. Sakeus is tall and lean, forty-nine years old, the father of twelve, with a slight beard speckled with grey in the chin whiskers. Sitting under a thorn tree for some protection from the sun, Sakeus talked about the history of wildlife around his village. Because of the springs, it had once been rich in wildlife. "When I grew up there was springbok, just beyond my village," he said pointing beyond a low hill. "Sometimes elephants came into our garden here," he continued, indicating a clump of thorn trees a hundred yards from where we were sitting. These days he doesn't see much game. "Those animals don't come around anymore," he said.

The "white men" shot the elephants, he said. "We found carcasses in the Hoanib River." The tusks and feet had been sawed off, but the meat had not been taken, left for the vultures and predators. The local people hunted plains animals for meat. "I could understand why people were hunting. There I was sitting at home watching the drought kill my goats and my cattle and we were hungry and this was why people turned to hunting." When asked how many animals had been shot, he said, "Ta, ta, ta, ta, ta," a common utterance, which in this case meant "a lot." He took out a straight-stem pipe, dipped the bowl into a pouch of tobacco, then lit it; a woman in a long dress of patchwork colors and a bright orange *ekori* walked by. Sakeus liked having the wildlife around; they were a natural part of his life, environment and culture. So, when Owen-Smith came along and discussed with Sakeus the community game guard concept, Sakeus was eager to join, and he played a key role in the capture of one of the worst poachers to operate in the Koakoveld since the end of the drought.

It happened while Sakeus was on a patrol with Save The Rhino Trust, a nonprofit organization. (In 1985 Owen-Smith lost the small amount of funding he had had and was forced to lay off some of the auxiliary guards; Sakeus had found a job with Save The Rhino Trust.) The group was not out looking for poachers but was monitoring rhino movements when

Sakeus spotted some barely perceptible human footprints. The Himba and Herero can spot footprints in the rocky soil where they are no more noticeable to an inexperienced eye than an individual cloud on an overcast day. "Those men were walking very cleverly—they were walking on rocks. They were avoiding the easy, sandy path next to the rocks," Sakeus recalled, and this is what made him and the others suspicious: people generally walk along the narrow paths worn by animals. It was late in the day and the group had to stop before following the human spoor very far.

What happened next mirrors the story of the conservation effort in most African countries. The Department of Nature Conservation office, in the town of Khorixas, was contacted by radio, and the next day government rangers tried to follow the tracks, but failed. What was needed was a plane to fly over the area. The Nature Conservation office had only one plane, and it was in Windhoek for service. A private pilot offered his services, but it took a week to get the necessary government clearances.

Eventually, flying over the area, the searchers spotted an elephant carcass; on the ground, the auxiliaries and government rangers found that it had been shot by poachers, and they intensified their manhunt. Next, they came across the carcasses of two rhino. The poachers had concealed them with brushwood, but hungry lions had pulled away the thicket. Even though it had been a week since the poachers' tracks had first been spotted, the auxiliaries were able to pick up the trail again. They followed the tracks for fifteen miles, to a small village. The villagers said that a man who was not from the area had been living among them, and they suspected that he was the poacher. He was, and the extent of his poaching was far more serious than anyone in Kaokoveld had realized—he had killed at least five rhino and three elephants. But here the tale is dramatically different from most African poaching stories: the man was arrested, charged, pleaded guilty and was sentenced.

The auxiliary's function is not to apprehend the poacher, but, as Sakeus had done, only to detect his presence, and then to alert the headman, Owen-Smith, or a government game ranger. In the battle against poachers, quick detection is critical, more important than military operations. "It doesn't matter if you kill or capture poachers," says Rowan Martin, a senior officer in Zimbabwe's wildlife department. He spent five years studying his department's anti-poaching efforts in the Zambezi Valley, where up to fifty gangs have operated and the rhino population has been decimated. Based on that study, Martin concluded, "What's critical is detection. You must find them as quickly as possible, so that you reduce the time between when they get into the park and when they start killing." Martin's conclusions have not been taken into account by the planners of most anti-poaching operations—another reason why they have been largely unsuccessful.

Zimbabwe and Kenya are spending millions of dollars for guns and ammunition and vehicles and even helicopters. The Kaokoveld auxiliary doesn't even always carry a rifle and performs his task of keeping alert for poachers while tending his cattle or going about his normal activities; he is, in effect, always on duty. It is often a carcass that sets the auxiliary on his search. Or in the case of one auxiliary, Ngevi Tjihako, it was the suspicious behavior of two young men he noticed walking through his area; he had then followed them for thirty-five miles.

Ngevi lived in one of the more remote and isolated parts of the already remote Kaokoveld, about a hundred miles from the Angolan border; to reach him, it was necessary to drive off the track, down a rocky riverbed, and over rough terrain. Poachers would be able to operate freely here were it not for the auxiliary guards. Before asking Ngevi to tell his story about catching the poachers, Owen-Smith, who had not been here in a while, inquired of Ngevi and his friends about their life in general. Several Himba men had gathered around a roaring fire, where a goat was stewing in a large kettle. The men had thick strings of cowrie shells around their necks and were wearing pleated skirts and Western T-shirts. Their muscles rippled. The style in which they wore their hair—piled on top of the head, then wrapped tightly in soft leather—signified that they were married. A sliver of moon rose in the clear sky.

The men told Owen-Smith that jackals and hyenas had been causing a lot of damage; recently a hyena had killed two cows. (I thought nervously about the goat carcass hanging in the tree not far from my sleeping bag.) They asked Owen-Smith if he could bring them poisons to kill the hyenas, which the government used to distribute to control predators. Owen-Smith explained that the poisons also killed other animals, so it was not good to use them. The oldest man in the group, a headman, said he understood, but, he added, "it still pains me."

I asked about other animals—lions, elephants, rhinoceros. Were there many around? The men said that there used to be a lot of these animals in the area, so many that people were afraid to come to the riverbed where we were now sitting. But they had disappeared largely because of the excessive hunting during the drought, and these men had mixed feelings about their decline. The headman told a story about an encounter with a lion. "The lion came to my house and took my dog and ran away," he began. He grabbed his rifle and followed. When he got close, the lion charged and jumped on him before he could shoot. The man's son started yelling, and the lion turned on him. Quickly recovering, the old man shot it dead. Asked how big the lion was, the man said simply, "It wasn't very thin."

The men said they were pleased there were no more lions. Owen-Smith reminded them that earlier in the discussion, Ngevi had said that God made all animals, so how could they think it was good that there were no lions?

The headman said that yes, God had made the animals, but it was still good that they were gone because they caused so much damage. Not only the lions, but also rhino and elephants. "I know God will be cross about what I say, but for me it is a matter of fear," the old man said.

Ngevi's ten-year-old son was snuggled next to his father, and I asked him if he would like to see an elephant. No, he said, because his mother had told him they are dangerous. Rural African women particularly do not like elephants because they trample the crops, which women tend, and linger near the watering holes where the women go to fetch water.

The discussion continued, with one man saying he thought children should see wild animals and not just hear about them from the elders. After listening further, Ngevi's son said that maybe he would like to see an elephant. But not a lion. He had seen a lion once, at the watering hole; he would not like to see another one, he said.

Although their numbers had declined, zebra, giraffes, gemsbok and springbok were still plentiful in the area, and this pleased the men. "They make the land more beautiful," the headman said. He also said, "I was their herder and when I was hungry I got meat from them." He is no longer able to hunt them, though he and the other men would like to.

Finally, Ngevi told Owen-Smith a story about poachers. It began one afternoon while he was tending to his cattle. From a distance he saw two teenage boys who seemed to be walking in a curious way, as if they did not want to be seen, and Ngevi's suspicions were further aroused that night when they did not call in at his house to sleep, as people passing through an area normally do. "I thought about it the next morning—why

didn't they come back to my house?—and I followed the tracks of the
two men," Ngevi said. He did not find anything.

The next day he took up the search again. After a while, he came to a
place where they had taken off their sandals and had begun walking
barefoot, which would make it harder for them to be detected. But Ngevi
was able to follow the faint footprints and eventually he found a .303
cartridge case. He thought, "If I was hunting, in what direction would I
shoot?" He went in that direction, and soon spotted zebra tracks and
blood on the ground. He followed this trail, and eventually came upon
a dead zebra. The boys had taken some of the meat and had cooked it on
a fire, but they had left a lot and vultures had been eating the carcass.
Ngevi returned home. "I sat and thought about what I should do now,"
he recalled. He decided he should find the two boys, and the next day,
he picked up their tracks from where he had found the zebra carcass and
followed them to the village of Okahanga. He had tracked the two boys
from very early in the morning until after sunset.

When Ngevi arrived at Okahanga, he went to the headman and told
him what had happened. The headman summoned the villagers, and
Ngevi said to them, "I have brought you together because there are two
of you who have gone all the way to my area and shot a zebra." The
villagers asked Ngevi to point out the two boys, and he did. The boys
admitted what they had done. Ngevi then asked their parents to take
them to the headman. The headman was "very cross," Ngevi remembered, but he said that he was not going to send the boys to jail because
they would just get free food and then come back. Instead, the headman
fined each boy one castrated male goat and ordered that they be given
eight blows with a whip. He summoned all the young men from the
village to watch the thrashing. "I have appointed people to look after
the game and they have been told to look out for people hunting," the
headman told the village. "Nobody must hunt."

"It is finished," Ngevi said when he had recounted the story. Then
he asked Owen-Smith if he had done the right thing. Yes, Owen-
Smith said; the punishment was better for the boys than going to jail,
because jail would only expose them to common criminals. On occasion, Owen-Smith has taken auxiliaries to observe a poacher's trial, so
they will understand how the legal system works and that it is fair.
More than a hundred men have been convicted for poaching in the
Kaokoveld since 1982. Whether as a percentage of the population or

of the poaching incidents, it is a record that probably no other jurisdiction in Africa can match.

After leaving Ngevi the next day, we drove across a vast gravel plain,
where in the summer (December and January at the bottom of the African
continent) temperatures reach 120 degrees. A springbok bounded into
the air in front of us and remained suspended in space as it floated across
the road before joining about twenty others pronking in the sun-goldened
grass. We passed a spring, then the track was enclosed on both sides by
rock outcroppings fifty to a hundred feet high. The centuries of alternat-
ing heat and cold have cracked the rocks into boulders, and their granite
surfaces have been worn smooth by thousands of years of wind. The
silence engulfed us, and our voices dropped in harmony.

            IT WAS NOT predestined that Owen-Smith would get men
like Ngevi to volunteer to protect the wildlife or that more generally he
would get the support of the Himba and Herero. After all, the essence
of what Owen-Smith was saying to them was that they should conserve
the gemsbok, the zebra, and other plains animals, but that they could
not hunt them, even to feed their families; that they should protect
elephants, rhino and lions, animals they consider dangerous because
they trample their crops and kill their stock. This is the essence of all
conservation programs in Africa.

Owen-Smith realized that if conservation was to be successful, more
would have to be done than enlisting committed people from the community to defend against poaching. There would have to be something
positive for the Himba and Herero, some benefits from the wildlife. And
so, in 1987, five years after first sitting under the trees with Joshua
Kangombe and other headmen and coming up with the auxiliary game
guard scheme, Owen-Smith met with the small community of Himba
and Herero near Purros, a spring in the lower Hoarusib River, and
discussed with them how they might benefit from tourism. This time
Owen-Smith was joined by Margaret Jacobsohn, an anthropologist who
was concerned about how the Himba and Herero would be able to
preserve their cultures in the face of increasing contact with Western
tourists. Before coming to the Kaokoveld, Jacobsohn, an attractive
woman with long brown hair and now in her thirties, had been a highly
regarded journalist in Cape Town, as a stringer for several Dutch newspapers, a reporter for the *Rand Daily Mail*, and then as an editor on the

Cape Times. She abandoned her career after the South African government imposed the state of emergency in 1985, which included heavy
censorship. "To practice honest journalism meant going to jail," she says.
She switched to anthropology and rural development. Jacobsohn had
visited Kaokoveld with her family in the 1970s and later as a journalist,
and in 1986 she took up what has become virtually permanent residence
to conduct field research, and work and live with Owen-Smith. As part
of a doctoral program she has studied how the Himba and Herero are
reacting to change in their culture, change brought about mostly from
the West.

Recalling those first meetings with the Purros community, Jacobsohn
says, "What emerged was they were negative on the return of the wildlife
and negative on tourism." Understandably.

Due to the successful anti-poaching program, wildlife had begun to
return to Purros. Three elephant bulls drank from the spring in November 1986, the first in five years, which frightened the women; and when
the young men and women took their cattle and goats out for grazing and
water, they began to encounter lions. By 1987, the Kaokoveld was also
beginning to experience something of a tourist boom—about ten vehicles
a day would pass through Purros in July, the high season. That is nothing
compared with Kenya, where forty vehicles will surround a lion pride,
but even the limited tourism was tearing at the social fabric of the Himba
and Herero.

They saw what Westerners wore and possessed, and began wanting
the same. But there was almost no way of earning cash in the Kaokoveld,
so the people began begging from the tourists. Young people who were
supposed to be tending their cattle were remaining behind at the village,
waiting for handouts from the tourists. The tourists were generally oblig-
ing, of course, taking pity on these "poor" people. Resentments developed. When several members of one Himba family who had been the
recipients of considerable "generosity" from a tour group—the tourists
had left some food, a water container and a broken deck chair—became
ill, the family accused another family of having put a curse on them out
of jealousy.

Jacobsohn suggested to the people of Purros that they make crafts and
sell them to the tourists, in order to earn money and not have to beg.
She was also appalled and angry at the way tourists would buy things
right off a Himba's person, such as necklaces and armbands, or march
into their homes and offer to buy gourds, baskets, even family heirlooms.

Still, when she raised the crafts idea with the people in Purros, they asked her, dumbfounded, "What can we possibly make that the whites want?"

Eight extended families make up the Purros community, living in huts scattered about the sandy earth, with mountains and sand dunes visible in the distant haze; for many months Jacobsohn lived here. When I visited Purros with Jacobsohn sometime after her suggestion had been implemented, a woman sat working in front of one hut, its cracked dung bleached to a light brown. Her back was straight, her legs stretched in front of her, ankles covered with several inches of silver-colored rings. A gourd was hanging on a rope from a tripod she had fashioned from two-foot-high sticks, and she rocked it back and forth to separate milk from fat. She would later mix the fat with ochre to make the substance women smear on their bodies. Later in the day, she was weaving a basket, which she would sell to tourists. Nearby several women sat on the ground in the shade of the gnarled limbs of a camelthorn tree. A Herero was wearing a long floral print dress, a white necklace and a turquoise *ekori*. Her Himba friend had calfskin covering her midsection, her hair was plaited and she was smeared in ochre; from a zippered pouch hanging on her left side, she pinched some tobacco and tamped it into a homemade metal pipe about four inches long, which she lighted with a stick she removed from the fire. The women admired two metal kitchen pots, both lidded, one deep and the other squat, which Jacobsohn had brought for them, and which they had paid for from the money they earned selling their crafts. The crafts market has had a side benefit for the women in Purros of giving them access to cash for the first time; as in the rest of Africa, the Kaokoveld women are routinely excluded from the few wage-labor jobs available.

When a well-built young Himba, seventeen-year-old Katondoihe, heard that Jacobsohn had arrived, he anxiously came in from the field, hoping she had brought him a pair of running shoes. She had, and his eyes brightened with delight. They were not a gift, however. Katondoihe purchased them with the money he had earned from selling tourists some armbands and four neck pillows, thick pieces of wood carved with a concave arch where a man rests his head when he lies on the ground. One of Katondoihe's friends, clearly envious, later gave Jacobsohn some money and asked her to buy him similar running shoes when she next went to Windhoek. (Jacobsohn suggested that the boys wanted them because they were lighter on their feet than sandals made of tire rubber, important for people who spend most of their days walking.)

The Purros community has discovered another significant source of money from tourism: it has levied a tax on all tourists who spend a night on their land. The justification for the levy is simple: it is the beauty of their land and the wildlife on it that attracts the tourists. The tour companies resisted, as hotels and safari operators throughout Africa have resisted similar proposals, but after lengthy negotiations, they agreed to pay the levy. The amount is about $10 per tourist, which isn't much for the tourist but is a considerable sum for Purros.

The Purros Conservation and Development Committee, composed of one representative from each of the eight families, has been set up as part of the community's new approach toward tourism. It decides how the tourist levy should be divided. Initially it made direct distributions to the families. Upon receiving his share, the oldest lineage head in Purros told Jacobsohn, "It is as if we are farming wild animals, but instead of getting meat and skins from them, we get the money that the tourists pay to see them. That is why we must look after our wild animals."

Jacobsohn has discovered that the Purros project, and particularly the levy, has had an unintended effect. "The whites come in with a different attitude toward these people," she says. The tourists no longer look on the Himba and Herero as beggars, and they know that the money they are paying makes them partners in a conservation project, that the community is taking care of the wildlife and this is what they are paying for. "It has made for much more dignified tourism," Jacobsohn says.

THE PROJECTS that Jacobsohn and Owen-Smith are developing in the Kaokoveld are certainly the least expensive and most cost-efficient conservation programs in Africa, as well as its most successful. The Purros project costs virtually nothing; indeed, it generates revenue. The total cost of the community game guard program in 1989 was $30,000, nearly all the money coming from the Endangered Wildlife Trust, a private organization in Johannesburg. The volunteer rangers were paid the equivalent of $25 a month, and received rations of maize meal, sugar, tea, coffee, tobacco, soap and milk powder. Owen-Smith earned about $8,000 in 1989. "Ludicrous, isn't it?" Jacobsohn said. Yes, when one considers that the expatriate directors of the international conservation organizations in Nairobi were being paid $50,000 and more. "It's not so bad," Owen-Smith said about his salary.

It seemed to me that what Owen-Smith and Jacobsohn were doing in the Kaokoveld should be a model for conservation in other African countries. I thought about Kenya, where the soldiers had burned down people's villages in an effort to control poaching near Kora, instead of enlisting the people in the anti-poaching campaign. I thought of the pittance that rural people who live near Africa's parks receive from the millions of tourist dollars that come into their country. Still, when I suggested to Owen-Smith that his program might be copied, he said, "I don't know. There's no holy grail. Ours is not a model for anybody—except for the principle that you have to involve the local people, that you have to have the support of the community." It is a principle few Westerners have absorbed.

When I was in Kaokoveld with Owen-Smith and Jacobsohn in July 1989, the movement to ban the trade in ivory was surging—the previous month the United States, Britain and most European governments had imposed unilateral bans on the importation of ivory into their countries, and the African Wildlife Foundation and World Wide Fund for Nature were lobbying hard for a worldwide ban. "In my opinion, it's a bad thing," Owen-Smith said about the ban. "The guy who is thinking only of the elephant is for the ban. The person who is thinking about Africa and Africans is against it."

In October 1989, at Lausanne, Switzerland, the countries that are parties to the Convention on International Trade in Endangered Species of Wild Fauna and Flora (CITES) declared the elephant an endangered species under the treaty, which meant that all international ivory trading was prohibited. It was the culmination of one of the most successful campaigns in the history of conservation—successful, that is, from the point of view of those who believed that an ivory ban was the way to save the elephant. The campaign was intense, with more effort given to slogans, sound bites and gruesome pictures of elephants with their faces hacked off than to good science and rational debate. Conservationists with impeccable scientific credentials who were opposed to a ban were overcome by the public pressure and emotion and concerns about money. Organizations discovered that embracing the elephant and calling for a ban brought in money like no other cause; conversely, organizations that failed to climb on this bandwagon risked losing members. Facts that rebutted the need for a ban were ignored, such as *growing* elephant populations in some African countries. Above all, Africans were ignored, overwhelmed, manipulated and outmaneuvered—by a conservation crusade led, orchestrated and dominated by white Westerners. It was all familiar, the latest chapter in the story of conservation in Africa.

TWO

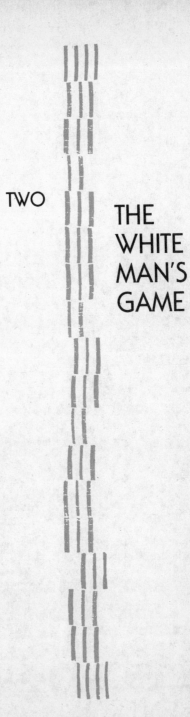

THE
WHITE
MAN'S
GAME

IVORY LUST

|||| DURING THE LAST quarter of the nineteenth century, the European powers were engaged in what has become known as the scramble for Africa, and when they finished, just about all of Africa belonged to everybody but the Africans. Once they controlled the continent, the imperialists wanted to set it right—at least in their own view. So in 1900 the foreign ministers representing the African colonial powers—Britain (whose properties included Uganda, British East Africa and Nigeria), France (most of West Africa and Madagascar), Germany (German East Africa and South-West Africa), Belgium (Congo Free State), Italy (Libya, Eritrea and Somaliland), Portugal (Angola and Mozambique) and Spain (small pieces of land in West Africa)—gathered in London. After several weeks of debate and discussion, they dipped their pens into ink and signed the Convention for the Preservation of Animals, Birds and Fish in Africa. It was the first international conservation treaty, and though it was never ratified by all the countries, it became the basis for most of the colonial wildlife legislation in Africa, and the forerunner of the Convention on International Trade in Endangered Species (CITES), which came into being seventy-three years later and is the most comprehensive conservation treaty today.

The 1900 treaty covered what was considered Central Africa, which meant all of the continent except for North Africa and South Africa. In these latter regions—in Algeria, along the Nile, in the Cape Colony—"the big game have almost wholly ceased to exist," *The Times* of London noted in its report on the final day of the conference. The newspaper went on to provide a concise and vivid summary of the situation:

> It is necessary to go far into the interior to find the nobler forms of antelope, and still further if the hunter wants to pursue the elephant, the rhinoceros, or the giraffe. It is perfectly clear that very soon those animals, unless something is done to prevent their extermination, will be stamped out as completely as the dodo. To some extent this process

is inevitable. The advance of civilization, with its noise and agitation, is fatally disturbing to the primitive forms of animal life. Commerce, moreover, discovers continually some new demand for the trophies of the chase. The horns, the skins, and the plumage of beasts and birds have an increasing market value. It is not surprising, therefore, that men of science have become alarmed at the prospect of the extinction of many of the most interesting and characteristic types of zoological development.

Most of the alarm was coming from Britain, which was the leader in conservation thinking at the turn of the century. Jeremy Bentham, the noted liberal philosopher, had set the foundations for ethical treatment of animals in the eighteenth century, and the British Society for the Prevention of Cruelty to Animals was founded in 1824, forty-two years before the first American chapter; the British parliament enacted a law restricting scientific experiments on live animals in 1876, a full ninety years before similar legislation was adopted by the United States Congress. The early British organizations and laws were concerned mostly about domestic animals, from cattle to pet cats, not wild species. But in 1903 the first international conservation organization was founded—the Society for the Preservation of the Wild Fauna of the Empire. The empire was Britain's. The society's objective was to prevent the destruction of wild animals throughout the empire, but primarily in Africa. In the United States, a conservation movement was in its embryonic stages. The Sierra Club had been formed in 1892 by John Muir, who was a disciple of Henry David Thoreau. In *Walden* Thoreau called on man to live in harmony with nature; though the book was published in 1854, it is likely that more college students read it in the 1960s than had in the previous hundred years, for it was only then that the American environmental movement came of age.

At the turn of the century, few conservationists in the United States or Europe were arguing that animals had rights or that man had an ethical duty to animals; nor were there even many like Muir who put forth the notion that man has an obligation to preserve nature for future genera-tions. The predominant conservation attitude at the time can be found in the preamble to the 1900 Convention. The European colonial powers were "desirous of saving from indiscriminate slaughter, and of insuring the preservation throughout their possessions in Africa of the various forms of animal life existing in a wild state which are either useful to man or are harmless." It is the last clause that is the most revealing. These conservationists were not concerned about saving all wild animals, only those that were not dangerous to man or which were of some value to him. Thus, complete protection was accorded to only a few animals— the giraffe, gorilla, chimpanzee, mountain zebra, white-bearded gnu, pygmy hippopotamus of Liberia and wild ass. Moreover, it was still permissible to shoot most other animals, including elephants, rhino, zebra and gazelle, though there were restrictions: no shooting of infants or females, and limits on the number that could be killed by any one hunter. In protecting "women and children," the treaty signers were not acting solely out of compassion, if, indeed, out of compassion at all. These animals had a value—ivory, horns, skins, meat—and protecting mothers and their offspring ensured a continual supply.

The men who gathered in London had a further motivation: they wanted to preserve the wildlife that was popular with big-game hunters. One of those who played a leading role at the conference was Sir Clement Hill, director of the African section of the British Foreign Office, who had hunted in East Africa. Hunting had long been (and still is) a sport popular with the British royalty and upper class—the first reserves were "royal" reserves where the "royal" game could be hunted, and in the first game reserves the British established in Kenya, game could be hunted with a license. When it came to conservation, the Society for the Preservation of the Wild Fauna of the Empire was founded by lords, viscounts, knights, and other upper-class figures of British society, nearly all of whom were game hunters, which quickly led to their being satirized as the "penitent butchers."

It was not only that the conservationists at the turn of the century permitted hunting. In sharp contrast to contemporary environmental attitudes, the 1900 treaty actually encouraged the killing of certain species. These included the lion and leopard, as well as the wild dog and spotted hyena. They were considered vermin by the British settlers. Sir Alfred E. Pease, a farmer and big-game hunter who was host to Theodore Roosevelt in 1909 and later acquired a reputation for his studies of lions, noted that lions were a particular menace to ostrich farming, a considerable commercial enterprise at the time; he had lost forty birds to lions in one night. "Most settlers would at present vote for their extermination," Pease said of the lion in 1911. A less articulate Kenya settler wrote years later, "Among our enemies I am afraid I must include the Lion, there are also those hardened criminals, Hyaenas, Leopards, Wild Dogs and Jackals."

The leopard was taken off the vermin list in Kenya in the 1930s and laws were passed against killing it. But it was not because of the moral crusade in the West that made wearing a leopard skin unconscionable and unfashionable—that did not come about until the 1960s. Rather, it was Kenyan farmers who first came to the leopard's protection. The farmers' crops and fields were being destroyed by the baboon and the bush pig, a nocturnal animal with knifelike tusks, and since the leopard fed on these animals, the farmers wanted laws against killing it; one district commissioner believed that each leopard kept alive meant the elimination of 250 pigs.

As the laws about vermin and the experience with the leopard indicate, when conservation clashed with the interests of farmers and economic development, the latter prevailed. One of the few early African settlers who had a broader, more philosophical, view of conservation was Keith Caldwell. He argued that the wildlife was a heritage to be held in trust for future generations. Nevertheless, Caldwell, who had come to East Africa during World War I and had remained, helping to establish the wildlife departments in Kenya and Uganda, made it clear that while the role of the game department was to preserve game, it was to do so "in such a way that it does not in any way retard or interfere with the economic development of the country, or place any difficulties in the way of stock-breeding or crop-growing." This is how many African governments feel today—that wildlife protection should not interfere with development. Back then the farmers about whom the government was primarily concerned were the white settlers. Thus the land set aside for game reserves was not in Kenya's White Highlands, where the British settlers had their tea and coffee plantations, but in places where the whites did not settle, either because of lack of good soil or enough water or because of the presence of the tsetse fly.

The colonists were not, of course, as solicitous of the concerns of the Africans. Throughout the continent, it was usually their land that was taken for parks and reserves. And although hunting was allowed, a license was necessary, and the white colonial administrators did not issue many licenses to Africans, who could not have afforded one anyway; moreover, for political reasons, the governments prohibited Africans from owning rifles. With the exception of a few tribes that were allowed to continue hunting as they traditionally had, Africans who shot wild animals for meat or sport or to protect their livestock became, ipso facto, poachers.

Hunter-gatherer tribes were the most severely hurt by the laws that prohibited killing wild animals. But most African tribes shot some wild animals for meat, if only to supplement their diet. Africans also had cultural and other uses for the animals. They fashioned capes from gazelle skins, carved ivory and rhino horn into snuffboxes and tobacco holders, wove wildebeest tails into fly whisks. The rhino's tough hide made excellent shields, capable of deflecting spears. When a woman of the Boran tribe, pastoralists who roam today in northern Kenya and southern Ethiopia, gave birth to a son, the father proudly carried a whip made from rhino tail. The Boran carved elephant tusks into bracelets, which some men wore on their upper arms—only those men who had killed a lion or an elephant or a rhinoceros or some other wild animal that it took considerable bravery to confront with a spear. Any man who wore an ivory bracelet was therefore respected. Today, any Boran wearing an ivory bracelet, or carrying a rhino-tail whip, would more likely be arrested. The Boran also shot giraffes and used the skin to carry milk. It was better than any other container—it didn't break or rust, which explains why even today a Boran will pay ten cows for one giraffe skin.

It has long been an article of faith among whites in Africa that if the white man had not brought his conservation laws to the continent the game would have disappeared. In 1897, Frederick Selous, the most renowned big-game hunter of his day (he led Theodore Roosevelt on his safari), wrote that "it is hardly too much to say that 997 out of every 1,000 elephants, whose tusks come to the London market, are killed by African natives," and that the white rhino had been exterminated in parts of southern Africa "entirely by native hunters." Africans may well have fired the bullets or arrows that killed these animals, but they were being paid by Arab and European traders who were selling the ivory and rhino in markets far from Africa for enormous profits. Yet Selous's condemnation of the Africans, which reflected the colonial mentality, has been accepted. In *Between the Sunlight and the Thunder: The Wild Life of Kenya*, a book published in 1962, Noel Simon, a British settler–turned–wildlife enthusiast, repeated Selous's statements and reinforced the indictment of Africans. The book was heralded at the time of its publication by the Conservation Foundation in New York as "an important piece of historical research." However valuable Simon's book is—and it is worth reading for its insights into animal behavior—it suffers from his bias against Africans. "Most Africans are born poachers," Simon declared. There were few whites at the time who did not share this prejudice. The journals of the Fauna Preservation Society, which published reports from the wild-life departments in Kenya, Tanganyika and Uganda as well as papers by conservationists, are replete with condemnations of African poachers for destroying the game; and the Americans and Europeans who founded the conservation organizations that came into being in the 1960s, such as the African Wildlife Foundation (AWF) and the World Wildlife Fund (WWF), acted out of a conviction that the Africans would destroy the wildlife.

There is, however, a polar opposite view about Africans and wildlife: that they lived in beautiful harmony and if the white man had never come, the peaceful coexistence would have continued into eternity. There is some truth to this belief. Many tribes had cultural taboos against killing too many animals. The Boran, for example, believed that a person who killed a bird of prey, such as an eagle, would go mad or die (a belief that still exists); and there were practical reasons for conserving the animals— the people needed them for food and clothes. Also, most African tribes were animists, and that means they worshipped animals. Christian mis-sionaries, on the other hand, brought the Bible, and in Genesis God commands man to exercise "dominion over the fish of the sea, and over the fowl of the air and over every living thing that moveth upon the earth." (This is still the prevailing Judeo-Christian ethic, though an in-creasing number of ethical and religious thinkers argue, stated most simply, that since God put man and animal on earth, He intended them to be treated equally.)

At the same time, however, the notion that before the Europeans came, Africans and animals lived in a state of natural peace is heavily influenced by modern Western romanticism, and is as creed-bound as the view that all Africans are poachers. To begin with, not all tribes had the same attitudes toward wildlife as the Boran. Some tribes killed large numbers of animals, by setting fires or digging huge pits, and then driving the animals toward them. The romantic notion also fails to recognize that not all Africans were hunter-gatherers or pastoralists for whom wildlife was not a threat; many were agriculturalists and therefore no more toler-ant of marauding herds of elephants or baboons than were their white settler neighbors. Ultimately, inevitably, the majority of Africans would have advanced from being hunter-gatherers and pastoralists to becoming agriculturalists and urbanites. By the 1950s, in East Africa, many Africans were engaged in wide-scale commercial poaching to supply meat and skins to growing urban populations. And they were no longer using only poison arrows, of course, but now had the bolt-action rifle and would soon be armed with the AK-47; as weapons became more sophisticated and potent—and more of them found their way into the continent during wars—the threat to the wildlife would become exponentially more serious. What might have come to pass, we will, of course, never know, for the white man did come with his laws. And at the time that he did, they were needed because he, and not the African, was destroying the game.

The 1900 Convention "had been necessitated by the unbridled hunting of game, by Europeans," Richard Fitter and Sir Peter Scott, two prominent British naturalists, wrote in *The Penitent Butchers*, a brief history of the Fauna Preservation Society. In Kenya at the turn of the century, lions were being slaughtered by big-game hunters, by settlers protecting their cattle, by the builders of the rail line from Mombasa to Lake Victoria. It was the European settlers in the Cape, at the southern tip of the continent, who were responsible for the first known extinctions of species in Africa, and they took care of two, the blaubok and the quagga, both of which existed in great numbers on the veldt when the settlers arrived. The blaubok, or bluebuck, was an antelope of the same genus as the roan and the sable; it was eliminated before 1800, primarily because the settlers took over the animal's grazing land for their cattle. The quagga, which looked like a stout pony, with an equine mane and zebra stripes, was gone by 1860. The Boers not only fenced the quagga out of their pastureland, but also hunted them for their skins, which they used for grain bags. (An exhibit in the British Museum of Natural History today raises the question of whether it might be possible to "re-create" the quagga using DNA.)

Recognition that the European settlers were responsible for the destruction of the game is found in a comment by the first governor of British East Africa, Sir Charles Eliot. "By a fortunate law of distribution white settlers have not hitherto much frequented the districts where there is most game," Eliot wrote in 1903. When they begin to move into those areas, he went on, "I do not think it will be found possible to make them observe" the laws against killing certain wild animals. He did not think any species would become extinct, however, but the reason was that "the greatest variety of forms, if not the largest herds, seem to be found near Baringo and between Voi and Taveta, neither of which localities are likely to attract Europeans."

THE STORY of the threat to the African elephant parallels the European conquest of the African continent and the growth of the white man's quest for ivory. It is a story marked by paradoxes and switchbacks—ivory greed threatening the elephant, then saving it, then threatening it again.

Ivory has been treasured going back millennia when women coveted it for combs and mirrors, and rulers used it to decorate their thrones and tombs; before the end of the first century A.D., the Roman Empire had exhausted virtually all of the African ivory it could find, denuding the northernmost reaches of the continent. In modern times, the Portuguese were the first to bring ivory out of Africa because they were the first to sail around the continent and establish trading posts, in Angola and Mozambique. The serious ivory trade, and alarming slaughter of elephants, began with the coming of the Boer and then English settlers to the southern tip of Africa. When the Europeans arrived in the 1600s, elephants were in abundance; by 1800, there was little more chance of seeing one around Cape Town and Port Elizabeth than there would be today in those modern coastal cities. Alarmed by the depletion of the elephant herds, in 1822 the British prohibited shooting an elephant, or a hippopotamus, in the Cape Colony without a license, the first major game protection law in Africa.

There was still an abundance of elephants in the interior, however, and the European hunters went after them, opening up the country as they searched for the huge pachyderms. In the 1870s, 100,000 pounds of ivory was exported from what is now Zimbabwe; that probably represented the death of two thousand elephants. One prominent hunter, William Baldwin, who traded with African chiefs for ivory and acquired his own by shooting elephants, accumulated 350 pounds of ivory on one trip and 100 pounds another time; he once killed eight elephants in a half hour, and during another expedition he shot six bulls, whose tusks weighed 250 pounds. Baldwin had a plethora of rivals who matched his voracious appetite for elephants and ivory, and by the end of the century, the elephant populations had been decimated between the Limpopo and Zambezi rivers; the elephant would recover in those areas, however, and in recent years some of the worst poaching has occurred in the Zambezi Valley.

It was a similar story in Central and East Africa. Ivory, in fact, was what lured the nineteenth-century explorers into the dark continent and what financed their getting there. European governments thought the continent harbored many El Dorados, but with the exception of Cecil Rhodes, who pushed up from the Cape in search of diamonds and gold, the resources coveted by the European entrepreneurs were not minerals from the earth—not cobalt or tungsten, and back then, not even copper or oil. Ivory was the lure. Belgium's King Leopold believed there was enough ivory in the Congo basin to finance the Congo Free State, an assessment his hired explorer, Henry Stanley, shared; but Stanley knew that to control the ivory in the Congo and beyond he would have to ward off other European countries and deal with Arab businessmen who controlled trading. The most notorious trader was certainly Hamed bin Mohammed, alias Tippu-Tib (also, Tibbu-Tib), who operated from the Indian Ocean island of Zanzibar. One of the first African explorers, he was described by Stanley as "a tall, black-bearded man, of negroid complexion, in the prime of life, straight, and quick in his movements, a picture of energy and strength." He was, Stanley exclaimed, "a remarkable man—the most remarkable man I had met among the Arabs, Wa-Swahili, and the half-castes in Africa." Tippu-Tib provided protection, guns and couriers for Stanley, and on one of his expeditions, Stanley negotiated with Tippu-Tib for 600 carriers "at £6 per loaded head" to carry ammunition from Stanley Falls to Lake Albert; on their way out, the men would haul seventy pounds of ivory each.

From deep inside Somalia, Sudan, Uganda and Tanganyika, as well as the Congo, ivory was packed out by long human trains. Then, it was shipped by dhow across to Zanzibar, before moving to India and Europe; later, after Britain colonized Kenya, the port of Mombasa became the major departure point for ivory, and so vital was the ivory trade to that city, continuing until the 1960s, that the city fathers erected two towering metal tusks, which still stand, four lanes of traffic passing under them. As Americans and Europeans grew richer with the rise of industrial capitalism, their consumption of ivory increased. In the last decade of the nineteenth century, the British imported about one million pounds of ivory a year and the Americans about half that much. It was used for cutlery, combs and billiard balls; but most of it was shaved into piano keys—American piano makers were turning out three hundred thousand units a year at the turn of the century—and pianists spoke about "tickling the ivories."

The craving for ivory was accompanied by fears that the elephant would be wiped out. In 1874, the secretary of the American Geographical Society, Alvan Southworth, traveled several thousand miles up the Nile, through the Sudan and into Central Africa. He was primarily interested in finding the elusive sources of the great river and examining the slave trade, but in his account of the journey, he commented on the ivory trade. "Ivory traders, wars and civilization" were eliminating the elephant, he wrote, "and it is thought that a few years more will suffice to extinguish the last vestige of the African colossi." The same warning was sounded by British explorer Joseph Thomson, who acquired fame for becoming the first European to cross Maasailand and for whom the Thomson's gazelle was named. "It may be safely predicted that in twenty years, the noble African elephant will be a rare animal," Thomson wrote, after leading a British Royal Geographical Society expedition to East and Central Africa between 1878 and 1880. A century later, Americans and Europeans who wanted a ban on ivory trading were expressing forebodings identical to those of Southworth and Thomson.

That the earlier fears proved to be unfounded does not in itself mean that current ones can be dismissed. First of all, a century ago, most of Africa's jungles had not been penetrated by the white man, so it was impossible for him to know that while the elephant, and other game, might be disappearing from the areas he explored, they were in abundance in areas still inaccessible to him. Moreover, actions to save the elephant were taken. But, in stunning contrast to the contemporary attitude that a ban on ivory trading is needed to save the African elephant, it was a desire to *promote* the ivory trade that was behind the early laws.

In 1888, the British government gave the Imperial British East Africa Company a license to operate in the vast region of East Africa that extended from the Indian Ocean to beyond Lake Victoria. The British had decided to exercise their control over the territory through this company rather than by making it a colony because there was little public support in Britain at the time for establishing colonies in Africa, largely because it was felt they would be a drain on the Treasury. Then, as now, wildlife was the region's most valuable resource, and just about its only exportable one. Consequently, the company imposed a 15 percent duty on ivory exports, along with a 10 percent duty on the export of rhino horn and hippopotamus teeth. The East Africa Company was an economic failure, and in 1894 Britain, now in a geopolitical contest with Germany, which was making advances in East Africa, established the Uganda Protectorate, and a year later the British East Africa Protectorate (Kenya).

Almost immediately, London enacted laws to save the elephant. Again, it was not acting out of a moral commitment to preserve a priceless heritage. It was a matter of economics. In the British East Africa Protectorate, ivory accounted for nearly half of export earnings, and the government feared that unless something was done, "no ivory is likely to be obtained after the next fifteen or twenty years," as a concerned British government official had warned in 1890. To stave off this economic catastrophe, the government prohibited the shooting of female elephants or any elephant whose tusks weighed less than ten pounds each. These regulations were the first wildlife conservation laws in Africa, outside the Cape Colony.

Then came the London Convention of 1900. Though the treaty dealt with all wild animals, the delegates were most concerned about the elephant. Still, the treaty did not completely ban the shooting of elephants. It only prohibited shooting infants, females when accompanied by their offspring, and elephants whose tusks weighed less than eleven pounds each. Behind these protections of "women and children" was some elephant biology: an elephant's tusks, which are actually protruding teeth, continue to grow throughout its lifetime, and in a male more rapidly in later years. This may not have been scientifically established in 1900, but European hunters had spent enough time in the field observing elephants to know that the bigger ones had bigger tusks. Thus the objective of the prohibitions was simple: keep elephants alive until they grow older and their tusks are worth more. The heaviest pair of tusks ever recorded weighed 440 pounds. They were taken from an old elephant killed on the slopes of Mount Kilimanjaro in 1898 and sold by Tippu-Tib for $5,000; ten feet tall, they were later on display in the British Museum of Natural History. Today it is unlikely that anything near that weight exists on the continent and even a 200-pound pair of tusks, which was common a century ago, is rare, because poachers kill elephants before they reach maturity.

The game regulations enacted in Uganda and Kenya in accordance with the 1900 Convention brought about the desired conservation almost immediately. "The most direct result of the Regulations has been to afford partial immunity to the large herds of elephants," a British colonial officer, Colonel Hayes Sadler, reported from Uganda in 1903. He noted a considerable increase in elephants along the western shore of Lake Albert, which, he added, offered "perhaps the best field in this part of East Africa to the sportsman anxious to secure a large pair of tusks." Sadler pointed out, however, that "whilst preserving the elephant, we have also to think of the people. Latterly, and as a practical result of protection, many complaints have been received of damage done to shambas and cultivation by elephants, plantations being destroyed, and, in several instances, habitations and villages being deserted." It would be necessary to shoot the elephants that were causing the destruction, Sadler said. Sadler's understanding of what the presence of elephants often means to Africans was generally lacking among the Western advocates of the ivory ban eighty years later, most of whom, unlike Sadler, had never been to Africa.

In Uganda, buffalo and hippopotamuses also thrived because of new game laws, and soon they were wreaking so much havoc that they were necessarily removed from the protected list and classified as vermin. What saved the elephant from that fate? Not a moral crusade. "Only the great demand for ivory prevented the necessity of following the same course with regard to the elephant," Theodore Roosevelt wrote in *African Game Trails*, the account of his 1909 safari.

Even progressive conservationists, men who posited an aesthetic and moral basis for preserving wildlife, thought it was permissible to kill elephants for their ivory. "There must be no general system of making money out of the destruction of game," Captain Caldwell said in a 1924 address to the Kenya and Uganda historical society. But he added, "An exception is made in the case of ivory." The sale of ivory financed the Kenyan game department. In 1923, for example, the department earned £16,000 from the sale of ivory; the cost of running the department was only £4,000. Though the price of ivory fell, largely because of the depression, in 1934 the department took in £9,709 from the sale of ivory and rhino horn (ivory accounted for at least 75 percent of that amount), while its total expenditures were just under £9,000.

The price of ivory remained relatively stable, and low, for several decades. In 1970, raw ivory brought only about $2.50 a pound. Then it soared, fetching $60 a pound by the end of the decade. No one seems certain why the price rose so dramatically, but it coincided with the oil crises and a period of financial instability brought on when the United States took the dollar off the gold standard. Many people, it seemed, bought ivory, like gold or silver, for its intrinsic value.

Whatever the causes, the price rise was accompanied by an escalation in poaching, and warnings were sounded. "Elephant poaching in Africa has reached such alarming proportions that it is feared the elephant may become extinct in the next five years," the African Wildlife Foundation wrote to its members in 1973; in Kenya alone, the organization said, at least 1,000 elephants were being poached each month. Fifteen years later, AWF would use virtually identical language when it called for a boycott on buying ivory. AWF's warning in 1973 had had little effect. Between 1973 and 1977, Kenya's elephant population fell from an estimated 167,000 to 59,000. The pursuit of ivory was not the only cause for the decline—a drought and increasing human population contributed— but it was certainly an important, if not the major, one.

Ivory trading was legal in Kenya, with government permits, but there was not enough legal ivory to supply the demand and between 10,000 and 25,000 elephants were illegally killed each year for their ivory, an official in the Kenya game department, Peter Jarman, concluded in 1973. Corruption was pervasive. In his thirteen-page confidential report, Jarman noted that prominent individuals were involved in the illegal trade, including two assistant ministers responsible for wildlife management. The same year, Ian Parker, a former game warden and active conservationist, was asked to look at the ivory trade by a wealthy businessman, Jack Block, who owned the popular Norfolk Hotel in Nairobi, and who was also chairman of the local WWF chapter. Parker discovered that traders arranged with poachers in advance to buy the ivory and that it was not only Kenyan elephants that were being poached; even more of the illegal ivory was coming from elephants killed in Tanzania and the Sudan, then smuggled into Kenya before being shipped on or carved in Kenya for sale to tourists. In a report that Block considered too sensitive to be made public, Parker said that "there are people of great political consequence in Kenya involved in the ivory trade." (He was careful not to name them.) In 1975, a cabinet minister told the *Sunday Times* of London that he had been instructed by President Jomo Kenyatta to issue a permit to export fifteen tons of ivory to one of the president's daughters, Margaret, who was mayor of Nairobi, and a permit for five tons to the foreign minister. The principal ivory trader was Mama Ngina, President Kenyatta's fourth wife.

Under pressure from the World Bank, which was giving money to Kenya for tourism, Kenya banned all hunting in 1977, and when that didn't achieve the desired goal of halting the poaching, the next year the government put an end to the sale of any wildlife products, such as zebra skins and impala horns, as well as ivory carvings, which was a blow to many small shopkeepers in Nairobi. Poaching nonetheless continued— there was simply too much money to be made and too much corruption.

In America, conservationists succeeded, in 1978, in having the elephant classified as a "threatened" species under United States law; therefore a permit was required in order to bring ivory into the country. The United States market, though, was not the most important one, and still isn't, contrary to the popular perception. In the debate preceding the 1989 ban on ivory trading, it was claimed by the advocates of the ban that Americans consumed one-third of the ivory. But it was a third of the *worked* ivory—that is, ivory already carved, whether into figurines or piano keys—not of the raw material. For most of the past two decades, Americans have consumed only about 10 percent of the ivory leaving Africa.

Since the 1970s, Japan and Hong Kong have been the major markets for ivory. In Japan, most of the ivory is carved into *hanko*—seals—which the Japanese use in lieu of signatures on checks and other important documents. Once only a small elite could afford a seal, but as the Japanese economy boomed and the middle class expanded, so did the demand for seals. The ever-richer Japanese also began buying more ivory figurines. Until 1970, the amount of raw ivory going into Japan rarely exceeded 150,000 pounds a year; during the seventies, it averaged 500,000 pounds annually, and in 1983, Japan consumed just over 1,000,000 pounds of elephant tusks. In the early 1980s, even more ivory was being shipped into Hong Kong—600 *tons* in 1983—where most of it was carved into figurines and sold to tourists—Europeans, Americans and, increasingly, newly wealthy Asians.

Since it was the greed in the developed world, West and East, that was contributing to the devastation of African elephant herds, it was fair to expect the developed world to take some actions to protect the elephant. But the actions it would take were as irresponsible as the greed.

PATRICIANS

IT IS ALWAYS difficult to define precisely when any movement begins, and when it is successful the task is compounded, because there is no shortage of individuals and organizations who will write the campaign's history in order to exalt their role in it. That has happened with the ivory ban crusade. Numerous conservation groups now boast in their fund-raising appeals that this was their victory, that they were the ones who pushed to have the elephant declared an endangered species and to have ivory trading banned; even some organizations that initially opposed a ban claim credit. Nonetheless, on close and objective examination, it can fairly be stated that the campaign that led to the prohibition on commercial trading in ivory at Lausanne in October 1989 began with actions taken a year and a half earlier by the African Wildlife Foundation, a relatively small conservation organization at the time with its headquarters in Washington, D.C., and a field office in Nairobi.

In February 1988, AWF sent out a message to its supporters. It was signed by the organization's president, Paul Schindler, and was couched in personal language. "With great sadness I find I must write to tell you that the plight of Africa's wild elephants is far more desperate than I could have ever imagined," Schindler began. Styled as an "Urgent Memorandum," the appeal was prepared by a California company skilled in direct-mail solicitation, and it was designed to shock and raise money; it succeeded in both. The two-page "memorandum" said that in Kenya the number of elephants had declined from 165,000 fifteen years before to 20,000; that all 5,000 elephants remaining in Kenya's Tsavo National Park—down from 30,000 in the 1970s—would be dead in seventeen months; that half of the 50,000 elephants in Tanzania's Selous Game Reserve (the largest protected area in Africa) had been killed in the last eight years; that in Uganda, 90 percent "of these beautiful animals have been wiped out"; and that in the Sudan, 10,000 elephants die each year, or "more than 27 a day, every day, for the last 10 years in just one country in Africa." AWF said it was the "insatiable greed of the ivory hunters" that was responsible for the "slaughter," and to stop it, the organization was declaring 1988 the "Year of the Elephant," and was mounting a public awareness campaign. The foundation asked for tax-deductible gifts of $25, $35, $50 or more to support its cause.

The money started coming in immediately, and three months later, the organization elevated its campaign with a press conference at the National Zoo in Washington, D.C.; for maximum emotional value, it was held in the yard of the zoo's African elephant, Nancy. AWF's vice-president, Diana McMeekin, told reporters that in 1977 there had been 1,300,000 elephants in Africa; now there were 730,000. McMeekin is a striking blonde woman who only a few months earlier had still worn ivory bracelets herself—because neither she nor AWF had seen anything wrong with buying ivory. Now, however, they were converts, and she issued the organization's plea: "Don't Buy Ivory." The public reaction to the press conference staggered the organization. Though AWF was well known in Kenya and Rwanda, where the organization's elephant logo marks its vehicles, few Americans knew of the African Wildlife Foundation; after the press conference, McMeekin was being heard around the country, appearing on twenty to twenty-five radio shows a week.

AWF wasn't asking for a complete ban on trading at this time. It only wanted consumers voluntarily to forgo buying ivory. Nevertheless, outside of AWF there were hardly any scientists or professional conservationists who thought that even a limited restriction of the ivory trade was a good idea. Above all, the world's wealthiest conservation organization, WWF, the one with the panda logo, did not. Eventually, however, in the face of public pressure, WWF would do a complete about-face and call for an international ban on all trading, as would AWF. Many organizations joined the ivory ban crusade, but these two were the most eminent and critical to its success. Though in 1989 WWF dwarfed AWF in terms of members, money and visibility, the two organizations—born in the same year, 1961, fathered by patricians who were convinced that whites had to act or the Africans would destroy the game—had much in common.

THE AFRICAN WILDLIFE LEADERSHIP FOUNDATION (AWF's original name) was conceived in the late 1950s by a tax court judge and his friends, wealthy men who were avid big-game hunters. The judge was

Russell E. Train, who today is recognized as the doyen of the mainstream conservation movement in America—he was the first chairman of the White House Council on Environmental Quality, has been head of the Environmental Protection Agency, and is now chairman of WWF in the United States. Train is the embodiment of commitment to public service and comfortably a member of the closest thing America has to an aristocracy. For many years he has been a member of one of the oldest and most exclusive clubs in North America, the Long Point Company, whose fewer than twenty members—Mellons and the like—own their own spit of land, which thrusts into Lake Erie. The "E" engraved on Train's cuff links and embroidered on his shirts is evidence that he can trace his lineage back to the fourteenth-century Scottish Erroll family who became part of the British royalty (though Train's family later dropped the last "l"). Train also married well, to Aileen Bowdoin, a descendant of James Bowdoin, a member of the Massachusetts colonial legislature; though Train was a devout Republican, Aileen Bowdoin was a bridesmaid when Jacqueline Bouvier became Mrs. John F. Kennedy. Train followed the pattern of his social class, beginning with an elite prep school (St. Albans in Washington, D.C.), and then on to Princeton University, from which he graduated in 1941 (the same year the playboy Earl of Erroll was shot in the head in Nairobi, the murder becoming the grist for gossip at the time and for the 1988 movie *White Mischief*). After service in the army during World War II, Train went to law school at Columbia. Then he embarked on a Washington career. At the age of thirty-three he was already chief counsel to the powerful House Ways and Means Committee, and in 1957 President Eisenhower appointed Train a federal tax judge; at thirty-seven, he was the youngest man on the federal bench.

On vacation a year earlier, Train had ventured to Kenya on a hunting safari. Several times he and his wife had to scurry up trees to escape charging rhino. "Never thought I could climb a thorn tree, but it's remarkable how well you can—my wife said I went past her," Train recalled with amusement thirty years later. He hunted along the Athi River, east of Nairobi, which was heavily populated with rhino then; today there are almost none. On Train's second safari, in 1958, he shot an elephant. Its left tusk weighed 105 pounds and the right one, 102. Bagging an elephant with tusks weighing more than a hundred pounds each has long been every big-game hunter's dream, and the feat earned Train a place in the "Hundred Pounder Club"—his name is third on a plaque that is now a historical item in the Nairobi offices of Ker & Downey, one of the oldest safari companies in Africa. Train is careful not to talk a great deal these days about his shooting an elephant, and the tusks are kept discreetly out of sight from most of his house guests, but he could not resist finishing his reminiscence by noting that Winston Guest, the international socialite, never bagged a hundred-pounder, even though, Train remembers with further relish, Guest had no less than Beryl Markham and Bror Blixen as his guides.

After his second safari, Train was invited to gatherings of the African Safari Club of Washington, an informal social club of men who got together over drinks and dinner to swap tales about their hunting exploits in Africa. On one such occasion, at the Roma Restaurant on Connecticut Avenue in Washington, D.C.—the owner of the restaurant was a member of the African Safari Club—it was suggested that the club should have a conservation program in Africa. Soon after, Train convened a meeting in his tax chambers, attended by, among others, Kermit Roosevelt, grandson of Theodore Roosevelt. The group came to an obvious conclusion—that if it was going to engage in conservation work in Africa, it would have to raise money. "That meant that we needed to have a nonprofit, tax-exempt organization, otherwise people wouldn't give the money," Train recalled. One day in March 1961, Judge Train gave his law clerk $12 and sent him a few blocks to file the articles of incorporation for the African Wildlife Leadership Foundation, AWLF, which would become the African Wildlife Foundation, AWF, in 1983.

The men who joined Train in establishing AWLF had much in common with the patriarchs of the Fauna Preservation Society, which had been the first conservation organization to focus on saving Africa's wildlife. For one thing, they were serious big-game hunters. The shooting editor of *Field and Stream* was on AWLF's original board of trustees, and the first issue of the *African Wildlife News*, the organization's newsletter, carried an advertisement for the Mark V rifle: "Now, White Hunters regard the Mark V as standard equipment for the safari whose sporting purpose is clean kills with a single shot." Like their British predecessors, but unlike most of today's environmentalists and Greens, the AWLF founding fathers were also politically conservative. On the walls of Train's office today hang expensively framed and warmly inscribed photographs of Train with Richard Nixon, whom Train served for his entire presidency; with Ronald and Nancy Reagan; and with George Bush. One of AWLF's founders and first board members was Maurice Stans, who had hunted in Kenya, Tanganyika, Ruanda-Urundi, Somalia and Angola and who belonged to the East African Professional Hunters Association. Stans was director of the budget during the Eisenhower administration and gained notoriety during Watergate, when he was Nixon's finance chairman; he was indicted but not convicted for receiving illegal campaign contributions. Another original board member was Kermit Roosevelt, who had hunted jaguar in Brazil, and ibex and mouflon in Iran; in 1953 Roosevelt had been in charge of the CIA's operation that toppled the government of Iran and put Shah Mohammad Reza Pahlavi on the throne. A third trustee, Edward Sweeney, was a member of the Subversive Activities Control Board, an association that AWLF listed first in its biographical sketch of Sweeney.

Given their political orientation, it is not surprising that Train and his friends were spurred to act by the independence fires then blazing through Africa. Their attitude is revealed in the editorial in the first issue of the organization's newsletter. "For better or for worse, the future of most of Africa's game country and the fate of its wildlife resources are in the hands of Africans themselves," Train wrote. There is little doubt that he and his colleagues thought it would be for worse. The editorial went on, "The political realities of present-day Africa are too plain to require spelling out here. The essential need is that we face up to that reality and do not fall back upon wishful thinking." The reality was that in just two years, 1960 and 1961, some twenty African countries became independent, and that meant whites would no longer dominate conservation, at least not in government positions. *"In Tanganyika alone, the government recently ordered 100 percent Africanization of the game service by 1966!"* Train wrote, his italics revealing the horror he felt. And he added, lest any doubt remain, "Replacement of European staff by untrained, unqualified men spells disaster for the game."

Train was right to fear that Europeans would be replaced by people without qualifications—virtually no Africans had been trained in conservation or wildlife management. In fact, most Britons who were working as wardens, rangers and park managers had had no formal training. They were, as Train notes, "dedicated amateurs." They were men who liked adventure and the outdoors; many were retired army officers who had come to Africa during the wars or to serve in the British colonial service, and had then stayed. Men like Captain Keith Caldwell, who had served in World War I; Myles Turner, who had served in the East African Reconnaissance Squadron in World War II and after the war had become a warden, first in the Serengeti and then in Kenya's Maasai Mara; George

Adamson, who had knocked about building roads and prospecting for gold before becoming a game warden at the age of thirty-two; or Noel Simon, who had come after World War II to settle as a farmer, became a wildlife enthusiast, founded the East African Wildlife Society, and wrote prolifically about conservation, as in his book *Between the Sunlight and the Thunder*. The British wardens and professional hunters hired Africans as trackers, gun bearers and cooks, but they did not promote them to any positions of responsibility.

Train and the other AWLF founders concluded that if Africa's game was to be preserved what was most needed was education and training for Africans. AWLF's first large grant was $47,000 to help establish the College of African Wildlife Management in Mweka, Tanzania—at the base of Mount Kilimanjaro; it was the first school in Africa to train Africans to become wildlife professionals, and today it is one of only two wildlife management colleges in all of sub-Saharan Africa. AWLF also brought Africans to the United States to study wildlife management. "I'll never forget the excitement I had when in response to a letter from me, Robert Maytag—he was head of the Maytag Company then—wrote me and said he would like to sponsor a student to come to the United States, and that turned out to be Perez Olindo," Train recalled. Train remembers the organization's first scholarship with particular satisfaction, because it provided Olindo, a Kenyan, with the academic foundation for a distinguished conservation career in and out of government; during the ivory ban debate, Olindo was a prominent and respected voice, often at odds with the organization that had first helped him.

For several years, Russell Train *was* AWLF. "I was sort of the chief bottle washer, everything else," he said. "I ran it out of my hip pocket." Train built the organization's membership primarily from wealthy Americans who had traveled to Africa on hunting or photographic safaris. Most of them were clients of Ker & Downey, which was founded soon after World War II by two professional hunters, and became the most prestigious of the safari companies, which it remains today. Ker & Downey, which had taken Maurice Stans and Train on their big-game hunting safaris, provided Train with a list of its clients, and Train wrote them to solicit donations. He rented a post office box—"P.O. Box 125, I remember it to this day," Train recalled three decades later—and it was in a building across from the tax court. "Every day at lunch hour I'd go and check P.O. Box 125, and when there was a letter or a check or something, it was quite exciting." In those days, tax court judges rode circuit, and as Train traveled the country, he called on individuals who had expressed an interest in Africa or its wildlife. He looks back on those early years of AWLF fondly. "In some ways it was probably the most satisfying thing I've done because it was purely a one-man show. It was fun. Very gratifying," Train said in 1991, sitting in the plush office, with a couch, coffee table and executive blue-grey carpet which he occupied as chairman of WWF of the United States. A man of patrician bearing, tall, and still trim at seventy-one, Train was wearing a blue seersucker suit and white shirt.

Train had left AWLF in 1969 to go into government—first serving as Nixon's Under Secretary of the Interior, then as the head of the Council on Environmental Quality, and finally moving to the larger and more powerful Environmental Protection Agency. When a Democrat, Jimmy Carter, was elected to the White House, the days of high-level appointments for Train were over, and he left government. Rather than join a law firm or become a lobbyist, Train remained in the nonprofit conservation field, which allowed him to combine his commitment to public service and his passion for the outdoors. He did not return to AWLF, however; that was still too small and insignificant an organization. Instead, in 1978 he became president of the better-known and more influential WWF. In 1985, he relinquished the presidency and became chairman.

After twenty-two years, in 1983 the African Wildlife Leadership Foundation dropped the "Leadership" from its name, a change that did not please Train. He still says "AWLF"—and when he reaches the "L," his voice strikes it like a tympanist. Train's reaction may be a manifestation of the proprietary interest that he had in the original name, or it may reflect his disappointment that the organization he had founded to provide leadership to Africans had, somewhere over the years, lost that as its guiding principle. It had become another garden-variety conservation group, funding Westerners to do research on wild animals, such as Dian Fossey on the gorillas in Rwanda and Cynthia Moss on the elephants in Kenya; their work was important, but it wasn't leadership.

AWF's current president, Paul Schindler, says the name change was needed because the longer name was ponderous and ambiguous. "The public wondered, 'Are you political? Religious? Bearded intellectuals?' " said Schindler, himself a sociologist (and bearded at the time). The public understandably wondered if AWF was a conservation organization. The top officials have lacked any conservation or scientific credentials—at best they, too, have been "dedicated amateurs." Train was replaced as president by a wealthy Texan, John Rhea, who made his money in real estate and oil and gas, and was a big-game hunter and member of the National Rifle Association. Following Rhea's retirement, AWF turned to diplomats, first Robinson McIlvaine, who had been an ambassador to Guinea and Kenya, and then Robert Smith, who had spent twenty-six years in the State Department, most of them in Africa. Schindler, who became president in 1985, has a doctorate in sociology and "has additional studies in philosophy, classics, business and history," according to his official résumé; for several years he was a professor of sociology at various universities and colleges in the Midwest.

At the time of AWF's thirtieth birthday, in 1991, the board of trustees was still dominated, as it had been from the beginning, by wealthy socialites, living in such exclusive and fashionable enclaves as Palm Beach; Lake Forest, Illinois; Portola Valley, California; Colorado Springs; McLean, Virginia. Many were also members of other nonprofit boards— the Field Museum of Natural History in Chicago; the Cleveland Zoological Society; the Cheyenne Mountain Zoo—and they included numerous celebrities such as John Heminway, the writer and documentary filmmaker, who was chairman of the board; George Plimpton; and Gloria Stewart, wife of the actor James Stewart.

Whatever the public thought about AWF, it did not think enough to provide much financial support. In 1988, when it launched its elephant campaign, AWF had a budget for that year of $2 million and a staff of only six working out of modest offices on the sixth floor of a building on Massachusetts Avenue. In contrast, across town, in an airy, expensively renovated building, the United States chapter of WWF had 450,000 members, a staff of 200, and a budget for 1988 of $23 million.

WWF IS NOT ONLY the largest conservation organization in the world, it is one of the largest charitable organizations in any field. It has five million members on five continents, and their donations now exceed $200 million annually. Though WWF's logo is the Chinese panda and its programs today stretch from Bhutan (helping to establish the first national park) to Israel (studying cave ecosystems) to Chile (controlling the trade in alerce wood), it is in Africa that the organization's history begins.

In 1960, Sir Julian Huxley, the eminent scientist and first head of

UNESCO, spent three months traveling around East, Central and South Africa, and wrote three long pieces for *The Observer*. Not since articles by John Muir eighty years earlier—which led to the foundation of the Sierra Club—had one person's writings had such a direct impact on organized conservation. And by the 1960s, Muir's ethical notions of preserving wild animals and space for their own sake were an influential strain in Western conservation, largely because urbanization and industrialization had destroyed so much of our natural heritage. Indeed, it was precisely because the developed world had done so poorly in conserving its own natural resources that it expected Africans to preserve theirs—and in many cases virtually demanded it.

Huxley's prose soared. "To see large animals going about their natural business in their own natural way, assured and unafraid, is one of the most exciting and moving experiences in the world, comparable with the sight of a noble building or the hearing of a great symphony," he wrote. "A processional frieze of antelopes moving across the African horizon rivals any theatrical spectacle. And I can testify that my first sight of a troop of elephants, old and young, making their way down to water to drink and bathe and play, and then composedly and majestically disappearing into the bush, was profoundly satisfying."

It was also sobering:

> Many parts of Kenya and Tanganyika and the Rhodesias which fifty years ago were swarming with game are now bare of all large wild life. Throughout the area, cultivation is extending, native cattle are multiplying at the expense of wild animals, poaching is becoming heavier and more organised, forests are being cut down or destroyed, means are being found to prevent cattle suffering from tsetse-borne diseases, large areas are being over-grazed and degenerating into semi-desert, and above and behind all this, the human population is inexorably mounting to press even harder on the limited land space.

One reader who was moved by Huxley's articles wrote back, "There must be a way to the conscience and the heart and pride and vanity of the very rich people to persuade them to sink their hands deeply into their pockets." The writer, a Victor Stolan, was not himself one of those rich. He was an immigrant from Czechoslovakia who as a child had acquired a love for animals. Stolan had some business experience—he had run a country hotel in England until gasoline rationing had so inhibited travel that it had to close—and he had some ideas about how to raise money, but he knew he was not the person to head the effort. So he asked Huxley to put him in touch "with somebody with whom ideas can be developed and speedily directed towards accumulating some millions of pounds without mobilising commissions, committees, etc. as there is no time for Victorian procedure." Huxley knew just the person, and he passed the letter on to E. M. (Max) Nicholson, who realized Stolan's dream.

Nicholson has received far less public acclaim for his contributions to the conservation movement than he deserves. His vision and energy led to the creation in Britain of the Nature Conservancy Council, and World War II had barely ended when Nicholson, Huxley and others began to think internationally about conservation, though as Nicholson recalls, "it seemed rather far-fetched" to be talking about conservation, given the war damage London and Europe had sustained. "Nineteen people were killed in that church by the same bomb," Nicholson recalled, motioning down the street, when we talked on a spring day in 1991 in the garden of his home in the Chelsea section of London. He was attired in a dark suit, white shirt, and tie, and though in his eighties, he had a remarkable memory for events decades past.

The end of the war was marked by a new spirit of internationalism, and Nicholson was one of the founders, in 1948, of the International Union for the Conservation of Nature and Natural Resources, or IUCN, which was to become the first lasting international conservation organization. IUCN thrives today and plays a critical role in conservation— though overshadowed by the more public relations–conscious WWF— but at the outset its future was perilous, as no financial base had been established. This was primarily because the organization was staffed by scientists, who as a breed are not particularly good at making appeals for money; besides, there was a general feeling in Europe that a scientist's work was tainted and compromised if it was linked to fund-raising. Nor were the IUCN scientists very effective in getting governments to adopt their conservation recommendations, which were formulated every three years at the IUCN assemblies. What was needed, Nicholson concluded, was an organization that would raise money for IUCN's scientific work in the field and conduct public campaigns generating pressure on governments to implement conservation measures. That organization would be WWF, and IUCN and WWF were married until the mid-eighties, when WWF-International forced an acrimonious split. (WWF wanted to build its own empire, which meant doing its own work in the field, as that was what people gave money for.)

The first international conservation organization may have been founded in Britain—the Society for the Preservation of the Wild Fauna of the Empire—but after World War II, the empire was crumbling (the society even dropped Empire from its name), and the United States was the democratic superpower, economically as well as militarily. Therefore, if an international conservation organization was to be successful, particularly one that was going to raise money, Nicholson knew that American conservationists had to be involved. In February 1961, two months after Stolan's letter, Nicholson went to the United States and met with the heads of the major conservation organizations. He ran into a combination of American provincialism and arrogance—international bodies were not needed and if anything was to be done to save African wildlife, Americans could do it best. The American conservationists were also worried that another group would just be a drain on their contributions, a jealousy that permeates and hinders the conservation movement to this day. "I was so depressed by the reaction I got in America that I thought I would have to report back to Julian Huxley that we couldn't get the support to do anything internationally," Nicholson remembered.

Then, at a meeting in York of the British Ornithologists' Union, Nicholson had a conversation with a friend, Guy Mountfort, the organization's honorary secretary and an ardent naturalist who was co-author of *A Field Guide to the Birds of Europe* and author of *Portrait of a Vanishing Wilderness* (about Spain's Costa Doñana); Mountfort would later write several more nature books. He was also the managing director of Mather & Crowther (soon to become Ogilvy & Mather). "I put this to him in about a ninety-second conversation on the stairs," Nicholson recalled, chuckling as he recounted what transpired. Nicholson told Mountfort about his disappointing experience in the United States and added that he saw no hope unless businessmen could be persuaded to support the cause with substantial donations. Would that be possible? Nicholson asked. "And he thought for about ten seconds, and said, 'I think it is.' And I said, 'Right, we're in business.' "

Encouraged by Mountfort, in the spring and summer of 1961 Nicholson chaired an elite group that included Mountfort, Huxley, Stolan, and Peter Scott, son of the legendary Antarctic explorer. Another amateur conservationist, Scott was beginning to develop his own plans to raise large sums of money for conservation. The group held nine meetings at 19 Belgrave Square, an elegant Victorian town house.

At the planners' sixth meeting, the committee took up the matter of a symbol for the new organization. Someone suggested the panda. The considerations were practical ones: it was recognizable no matter how small it was printed, so it could be used on everything from stationery to lapel buttons, and it looked like the real thing when printed in black and white, another critical factor in those days. The discussion was brief. "One of the most valuable trademarks that has ever been devised, and it took about twenty minutes," Nicholson recalls. Scott, a painter, executed the design that was finally adopted.

Nicholson's group worked in extraordinary secrecy. Minutes were marked "strictly confidential," and even when Scott sent a draft of the proposed constitution to Prince Philip, whom the founders were hoping to recruit to the cause, Scott wrote to Nicholson, "I hope this was all right in spite of its *most confidential* heading." The primary reason for the secrecy was a competitive one. The African Wildlife Foundation had just officially come into existence, "and this made us realize the full horror that within two years there might be a dozen competing wildlife funds, all going for the same source," Nicholson said. It did not happen within two years, but it would within twenty.

WWF had its de facto launch in Arusha, Tanganyika, in September 1961. The occasion was a conference that had been called by IUCN to persuade the leaders of the newly independent African governments about the importance of conserving their wildlife. "This was no doubt patrician," says Nicholson, who was instrumental in organizing the conference. Indeed, the founders of WWF were patricians and paternalistic, as were their counterparts at AWLF. Livingstone, Stanley and other explorers and missionaries had come to Africa in the nineteenth century to promote the three C's—Christianity, commerce and civilization. Now a fourth was added: conservation. These modern secular missionaries were convinced that without the white man's guidance, the Africans would go astray. "We felt that under the new African governments, all prospect of conservation of nature would be ended," Nicholson says. It would have been hard to find a white person working in African conservation at the time who was not convinced that independence would bring the end of the game. "The notion of conserving the creatures of the wild to ensure their continuance into the future is alien to the African," Noel Simon wrote in *Between the Sunlight and the Thunder*.

Nicholson wanted to launch WWF with a "Declaration of a State of Emergency," which would be signed by new African leaders as well as scientists and conservationists in Europe and the United States. The proposed declaration was sent to Tanganyika's Julius Nyerere, leader of the independence movement in his country and already an international voice for Africans. Nyerere balked. He felt conservation was important but given what the new nations were facing, it was hardly an "emergency." Peter Scott described Nyerere's reaction as a "bore," but added that something should be done to accommodate him. The WWF founders then persuaded Nyerere to issue a conservation proclamation in his own name, and he opened the Arusha meeting with a brief statement: "The survival of our wildlife is a matter of grave concern to all of us in Africa. . . . In accepting the trusteeship of our wildlife we solemnly declare that we will do everything in our power to make sure that our children's grandchildren will be able to enjoy this rich and precious inheritance."

Nyerere's three-paragraph declaration has been heralded over time. "The Arusha Manifesto can justly be described as a beacon in the history of wildlife conservation in Africa," the chief game warden in Tanganyika at the time, a British citizen, has written (condescendingly). The manifesto is often cited today by Africans to display their commitment to conservation. It was written by Europeans, including Nicholson and Ian MacPhail, an advertising executive hired by WWF; they even titled it the Arusha Manifesto. Nyerere accepted what the Europeans had given him without any changes, but he insisted on delivering it himself, whereas the Europeans had wanted all of the African leaders attending the summit to sign the declaration. (Nyerere's conservation manifesto at Arusha in 1961 is not to be confused with his more famous Arusha Declaration, which he issued in 1967, setting out the country's socialist course.)

A month after the Arusha meeting, WWF exploded on the public, in a "Shock Issue" of the *Daily Mirror*, which at the time had the largest circulation in Britain, and perhaps in the world—five and a half million readers. The tabloid's front page shouted:

> DOOMED—to disappear from the face of the earth due to Man's FOLLY, GREED, NEGLECT

Beneath that was the photograph of a rhino, a peculiar-looking one. Rather than a short horn that arched upward from the snout, this rhino's horn extended almost parallel to the ground for four and a half feet. The rhino, Gerti, lived in Kenya's Amboseli park. The text in the *Daily Mirror*, six pages altogether, continued:

> UNLESS . . . unless something is done swiftly animals like this rhino and its baby will soon be as dead as the dodo.

On page 2 was an elephant, with its trunk raised.

TRUMPET CALL FOR HELP—will YOU answer it?

Bags of mail poured in and most letters contained contributions. "At one point, we had £10,000, in this very house," recalls Ian MacPhail, WWF's first paid employee and the man behind the *Daily Mirror* promotion. There were "dirty, ten-shilling notes," a donation from Winston Churchill (£50, MacPhail believes), contributions from pensioners and convicts; the letter MacPhail remembers best was from a woman who wrote, "I was saving up to buy a pair of shoes, but I think the elephants need it more." Nicholson and Scott had both thought that the most effective way to support the organization was with large donations from the wealthy, and Shell International and a millionaire London property owner, Jack Cotton, did donate £10,000 each. But the *Daily Mirror*, a liberal working-class newspaper, raised £30,000 (the equivalent today of £200,000, or more than $350,000).

To attract donors, large and small, as well as media attention, Nicholson, Scott and the founding fathers of WWF wanted the royal family to lend their name. They approached Prince Philip to be president. Philip was an avid outdoorsman and hunter—in January 1961 he had bagged a Bengal tiger in India—and he and Queen Elizabeth had been to Kenya, on a safari best remembered because King George VI died while they were watching wild animals and Princess Elizabeth had become Queen. Scott sent Philip a draft of the proposed charter. Philip read it carefully, replying that one provision was "unctuous," and another "too wordy." This careful reading was not what Scott had expected. It is "a great bore that he suggests so much alteration," Scott wrote Nicholson. The founding fathers had wanted the Prince only as a figurehead. Philip agreed to head up the British chapter of WWF, but he turned down the presidency of the International and suggested his friend Prince Bernhard for the post. The men were alike in many ways. Both had been born into European royal families, but not very distinguished ones, and had acquired their status and string of titles when they married—Bernhard to the future Queen Juliana of the Netherlands. The two men were handsome, dashing, and staunchly conservative politically.

Scott, who liked consorting with royalty, made the pitch. "Prince Philip (who was sailing with me at Cowes in the 12 metre 'Sceptre' on Saturday) . . . told me that he was very keen that you should 'head-up' the international Trustees," Scott wrote to Bernhard. "Please may I ask

Your Royal Highness to say that you will be President of the Trustees of The World Wildlife Fund." Prince Bernhard eventually said yes, and he served as president until 1976, when he was forced to resign after it became public that he had solicited more than a million dollars in "commissions" from Lockheed in exchange for Lockheed's receiving contracts to build warplanes for the Netherlands. (At one point after the scandal broke, Bernhard said that he had intended to give the money from Lockheed to WWF; a member of the board at the time insists this is not true.)

Bernhard remained active behind the scenes in WWF, but a couple of years after he resigned, Philip became president of the International, and though it was thought he would serve for only a few years, he is still in power. The Prince is a committed conservationist and he undoubtedly has given prestige and visibility to WWF around the world. At the same time, however, many in the Third World have questioned whether he is the right person to head an organization that does most of its work in developing countries. At a meeting of the Commonwealth heads of state, most of them from the Third World and black, Philip said to an aide, "You wouldn't think the peace of the world rested on this lot, would you?" On another occasion, he referred to the Chinese as "slitty-eyed."

WWF WAS SET UP to raise money, but in spite of the initial successes, it did not prove very effective. Nicholson had said that $1.5 million each year would be needed for conservation, which Scott thought he could easily raise; indeed, he anticipated coaxing $25 million from the rich. Scott discovered that socializing with the elite was one thing, getting them to part with their money quite another, and it was several years before the total of WWF's revenues reached $1 million.

WWF's financial fortunes began to change dramatically after a hard-driving South African businessman, Anton Rupert, joined the board. An Afrikaaner from the Cape, Rupert had already made millions as the owner of Rothmans International tobacco company, the foundation of the Rembrandt Group, his wholly owned business empire. When Rupert expanded beyond South Africa, he bought Dunhill and Cartier, and eventually he became one of the richest men in South Africa, rivaled only by Harry Oppenheimer, the gold and diamond industrialist. Rupert had long been interested in conservation, including the restoration of historic buildings, and in 1968 he joined the WWF board of trustees; he stayed on the board for twenty-two years, in spite of a provision in the organization's original incorporation documents that limited members to two three-year terms, a provision that was routinely ignored for the benefit of several other influential members of the board as well. Rupert brought a considerable amount of his own money to WWF, but, more important, he conceived a plan that would raise millions.

Rupert's idea was the "1001 Club." The "one" was Prince Bernhard. The other one thousand were wealthy individuals who could be persuaded to part with $10,000. The one-time donation brings lifetime membership, and the names of the generous patrons are kept secret by the organization. According to these secret lists, American givers have included August A. Busch, Jr., of the beer company; Henry Ford II; Peter Grace; Nelson Bunker Hunt, the silver trader; Mrs. Geoffrey Kent, of Abercrombie & Kent; Robert S. McNamara; Cyril Magnin; Lew Wasserman, of MCA; Thomas Watson, of IBM. Many of the donors understandably wish to remain anonymous (in part to avoid being badgered by other charities), but it is also understandable why WWF does not want the list made public. It has included many less-savory individuals—Zaire's President Mobutu Sese Seko, one of the most corrupt leaders in Africa; Daniel K. Ludwig, the reclusive American billionaire, whose companies destroyed thousands of miles of the Amazon rain forest; Agha Hasan Abedi, the founder of the Bank of Credit and Commerce International (BCCI); Robert Vesco, the financier who fled the United States in the 1970s to escape trial on charges of fraud, embezzlement and obstruction of justice; Tibor Rosenbaum, founder of a Swiss bank that laundered billions of dollars of organized crime money and who was accused of embezzling Israeli deposits in the bank; Thomas Jones, who was forced out as chief executive of Northrop after it was revealed that the company paid $30 million in bribes to government officials and agents around the world in exchange for contracts; Lord Kagan, a British businessman convicted of theft and conspiracy to defraud the British tax service; a Norwegian shipowner convicted of taking a £1 million bribe; an individual who was the conduit for the money from Lockheed to Prince Bernhard.

There has been another remarkable feature about the 1001 Club—the number of South Africans. On the 1989 list, at least sixty individuals were from South Africa, including seven of Rupert's relatives. Many were also members of the Broederbond, the secret, conservative Afrikaaner society that has traditionally wielded immense political power in South Africa. Only five countries had more donors, and as a percentage of their population, South African whites had three hundred times as many members as the United States. It is easy to understand why so many South Africans have been willing to part with $10,000 to join the 1001, and not all of it has to do with conservation. Not many international clubs welcomed white South Africans, and membership in the 1001 provided them an opportunity to mingle and do business with tycoons, as well as with Prince Philip and Prince Bernhard. What else they may have gained from the membership is unknown, in part because so much of what WWF-International does is kept from the public and even from the organization's own trustees. Because of the secrecy and closed nature of the WWF club, it is also difficult to know the extent of the influence that so much South African money has had on the organization's conservation work. There can be little doubt, however, that WWF-International's initial opposition to the ivory ban reflected South African power on the board—South Africa was adamantly opposed to the ban, because its elephants were not being poached and it made money from selling ivory.

One place where South Africa's clout has been felt is in the office of the director-general, the man who runs WWF. Since 1977 that man has been Charles de Haes. Much of de Haes's past is vague, which seems to be by design: he has chosen to reveal very little about his background and some of what the organization does say publicly about him is at odds with the facts. On WWF's public list of officers and trustees, de Haes is identified as being from Belgium, and he was born there, in 1938. But as a young boy, he moved with his family to South Africa. After graduating from Cape Town University with a law degree, he got a job with Rothmans International, Rupert's tobacco company. De Haes's official résumé—that is, the one WWF distributes—makes a point of noting that he went to work for the tobacco company "although himself a non-smoker." It then says de Haes "helped establish companies" in Sudan, Kenya, Uganda and Tanzania. What it does not say is that these were companies that sold cigarettes. Maybe de Haes didn't smoke, but he made money by encouraging others to do so.

De Haes was brought to WWF through the back door by Anton Rupert in 1971. He was first assigned to be personal assistant to Prince Bernhard. One of his tasks was to implement the 1001 Club project. He was tremendously successful. Ten thousand dollars was worth even more back then, yet it took de Haes only three years to find one thousand donors. Prince Bernhard provided the letters of introduction, but de Haes was the salesman who clinched the deals. Even de Haes's fiercest critics—and they are many—use the word "brilliant" when describing his fund-raising skills.

In 1975, with the backing of Rupert and Prince Philip, de Haes was named joint director-general of WWF, and two years later he had the top position to himself. De Haes had no education or experience in conservation, other than his few years at WWF, yet he was now in charge of the most prestigious and influential conservation organization in the world. It was a position that would have appealed to the most qualified and eminent individuals in the field, yet no effort was made to recruit any of them.

WWF may have taken on someone without conservation experience, but then, it cost the organization nothing: Rupert agreed to pay de Haes's salary—which, according to a British trustee, goes far in explaining why de Haes got the job. WWF never said at the time that Rupert was paying de Haes, and it still tries to conceal this fact. The organization's chief spokesman, Robert SanGeorge, stated emphatically during an interview in 1991 that de Haes had not been seconded from Rothmans to Prince Bernhard and WWF during the early years. But an internal WWF memorandum signed by the organization's executive vice-president in 1975 talks specifically about "Mr. de Haes's period of secondment to WWF." What this means, of course, is that de Haes was still employed by a South African corporation while working for WWF. "I thought it was a scandal," says a former board member from North America, who added that it was only by accident that he learned that Rupert was paying de Haes. This board member did not like the arrangement. "Who does the director-general serve? Is the interest of a South African tobacco company synonymous with the world conservation movement?" Even more troubling to this director was the fact that it was kept a secret. "If it was such a good thing, why weren't they willing to say so in the annual report?"

In a similar vein, the organization treats as a state secret the question of who paid de Haes after he became director-general. It was "an anonymous donor," SanGeorge says. Even board members have been in the dark. When on occasion one asked, he was told that the donor wished to remain anonymous.

It is unlikely that any other charitable organization that depends on public support operates with such little accountability and in such secrecy as WWF has under de Haes. It is easier to penetrate the CIA. And when WWF has been caught in embarrassing conduct, it has engaged in damage control and cover-ups of the kind that might be expected from a company whose products have caused injury to consumers or the environment. Under rules de Haes promulgated, WWF employees are prohibited from talking to anyone outside the organization about anything except what the organization has already made public; the obligation to secrecy binds the employee even after he or she has left WWF. Few are willing to break this code of silence—given their fear of de Haes and, in the case of current employees, the generous salaries and pleasant living conditions in Switzerland.

It may well be, as one senior WWF officer put it somewhat defensively, that a dollar given to WWF is still a dollar well spent for conservation. But, as this person added, "imagine what the organization could be with better leadership."

Over the years there has been increasing dissatisfaction with de Haes's leadership. One of the most serious challenges to his rule came in the early 1980s, when the heads of the WWF organizations in Britain, the Netherlands and Switzerland began to discuss among themselves changes they thought were necessary in the organization. These organizations should be able to effect change because they provide most of the funds for the International—WWF-UK alone contributes nearly one-third of the International's budget, and Switzerland and the Netherlands rank second and third. The way WWF was set up, two-thirds of the money raised by the national organizations goes to the International, while one-third remains with the national organization. The "dissident" leaders of the three national organizations objected to this because there was no accountability over how the International spent the money. They also did not like the fact that the WWF-International board of trustees doesn't represent the national organizations. The board is a self-selected body—that is, those on the board decide whom to place on it—and the national organizations, even though they give the money, have no right of representation. In short, the heads of the British, Dutch and Swiss organizations felt that too much power was concentrated in Gland—the Swiss town where WWF-International's headquarters is located—and that the local organizations should have more autonomy.

Sir Arthur Norman, the head of WWF-UK at the time, was particularly disturbed by the manner in which WWF-International set up chapters in other countries. He thought they should "be triggered off by local people, local enthusiasm, and not by someone in Gland saying it's time to set up one in China and then finding the people to run it." He describes the difference in approach as "imperial corporate rule versus liberal grass roots development." Norman was one of Britain's most successful businessmen—for more than twenty years chairman of the De La Rue Company, which printed currency certificates, and an early president of the Confederation of British Industries (CBI), Britain's most powerful business association.

Sir Arthur was the person who convened the meetings with the leaders from the Netherlands and Switzerland. "It was these meetings that angered de Haes," says one of them. "The idea that parts of the whole should talk with each other and not with the center—Gland—was not acceptable to him." Norman says that he and the other directors were not after de Haes personally—the "struggle was one of ideas." They knew, however, that de Haes would be unwilling to make the changes, to surrender power, so that if the changes were made, de Haes would have to go. De Haes had an important ally: Prince Philip. Philip spoke to Norman; de Haes remained as head of WWF-International. Norman gave up his reform campaign, and the organization continued to operate as it always had. "It still has the same patronizing approach," says one former WWF board member who sided with Norman. "It is run like a private country club." Not even the United States chapter of WWF, which has more members and raises more money than nearly all of the other national organizations combined, has been able to budge de Haes and Philip.

Even though American conservationists had initially been cool to Nicholson's idea, once WWF was a reality, they were quick to get on board. The launching of WWF-US was a black-tie dinner, on June 7, 1962, in the Grand Ballroom of New York's Waldorf-Astoria. President Kennedy lent his name to the cause—as honorary chairman of the dinner. The dinner committee was chaired by Winston Guest, the socialite who had been disappointed because Beryl Markham had not been able to find him a hundred-pounder to shoot. An international polo player—his teammates included King George VI—Guest was the godson and second cousin of Winston Churchill, and his grandfather on his mother's side, an American, had been a partner of Andrew Carnegie. It was a major social event—the New York Times even put it on the front page, with a picture of Prince Philip and Prince Bernhard, who flew over for the gala. One thousand five hundred persons paid $50 (roughly $1,000 today) to attend. Among the socialites, the politicians and the merely wealthy who dined off Wedgwood plates depicting African wildlife, specially made for the occasion, were Bernard Baruch, Nicholas Duke Biddle, Henry F. du Pont, William Randolph Hearst, Jr., Cornelius Vanderbilt Whitney, Mrs. M. de Kuyper, Dr. Baron Stefan de Schill, Marshall Field, Jr., Senator Jacob Javits, Paul Mellon, William Paley, Richard Scaife. The drawings on the large-size program with gilded letters were by Peter Scott, and the program noted (in a sign that those were different times), "The Brown and Williamson Tobacco Corporation have been kind enough to provide their Viceroy Cigarettes."

Until the mid-1970s, WWF-US remained a modest organization. It did not have a staff of scientists or conservationists and was in effect a foundation that gave money to individuals and other groups. Then Russell Train became president, in 1978. He set about building an empire, merging WWF with The Conservation Foundation, a mainline organization that had been founded in 1948, and launching a joint fund-raising scheme with his former organization, AWLF, the first step in what he hoped would be a takeover, but which eventually failed. Train brought scientists and fund-raisers into WWF-US and membership rose from fewer than 50,000 when he arrived to more than 300,000 when he stepped down as president in 1985 to become chairman. It was almost inevitable that WWF-US and the International would collide, that the Americans would not tolerate being the child of a Swiss parent.

Conservation projects in the field were supposed to be run out of Switzerland, but the Americans wanted to conduct their own. When WWF-US launched its own programs in Latin America, the International reluctantly acceded to a kind of Monroe Doctrine of conservation. But under Train, the Americans also expanded into Africa and Asia without asking the International or even caring much what the International thought. During one meeting of WWF-International's executive committee, at the Gland, Switzerland, headquarters in April 1990, a WWF vice-president complained that WWF-US was too independent, that it "continued to make decisions which came as surprises to WWF International" and that it hired field staff in Asia and Africa without prior consultation with Gland. According to the confidential minutes, Train replied that WWF-US "was not willing to take directives from Gland."

Even more contentious, not surprisingly, was the matter of money. WWF-US has never gone along with passing on to the International two-thirds of the money it raises, as the other national organizations do. In part this is because of U.S. tax laws, but the U.S. organization has not even been willing to give to the International what the tax laws permit. By 1991 the International said the American chapter owed $3 million; the Americans agreed to give no more than $700,000. "In principle we are not opposed to giving more money to the International," a senior WWF-US official said. "But we will not put one dime into the International until there is a system of financial accountability and a control of expenditures. There is absolutely no accountability." A man who served on the WWF board for more than a decade during the seventies and eighties, and who is not from the United States, agrees. "It is not accountable," he says of WWF-International. "Its financial accounts are not subject to the same examination as they would be in, say, the United States. It's really a club that is not democratically representative of its constituency nor accountable to it."

The feud between WWF-US and the International was out of public view, but by 1991 it had become a bitter one. The Americans threatened to leave the International; the International countered by threatening to expel them. It was like a messy and acrimonious divorce proceeding. At issue were the panda and the WWF name. The International said that if the American chapter left the International, it could not use the panda and the WWF name; the Americans said they had rights to both. The International retained a prominent American lawyer, Abraham Sofaer, who had been the senior State Department attorney during part of the Reagan administration, and it took delight in keeping the hiring secret from Train and WWF-US for several months.

There were high-level transatlantic negotiations, often involving Prince Philip and Russell Train—inherited royalty versus democratic aristocracy. They were appropriately civil to each other, but the animosity was deep. "He seems to have nothing better to do than pester us," Train once remarked about Philip, referring to the perpetual flow of faxes from Buckingham Palace to the modern WWF offices on Twenty-fourth Street in Washington, D.C. As for de Haes, Train described him as being consumed with power. "He has an instinct for the jugular," Train has said. "No one here [at WWF-US] trusts that guy at all." During the WWF-International executive committee meeting at Gland in April 1990, Train sought to curb de Haes's power. In a closed session of the executive committee—closed at Train's request—Train suggested that in the future the director-general should have only a one-year contract, instead of a three-year contract as had been the practice. The executive committee, chaired by Prince Philip, rejected the proposal. A year later, in July 1991, Train told Philip politely but firmly that he thought de Haes should leave. He had been encouraged to take this action by Sir Arthur Norman—not that he needed any prodding. Like Norman, Train lost. "If he goes, I go," Prince Philip said of de Haes. "Some of us felt, 'That's fine, too,'" recalled a senior WWF-US official. De Haes and Prince Philip stayed.

In early 1992 the International and the United States chapter signed an agreement that will keep the two organizations working together— however inharmoniously—until 1994, when both sides fully expect the battle will be rejoined, though perhaps without as much personal animosity.

At the WWF meeting in November 1992, in Buenos Aires, de Haes was finally ousted. Trying to put the best face on it, WWF-International issued a press release saying that de Haes had announced he would "retire." In truth, he had been forced out. The successful coup was led by the British, Dutch and Swiss national organizations, and at one point they had several other signatures on a letter they were circulating calling for de Haes to be dismissed. "On Monday, he was told he'd be fired on Friday," said a senior WWF-US official. "He headed it off with his resignation." Still, de Haes was given eighteen months before his resignation would become effective—on June 30, 1994. Many national organizations thought that was far too long, but once again de Haes had Prince Philip's support, and Philip continued to irritate the Americans.

With the announcement of de Haes's "retirement," a formal search began for his successor. One of the early prime candidates was William Reilly, who has had a long and distinguished career in conservation, including sixteen years as president of WWF-US, from 1973 to 1989, and who served as head of the Environmental Protection Agency during the Bush administration. But Reilly's chances were jeopardized by Prince Philip's opposition. "Philip considers him an uppity American who can't stand royalty, who is not sufficiently deferential," said a WWF-US official who has worked with Philip. Whoever is the next head of WWF-International will have to devote considerable time to repairing some of the damage of the past.

IN 1987, someone decided that it was time to take a look at WWF-International on its twenty-fifth birthday. The organization refuses to say who asked for the evaluation, but it was the sagacious Anton Rupert who thought it necessary. He paid for it as well, roughly $100,000, though the organization won't acknowledge this either. John Phillipson, an ecologist who had headed the animal ecology research group at Oxford from 1967 until his retirement in 1988 and was not part of WWF, was retained to conduct the audit. In broadest terms, the issue as Rupert posed it to Phillipson was, "We've been in existence for twenty-five years, how well have we done?" More specifically, Phillipson was to look at field projects—at how efficient and effective they had been and what had been their long-term results. Phillipson, and four consultants he brought on, scrutinized the International's programs in some thirty countries in Asia, Africa and Latin America.

Based on a complex system of scoring projects, he ultimately concluded that 73 percent of the projects had accomplished their immediate aims—this might mean that if a project as initially proposed and funded was to get a vehicle, the vehicle was delivered. It was harder to come up with empirical evidence to score the longer-term success rate of projects, but in general Phillipson concluded that it wasn't as high.

More seriously, Phillipson observed that the people working in WWF offices in developing countries "resent not being consulted about, or informed of, the conservation initiatives in their own countries" that the International and WWF national organizations, principally in the United States and Britain, embarked on. This was the attitude and approach that Sir Arthur Norman had tried unsuccessfully to change. If WWF employees in the Third World were not consulted and resented it, one can easily imagine how WWF treated those in developing countries who did *not* work for the organization, and how they felt about it. Another of Phillipson's criticisms was that "WWF is seen not to acknowledge sufficiently the contributions to conservation of either national institutions or other international organizations," and this led to accusations of "egocentricity and neo-colonialism." (The same criticism could be leveled fairly at most conservation organizations working in the Third World.)

When Phillipson's report was circulated internally among the staff of the International for their comments, most were angry; they charged Phillipson with making factual errors and failing to understand the organization and seeing the changes that had been made. But one senior officer at WWF, Timothy Geer, found the report to be "by-and-large on target." In a confidential memorandum Geer said, "Picking holes on minor factual errors is time spent looking at the hole and not the doughnut." A graduate of Beloit College, a small, distinguished liberal arts school in Wisconsin,

Geer had earned a doctorate in zoology from Oxford. He had worked on Madison Avenue—where he planned the advertising for, among other things, "Cool Whip Pies"—before joining WWF-International in 1983. Geer was no in-house goody-goody; indeed, he had once secretly tape-recorded a meeting with officials of WWF-US. But he felt it was important to look at "the big picture":

> WWF doesn't want to be specific about what it does and doesn't do; we shroud ourselves in a veil of vagueness and do little in a straightforward manner. WWF is not good at the people business; we communicate poorly, take people for granted, and claim cooperative victories as our own. We have a conservation agenda that differs from the local ones; while there may be reason for this the people at the other end don't know why and it is not explained to them. We don't operate according to a clear set of principles, but according to whim and the path of least resistance.

And if WWF's projects were 73 percent effective—"Not bad," Geer noted. "So let's be positive. This is the time to learn and not to cover our asses."

Prince Philip and de Haes felt differently. Immediately upon reading Phillipson's report, Prince Philip sent a fax to de Haes: "You may remember that I was not altogether enthusiastic about this project, but I had no idea that it might land us in such a pickle!! Whatever we do with it, we are bound to get into trouble. If we don't publish it in full, we are bound to be accused of trying to 'cover up' something. If we do let it out, all the mischief-makers will have a field day!"

Philip, who doesn't have much time for journalists (understandably, perhaps, given the way the British press hounds the royal family), and de Haes opted for the "cover-up." De Haes had all copies of the report numbered, and he and Prince Philip agreed that the full report should not be distributed to the board. Philip also urged de Haes to ask Phillipson to "modify his language," and if Phillipson would not do so, Philip told de Haes, "you will have to seriously consider doing some sort of 'editing,' particularly of the Executive Summary."

Phillipson has acknowledged at least one change. Initially he wrote that the management of projects, including financial accountability, was "appalling." That was changed to "leaves much to be desired."

There was more "editing." Phillipson's report was 208 pages. WWF released a 9-page summary. Among the many things left out of the public summary was Phillipson's finding that "a diligent auditor set among the project account files in Switzerland would surely open a cupboard full of skeletons." He was referring to the International's field projects—from some there were no reports at all, and many others had made no accounting of how the money was spent. Phillipson's conclusion that WWF's attitude engendered accusations of "neo-colonialism" remained in the summary.

Occasionally other skeletons got out, and when they did, it became clear that WWF had lost its ethical way, at least in carrying out its conservation work in Africa. In the late 1980s, for example, WWF provided Zimbabwe's Department of National Parks and Wildlife Management with funds to buy a helicopter for its anti-poaching operations in the Zambezi Valley, where the black rhino was on the verge of extinction because of poachers. The department used the helicopter to deploy anti-poaching units when it received reports of poachers in an area. At least fifty-seven poachers were killed in the helicopter-supported operations, and the WWF office in Zimbabwe reported that the helicopter "has made an enormous difference to staff morale and efficiency" in the wildlife department.

That WWF was involved was not known publicly until the environment correspondent of the British newspaper *The Guardian*, Paul Brown, broke the story. WWF responded with a statement saying that it had provided the funds for the helicopter "on the strict understanding that the helicopter would never be used as a gun-ship," and that it was "official WWF policy not to use any of its funds for purchase of arms or ammunition." The truth is the organization knew that the helicopter would be used in operations in which poachers would be killed. Indeed, there had been a long and fierce debate within WWF about the project, and many on the staff were opposed because Zimbabwe's policy was "Shoot first, ask questions later," as one of those involved in the debate puts it. Providing the helicopter "made the policy more effective," he said. As for WWF's statement that it did not provide funds for arms or ammunition, the organization's internal documents show that it was doing precisely that for at least one project in Tanzania in 1987.

De Haes and WWF-International had to work harder to cover up another scandal in Africa, this one involving mercenaries, intrigue, high-level WWF officials and Prince Bernhard. The mercenaries were former British commandos who worked for KAS Enterprises, a company headed by Sir David Stirling, the legendary founder of Britain's Special Air

Services (SAS), Britain's most elite commando force. Stirling, who died
in 1990, engaged in clandestine activities throughout the world, setting
up ostensibly private companies that were in fact covers for Britain's
MI-5 and MI-6. In Africa's conservation wars, in the late 1980s KAS, as
part of its arrangement with WWF officials, trained anti-poaching units
in Namibia, which was then still under the control of South Africa, as
well as Mozambicans in South Africa. (The South African government was
trying to destabilize Mozambique.) KAS also set up a "sting" operation to
catch traffickers in ivory and rhino horn. The project was code-named
"Operation Lock," Lock being the maiden name of the wife of a former
SAS officer, Lieutenant-Colonel Ian Crooke, who was in charge of it.

Some of KAS's anti-poaching activities were exposed in July 1989 by
Robert Powell, the Reuters correspondent in Nairobi. Powell, however,
was unable to link WWF to the operation, and so WWF remained silent
when Powell's story appeared, and continued working with KAS. But
Powell's article provoked Stephen Ellis, editor of *Africa Confidential*, a
fortnightly newsletter published in London, to probe further. Ellis, also
a freelance journalist, got an assignment from *The Independent* to write
an article about Operation Lock. In the course of his reporting he called
WWF and talked with Robert SanGeorge, the organization's chief spokesman. SanGeorge, an American, had come to WWF-International in 1990
along with his wife, a tough lawyer who became executive assistant to
de Haes. Without telling Ellis, SanGeorge, who has been seen with a
recording device attached to his phone, made a verbatim transcript of
their conversation, which he passed on to de Haes—SanGeorge even
noted when Ellis "paused to fetch a cup of coffee he had left in another
room."

A few days later, SanGeorge faxed a statement to Ellis. The statement
began: "It is, and always has been, the policy of WWF not to engage in
clandestine or covert operations which might be considered unethical by
governments, the public, or supporters of WWF." The organization then
went on to lay the blame for the covert operation on John Hanks, head
of the Africa Programme at WWF-International. It said that Hanks had
initiated the project "without the knowledge or approval of WWF-International's management." Six months earlier Hanks had been forced out
of WWF by de Haes and had gone to South Africa as director of the Southern African Nature Foundation, the name of WWF's affiliate in South
Africa. Not wanting to cross de Haes again and being loyal to WWF,
Hanks signed a statement assuming responsibility for Operation Lock.

Ellis wrote his story, and the day it appeared, SanGeorge sent a memorandum to all WWF national organizations. The memo reiterated what SanGeorge had told Ellis, and emphasized that Operation Lock "was initiated without the knowledge or authority of the Director General" and that "no funds for the Operation were channeled through WWF-International's books." It was a carefully crafted statement, befitting the work of a lawyer who wants to keep his client out of jail. But it was hardly an honest explanation befitting a charitable organization.

The truth, which has never come out publicly, is found in a series of communications from Frans Stroebel, executive director of WWF's South African affiliate when Operation Lock commenced and the man who had introduced Lieutenant-Colonel Crooke to senior police and conservation officials in South Africa. Stroebel wrote Prince Philip:

> I have given Mr. de Haes a number of comprehensive briefings on the project since I first became involved. In May 1989, I gave him *full* details. He then went to HRH Prince Bernhard to confirm that Prince Bernhard was indeed the sponsor. Mr. de Haes satisfied himself with the developments, and in subsequent discussions with me he never expressed any concern about my involvement, or, for that matter, the covert programme itself.

As for the funds for the operation, Stroebel said, in another letter, "The funds for Operation Lock *were actually WWF funds*." The money had come to WWF-International, then was channeled back out to Bernhard for Operation Lock in a series of strange transactions. First, in December 1988, Sotheby's auctioned two paintings owned by Bernhard—*The Holy Family*, a seven-by-five-foot oil by Bartolomé Esteban Murillo, and *The Rape of Europa*, a four-by-five-foot oil by Elisabetta Sirani. Together they brought in £610,000. On Bernhard's instructions the proceeds were donated to WWF-International; Sotheby's had noted in its catalogue that they would be. But if the buyer—who remains anonymous—thought the money was going toward WWF's general conservation work, he was mistaken. Within a few weeks after the sale, Bernhard called the administrator of the 1001 Club and asked her to transfer £500,000 from the 1001 Club account to Queen Juliana's (his wife's) account in the Netherlands. The £500,000 was needed for Operation Lock, according to Stroebel, and de Haes "agreed to the use of these funds as requested." (Bernhard told WWF it could keep the remaining £110,000, which at the time was worth a little less than $200,000.)

After Ellis's story appeared, many Western conservationists working in Africa were embarrassed, because Operation Lock had been exposed—not because they thought it was wrong to engage in a covert operation to stop the illegal trade in rhino horn and ivory. Indeed, the possibility of covert operations had often been discussed by elephant and rhino specialists. On one occasion, at a meeting attended by conservationists from WWF, AWF and other organizations, Hanks outlined what he had in mind and the general response, as described by a person who attended, was "Get on with it. Don't tell us what you're doing, but get on with it." Government officials in Zambia, Tanzania and Kenya did not feel quite the same way. They declined offers of assistance from KAS.

THAT THERE was a schism as big as a canyon between the approach to conservation taken by the Africans on the one hand and the conservation organizations on the other was not surprising, not when one looked at the conservation organizations: they were the monopoly of white Westerners. Whites headed them, hired whites to staff them, and implemented programs that reflected Western values.

WWF-International has its headquarters in Gland, a quintessential Swiss town—small, quiet, neat, and white. It carries out programs around the world, most of them in the Third World, yet one has rarely seen other than a white face in the Gland offices. For thirty years, not a single African, and only a handful of Asians and Latin Americans, were ever hired by WWF-International. Only one black has ever held a professional position in the Africa section of WWF-US, and he was not hired until 1991. In the field—that is, in Africa—walk into the organization's offices, and it is like colonial days: white at the top, blacks in the inferior positions. WWF's major presence in Africa has been its regional office in Nairobi, which in various incarnations has existed since the 1960s; it has always been headed by whites, and not until 1989 was there a single African in a professional position. Only one WWF program anywhere on the continent has ever been headed by an African.

As AWF—the *African* Wildlife Foundation—celebrated its thirtieth birthday, it had yet to have a single African-American on its board of trustees or working in its Washington headquarters. The Nairobi office had fourteen people with conservation portfolios in 1992—the top four, and ten altogether, were white expatriates. The organization also had nine senior associates. Eight were white. The director of AWF's program in Tanzania was an American; the director in Uganda was British.

"It's overly white," Mark Stanley Price, the director of AWF's Nairobi
office, acknowledges about the conservation movement in Africa. Since
taking over in 1987, Stanley Price, a British citizen, has brought more
Africans into the AWF office in professional positions than his predecessors did in the previous two decades, but still he defended the almost
complete absence of any in senior positions. "We're trying to run a
Western-type organization. It needs Western-type skills," he said.
"We're accountable to an American constituency, we're dealing with
Western donors." The more whites in the organization, the easier it was
to raise money from donors, he noted, adding, "That way we are able to
support more Africans." In other words, Americans and Western donors
do not feel as comfortable dealing with Africans as they do with white
Americans and Europeans. He is right.

It may have been understandable why there were few Africans working
in the conservation organizations twenty, or maybe even ten, years ago.
The colonialists didn't educate Africans to be biologists or zoologists, and
the jobs they gave them in wildlife and national park departments were
at the lowest levels. "Wildlife was a white man's game," says David
Western, one of the most prominent and qualified Nairobi-based conservationists, who was raised and educated in East Africa. In the immediate
post-independence years, a career in conservation wasn't one that many
Africans attending university considered. In Africa, traditionally, formal
structures weren't necessary to protect the environment—conservation
was part of the culture of many African tribes; they didn't hunt wildlife
to extinction, because they needed the animals. Moreover, immediately
after independence, government priorities were—and remain—health,
education and basic infrastructure projects, like roads, not conservation.
Western remembers that when he was studying zoology at the University
of Nairobi in the late sixties, a few years after Kenya's independence,
and a student in the department would say, "I work with animals," the
response was often, "Why don't you do something productive for the
country?" Students wanted to become engineers, teachers, nurses, doc-
tors, lawyers, agriculturalists.

That was a generation ago. Today there are enough qualified individuals to fill many of the positions in the conservation institutions in Kenya.
Western knows this. Since 1986 he has been the director of the African
office of Wildlife Conservation International, the field research arm of
the New York Zoological Society, and the office has looked markedly
different from the other conservation offices in Nairobi: it has been mostly

African—indeed, Western has been the sole white. Western is also a Kenyan citizen, which further sets him apart from the heads of the other major wildlife groups in Kenya, all of whom have been expatriates. (There is one conservation organization in Nairobi headed and staffed by Africans—the East African Wildlife Society. It is supported by two hundred corporate donors, and though it puts out a monthly magazine—*Swara*—its voice, unfortunately, is extremely quiet.) Though British by birth, Western moved to Tanzania when he was three years old—his father worked for the colonial government as a city planner, but he was an avid hunter and conservationist—and to Kenya in the 1960s. After several years Western gave up his British passport and became a Kenyan citizen, something very few whites do. Perhaps it was because he grew up in Africa that Western is more comfortable with Africans than the expatriate conservationists are. Or maybe it is because he realizes that Africans must be involved in conservation if Africa's wildlife is to be saved. Whatever the reasons, Western goes to the Kenyan universities in search of students who are interested in conservation; he encourages them in their studies, then hires them if he can.

It is not only that other organizations don't make this kind of effort to recruit Africans: more disturbing is that they actually turn away qualified Africans who come to them looking for positions. That is what Perez Olindo, one of the most eminent African conservationists, discovered.

Olindo's story is that of Africans in conservation, at least for his generation, the one now in position to provide leadership. It was fortuitous that he got into conservation. When he was in secondary school, he liked science and math and thought he wanted to be a doctor. "Then I got a very strong botany teacher, and he talked to us about student-teacher relationships in American universities and about 'pen friends,' " Olindo recalls. The botany teacher gave his student the name of an American professor who had been a Fulbright Scholar in Kenya. He happened to be a professor of wildlife management, and in the course of the correspondence between the African student and the American professor, the professor asked Olindo if he had ever thought about a career in that field. "I wrote back to him, 'What is wildlife?' " Olindo, one of eight children, grew up in western Kenya, where the human population was so dense that the animals had disappeared long before. "There wasn't even a hare," he recalled. His first exposure to Kenya's wildlife came when as a teenager he participated in an Outward Bound climb up Mount Kilimanjaro. On the way to the base of the mountain, he passed through some of the richest wildlife country in Kenya. "I saw all these animals, but I had no idea which was what. I was amazed," he said, eyes widening even thirty-four years later. Contrasting what he saw in this region with the absence of game in his own, he began to think that he should try to do something about the decline of the wildlife. "I didn't know how I was going to achieve it, or if there was even a way."

In 1960, Olindo set off for the United States, enrolling at Central Missouri State University, which he had heard about from a Kenyan who was a student there. Then he came to the attention—he doesn't know how—of Robert Maytag, owner of the home appliance company, who recommended him to Russell Train at the African Wildlife Leadership Foundation, and Olindo had the first AWLF scholarship. He transferred to Michigan State University, where the professor who had first written to him about wildlife was teaching, and Olindo earned a degree in zoology and wildlife management. Returning home, he embarked on a career in public service, starting as a biologist in the wildlife department; within two years he had become director of Kenya National Parks, in 1966. He held the post for ten years, doing such a good job that in his last year the department had an astonishing surplus of almost $3 million. When the parks and wildlife departments were merged and the senior position was given to the corrupt head of the wildlife department, Olindo left. He spent the next decade in a variety of conservation-related work, including six years as chief ecologist in the Ministry of Energy and Regional Development. In 1988, WWF-US awarded him the J. Paul Getty Wildlife Conservation Prize, the Nobel Prize for Conservation—which in addition to the honor bestows $50,000, at the time the largest monetary recognition for conservation work. Olindo also has a private pilot's license, which field conservationists in Africa deem essential.

When AWF was looking for a new director for its office in Nairobi, in 1987, Olindo applied and was confident he would get the job. Mark Stanley Price was hired instead. Stanley Price's scientific credentials are unassailable—he has an undergraduate honors degree in zoology and a doctorate from Oxford, and has conducted extensive wildlife research in Africa—but if the *African* Wildlife Foundation thought perhaps an African should head their operations, at least in Africa, Olindo was surely their man. In 1989, the WWF office in Nairobi was looking for a new director, to replace Hugh Lamprey, a Brit who had a long and varied career in conservation in East Africa, but hadn't hired Africans in any senior positions—"he didn't think Africans were capable," says an Ameri-

can who worked with him. Olindo expressed interest in the job. He
didn't get it. An American, Ed Wilson, who had no scientific training or
significant conservation experience—he had been Lamprey's *administrative* assistant for many years—effectively replaced Lamprey. Three years
later, Wilson decided that he wanted to move to Switzerland, in part for
the benefit of his children's education. He was given a job in the African
section of WWF-International. And the International sent a Belgian to
Kenya to become the head of the WWF office there. Again Olindo was
considered by Gland but passed over.

Olindo is a measured and cautious man, and he is reluctant to accuse
the conservation organizations of discrimination. Asked why there are so
few Africans working for the conservation organizations in Nairobi, he
said, "I think it's partiality in appointment." Didn't he mean discrimination? "Partiality in appointment—call it what you like," he said. Slightly
more boldly, he added, "If Kenyans—non-whites—are heads of these
organizations, I don't think the animals are going to die overnight."

Aside from the moral issue, failing to bring more Africans into conservation doesn't make for very good conservation. As many Africans see it,
white people are making rules to protect animals that white people want
to see in parks that white people visit. Why should Africans support these
programs? In 1979, WWF put half a million dollars into a project to save
the rhino in Zambia's Luangwa Valley. It was just about the biggest
investment WWF had ever made in a single project. Within a few years,
poachers had virtually wiped out the rhino. The project failed because it
was "administered predominantly by the white community," concluded
Zambia's Department of National Parks and Wildlife Services, an analysis
shared, and underscored, by the Wildlife Conservation Society of Zambia, a nongovernmental organization made up largely of whites. Their
analysis also noted that the local people were not involved in planning
or implementing the project, so they viewed it as they viewed programs
forced upon them during the colonial era.

It is a critique that fits the ivory ban movement as well. AWF launched
its "Don't buy ivory" campaign without consulting Africans—or if it did,
it ignored them. The organization felt it was "arrogant" for Westerners
to tell the Africans what they could do with their ivory—which is why it
didn't initially call for a comprehensive ban—then went right ahead and
told them. WWF professed to care about what the Africans wanted, but
then tried to manipulate them into doing what the Westerners wanted;
and those Africans who couldn't be brought into line were ignored.

During the ivory ban debate throughout 1988 and 1989, committees made up largely of whites commissioned studies, which were written by whites and then discussed at conferences dominated by whites. At the end of the twentieth century, the conservation movement in Africa was nearly as white, elitist and patrician as when the Society for the Preservation of the Wild Fauna of the Empire was founded at the beginning of the century.

WHAT DO WE
BELIEVE IN, AND
WHAT ABOUT
THE BAOBAB?

||||| AT THE OUTSET, when the African Wildlife Foundation sent out its "Urgent Memorandum" (in February 1988) and then held a press conference in order to call attention to the plight of the African elephant at the hands of poachers, the organization was actually proceeding with some caution: it was not asking for a ban on ivory trading. "We just wanted to educate people, nothing more," says Diana McMeekin, the AWF vice-president. It wanted to make Americans aware that ivory products come from elephants, which many purchasers apparently do not realize—an ignorance of the facts that was underscored when, in response to AWF's campaign, some housewives from Louisiana asked the organization if they could continue buying Ivory soap. And once Americans knew that ivory comes from elephants, AWF wanted Americans to stop buying it. To have gone beyond that educational purpose would have put AWF on "the slippery slope to an extreme position," McMeekin said. The extreme position, she explained, was a total ban.

She said that the advertising firm that had prepared the Urgent Memorandum and conducted AWF's direct-mail solicitations was "screaming" for the organization to advocate a ban because it knew it would be good for fund-raising. AWF resisted, according to McMeekin. "Our sensitivity is a very African sensitivity," she said, explaining why. "We felt that it would be arrogant and inappropriate for outsiders to tell Africa what to do about a natural resource of theirs."

AWF was not alone in thinking a total ban was not the best solution. In early 1988, it would have been hard to find a conservationist with any zoological background and experience in Africa or with elephants who believed that a ban on the ivory trade was the way to save the African elephant. Indeed, David Western declared unequivocally at the time, "A majority [of conservationists] feel that outright bans would not solve the problem." Moreover, he added, a ban "would exaggerate the problems with wildlife in Africa because African nations use the revenue from ivory to help finance their conservation programs."

If Western, who holds a doctorate in ecology, was the most scholarly of the conservationists in Africa who did not believe in a total ban on ivory trading, the most popular conservationist who shared that view was surely Cynthia Moss, whose *Elephant Memories: Thirteen Years in the Life of an Elephant Family* was published in early 1988. It was Moss who had approached AWF with the suggestion that it launch a campaign to alert people that buying ivory was killing elephants, and she accompanied McMeekin at the AWF press conference at the National Zoo in May 1988. Moss was already well known to Westerners going on safari to Africa, for many of them carried a copy of her book *Portraits in the Wild: Animal Behavior in East Africa*, which was first published in 1975, updated in 1982, and is the best guidebook for tourists who want to do more than ooh and aah when they see wild animals—who want to know about their eating habits, social structures, mating habits and more. Moss first came to Africa in 1967, on a long vacation, as a philosophy graduate of Smith who was working for *Newsweek*, drawn by a love of the outdoors and concern about the environment before it had become fashionable. "I wanted to see one of the last wildernesses before it went away," she says. "I was an environmentalist, I guess, one of the few members of the Sierra Club from the East Coast." In her twenties, with long blond hair, she traveled in Uganda, Tanzania, Ethiopia and Kenya, and like so many young Western women, from Isak Dinesen and Beryl Markham to Dian Fossey and Jane Goodall, she was enchanted by the continent. A year later Moss returned to Kenya, and she is still there. She began her studies of elephants in Kenya's Amboseli park in 1972, and they became her family. She named them—Slit Ear and Torn Ear, Teddy, Tonie and Tilly—watched them frolic, mate, become parents and die.

Because she wanted other people "to know them, enjoy them, and care about them," she wrote *Elephant Memories*. Reflecting the West's romantic enthrallment with elephants, the book sold out its U.S. printing and was published in paperback; it was also translated into French, German, Italian, Dutch, Finnish, and became a best-seller in Sweden. Moss ended her book with a look to "Future Generations." It was grim. Poaching was going on at a far greater rate than anyone had realized. Still, she wrote, "The situation is depressing but it may not be irreversible." What was needed to reverse it was a "worldwide campaign to reduce the demand for ivory." Even that, however, was too much for many conservationists.

When she was in the United States doing the final editing on her book, Moss called on WWF. She was accompanied by Joyce Poole, an American who had begun as Moss's student in Amboseli and had gone on to earn a Ph.D. in zoology from Oxford and an independent reputation for elephant research. At WWF, they met with Curtis Bohlen, the organization's senior vice-president, and Jorgen Thomsen, a senior biologist with TRAFFIC(U.S.A.). Moss and Poole were not asking for a total ban on all ivory trading. Still, they could not even get Bohlen and Thomsen to agree to a public awareness campaign. "We came away really depressed," Moss recalled three years later. "Their attitude was one of patting us on the head and saying, 'There, there, but we really know better.' "

Both Bohlen and Thomsen would become ardent converts to a total ban on trading, but they had to fight hard, and often covertly, before they could get their own organization on board. Once the United States chapter of WWF joined the cause, the International, which had been even more strongly opposed to a ban, capitulated.

A SENSE of the battles that were to come, and to become more fierce, between Westerners and Africans and among Western conservationists themselves, surfaced at a meeting WWF-International convened in Lusaka, the run-down capital of Zambia, in April 1988. The meeting had been called on short notice, and in his opening remarks, John Hanks, director of Africa programs at the International, explained that the reason for the "urgency" was pressure from organizations in the United States (AWF primarily) and Europe—"none of which seem to have consulted with Africans," he noted. The purpose of the meeting, which was really two days of workshops and plenary sessions, was to discuss what WWF's elephant conservation policy should be in view of these pressures. WWF wanted a frank discussion of the increasingly emotional issue, so the press was not invited, and no statement would be issued afterward, Prince Bernhard, co-chairman, told the delegates. Closing the meeting seemed to work. Delegates said things they wouldn't say publicly, and in some cases made statements that were contrary to what they said publicly. In addition to officers from WWF-International and six WWF national organizations—from those in the United States, the United Kingdom, South Africa, France, Japan and Hong Kong—the meeting was attended by representatives from the wildlife departments of Kenya, Tanzania, Zambia and Zimbabwe. Inviting these African officials (others had been invited but were unable to attend) suggested that WWF wanted to listen to Africans, and in a post-meeting report, WWF said that the views of the African wildlife officials were "of particular significance." WWF was being disingenuous or condescending—or both—or at least it is hard not to come to that conclusion considering that, as the debate about a ban intensified, when the views of African officials did not coincide with those of WWF, the African views were not considered of any significance at all.

At Lusaka, however, the WWF conservationists and the African wildlife officials agreed on just about everything, starting with their opinion— it was scathing—of AWF's Urgent Memorandum. The AWF mailing was singled out by the delegates as an "example of emotional and inaccurate reporting on the elephant situation in Africa."

When reports of that criticism reached Washington, AWF's president, Paul Schindler, took offense, and rather than let the incident pass—it is unlikely that it would have done any harm to the organization—he wrote to John Hanks. Schindler often put his intemperate views on paper when he probably would have been wiser to let his temper cool, and this time he sent his letter to everyone who had been at the Lusaka conference. Schindler told Hanks that he felt his own reputation had been "sullied" and that AWF had been "virtually slandered." In defense of the Urgent Memorandum, Schindler wrote:

> None of us may like the hyperbole that has insinuated itself into the direct mail business, but Americans are all too familiar with it.
>
> A random sampling of U.S. direct mail appeals will inform you that the last rhinos alive now are headed toward extinction, or that your children's children will have to learn about whales, pandas, etc. from books, because none will exist unless you send in some dollars.

Schindler noted that when he had come on as AWF's president, he had been given some friendly and collegial advice by Russell Train, the AWF founder who was now chairman of WWF-US. The direct mail consultants to WWF had advised Train that "although he wrote beautifully, he would do WWF a favor by merely signing direct mail appeals, but not writing them," Schindler informed Hanks. "He complied and those ghost-written letters have raised millions."

Schindler's defense was, in effect: Yes, we may be guilty of using hyperbole to raise money, but everyone does it. Indeed, most nonprofit groups dependent on public donations know that the best way to get those donations is with appeals to emotion; humanitarian organizations have hyped the number of potential famine victims in Africa for that purpose, for example. Besides, what is wrong with a little exaggeration when it is all for a good cause—to raise money for wildlife projects in Africa, Schindler asked. These were about the only defenses he could muster because the Urgent Memorandum fund-raising appeal was indeed misleading.

It was true that Kenya's elephant population had declined dramatically, to about twenty thousand. But given Kenya's human population and its need for land on which to grow food, that is the maximum number of elephants the country can tolerate, and it is more likely that their number will have to be reduced to less than 18,000. Moreover, in some parts of Kenya, there are too many elephants. One of the largest elephant populations in Kenya is in Laikipia, an agricultural district, where in 1992 the government had to erect electric fences to keep them from doing damage to farms, large and small, whose owners wanted the elephants shot. In Amboseli National Park, the very place where AWF's Cynthia Moss was doing her research, there are also too many elephants. They have destroyed the woodlands and the habitat for other animals, and among the proposals being considered by Moss and other conservationists to reduce or at least control the size of the elephant population are some form of birth control. AWF conveniently neglected to mention these facts in its urgent plea, and they weren't generally known to the public during the ivory ban crusade.

From the perspective of giving people who are concerned about wild-life in Africa an accurate and honest basis on which to act, the most egregious omission from AWF's appeal was fair recognition of the situation in other parts of Africa, particularly southern Africa. What was happening in East Africa—particularly Kenya and Tanzania—where poaching was out of control and the elephant numbers were declining, was not representative of all of Africa. In Botswana, in Zimbabwe and in South Africa, poaching has not been serious, elephant herds have been well managed, and the elephant, far from being endangered, has been increasing in numbers. World attention focused on Kenya, but the greatest concentration of elephants in east or southern Africa today is in Botswana—around 56,000, which is double the number of elephants that existed there a decade ago. Zimbabwe's elephant population increased from 30,000 in 1979 to 50,000 today, which is more than double Kenya's elephant population, and Zimbabwe is considerably smaller in area. In South Africa, which has the best-run wildlife department on the continent, the elephant population has remained stable, and poaching has been negligible. These three countries were adamantly against a ban. They made money from selling ivory, as well as hides, which were highly valued by Texas bootmakers, and some of it was returned to conservation—not a great deal in absolute dollars or even as a percentage of what was generated, but for wildlife departments severely strapped for funds it was a meaningful amount. But the southern Africans had a difficult time getting their case heard in the West, and an even more difficult one getting it understood in the emotionally whipped-up shouting for an ivory ban.

Though the southern African countries had the best case against the ban, at the Lusaka meeting it was no less than the head of Kenya's wildlife department, Perez Olindo, who took the lead in making the argument. Olindo's views carried weight not only because he is from Kenya, but because he is a personable man with great warmth and is widely respected in conservation circles. In all of Africa there are probably only a handful of men of his generation with credentials comparable to his. Olindo was opposed to a ban on ivory trading for several reasons. People had valued ivory for centuries, he noted, and ivory comes not only from poached elephants but from elephants that die naturally. Though Kenyans had not traded in ivory since the mid-1970s, they realized its value, and looked forward to the day when they would sell it again. Above all, Olindo looked upon Kenya's wildlife as a resource, a resource to be used—used wisely, but used—with some of the proceeds going to local people and conservation programs.

Olindo was on a committee of scientists and conservationists, the African Elephant and Rhino Specialist Group, which had been set up (by IUCN) in the 1970s to address the alarming declines in elephants and rhino. The group's most recent report was discussed at the Lusaka meeting. It included data showing that the African elephant population had fallen from just over 1,000,000 in 1981 to 700,000. "There can be no doubt," the report said, "it is the ivory trade that is reducing the population of the species most severely." This conclusion was a critical one because for many years ivory traders and even some conservationists had been arguing that it was not the ivory trade but increasing human populations and the concomitantly shrinking space for animals that were primarily responsible for the decline in the number of elephants on the continent.

Even with these findings and conclusions, however, as well as their own personal knowledge of the horrendous poaching problems they faced, the other wildlife officials who were at Lusaka—from Tanzania, Zambia and Zimbabwe—agreed with Olindo: they did not want a ban on ivory trading. They were unanimous and unequivocal about this. It was not that they did not care about the elephant. They believed strongly that something had to be done. But the leaders of the African wildlife departments said that what they needed to stem the poaching and save the elephant was money for their departments and conservation programs. They were not beggars, looking for handouts from the international community. They were realists.

All discussions about Africa must begin and end with a recognition, however grim, of the continent's underdevelopment and poverty. Of the world's thirty-six poorest countries, twenty-nine are in Africa south of the Sahara; nine out of every ten Africans live in absolute poverty. Infant mortality in black Africa is the highest in the world: one out of every seven children born won't live to celebrate his or her first birthday. Everything—including important projects like saving elephants—must be considered in that light. Impoverished African nations simply do not have the money that is needed to protect all their wildlife, not given their paltry resources and the human demands—for schools, roads, health care and other essentials of life.

Tanzania could only afford to pay its game rangers about $30 a month, the head of Tanzania's wildlife department said during one discussion at the Lusaka conference. To which his counterpart from Zambia interjected that his country's rangers earned less than $20 a month. Olindo spelled out what the low wages meant. Experienced Kenyan rangers were paid $70 a month, he said, "so it is not surprising they can be bought."

Kenya is better off economically than most sub-Saharan Africa countries, and tourism is a major source of income for the nation, yet the amount the government spent on parks and wildlife in the 1980s was about half of what was needed. In Tsavo, where poaching was so severe, the government was spending $10 per square kilometer in the late 1980s, less than one percent of what was needed to do the job.

Conservationists have concluded that at least $200 per square kilometer, and probably closer to $400, must be spent in order to protect elephants and rhino against poaching, and that at least one ranger per 50 square kilometers is required. Zambia had one scout for every 400 square kilometers. The country had fewer than 600 rangers; it needed at least 5,000. It had six working vehicles and one working aircraft—to patrol 241,000 square miles. Zambia lost more than 100,000 elephants between 1981 and 1987, and its black rhino population was virtually wiped out. Tanzania's Selous Game Reserve had 400 rangers to cover an area nearly as large as Massachusetts, Connecticut and New Hampshire combined; the elephant population, which had numbered more than 100,000 in the late 1970s, was down to fewer than 50,000 by 1988.

So, if you want us to save this priceless world heritage, Africans said, give us the money to do the job. And above all, do not take away one source of income that we do have—the sale of ivory.

WWF agreed, for a variety of reasons. Without any doubt, the power of Anton Rupert and all the South African money was one. But there were also legitimate reasons for being opposed to a ban. The status of the elephant was foremost among them.

It was true that declines had been cataclysmic. Nevertheless, the species "is not yet endangered," two senior conservation officers at WWF-US wrote in an internal memorandum in May 1988.

This determination that the elephant was not endangered, an opinion held by the experts at the African Elephant and Rhino Specialist Group as well, was more than critical to the ivory issue. It should have been dispositive of the debate. The only legal basis for an international ban on ivory trading is the Convention on International Trade in Endangered Species (CITES), and under that treaty trading is prohibited only in a species which is "threatened with extinction"—endangered, in the common parlance. The endangered species are listed on Appendix I of the convention, and over the years they have included the leopard, snow leopard, rhinoceros, gorilla, blue and fin whales, Tibetan brown bear, California condor, and orange-bellied parakeet, as well as scores of plants. On Appendix II are those species that are not yet endangered, but might become so if trading is not controlled. The African elephant was placed on Appendix II in 1977. The advocates of the ban wanted it moved to Appendix I.

WHILE THERE are international agreements to protect seals and polar bears, whales, birds, vicuña and waterfowl habitat, CITES is the most comprehensive international conservation agreement. It seeks to protect all fauna and flora. It was first proposed in 1963, but only after twelve years of debate and lobbying was it finally ratified by enough countries and put into effect. In large measure, the world was prompted to act by an alarming increase in the trade in wildlife products: in a single year in the late 1960s, the United States alone imported the skins of more than 5 million crocodiles, 13,000 jaguar, 9,000 leopards and 1,000 cheetah.

The treaty's preamble says that "wild fauna and flora in their many beautiful and varied forms are an irreplaceable part of the natural systems of the earth which must be protected for this and the generations to come." Not long after its adoption, the treaty was heralded by one prominent conservationist as "the single most important conservation measure ever agreed upon." Today, most conservationists would argue that CITES has failed to live up to its noble intentions. Part of the responsibility for the failure lies with the secretariat, which has been far too favorably disposed toward traders. But the governments of the world, including the 117 that have signed the treaty, bear more responsibility. To begin with, the signatories have given no enforcement powers to the secretariat. Nor have they given the secretariat, which administers the treaty from modest offices in Lausanne, enough money to control the trade or even to monitor it effectively. The 1989 budget for the secretariat was $2.6 million (as with other United Nations organizations, the United States contributes the most, 25 percent), and the staff, of just sixteen, including secretaries and messengers, was responsible for the more than eight hundred species covered by the treaty. Consequently, if the treaty's goals are to be realized, individual nations must enforce its provisions. Most have lacked either the ability or the desire—or both—to do so.

So, in spite of CITES, poaching and the trade in ivory increased, as traders and governments took advantage of loopholes. First, countries that did not sign the convention became the entrepôts for illegal ivory. In the early 1980s, Belgium imported, then promptly exported, nearly 500 tons of tusks. Then it joined CITES. With that, the trade shifted to the small city-state of Singapore, which exported 250 tons of ivory in 1985. In 1987, Singapore became a CITES member, whereupon Burundi, a tiny Central African country, became the major entrepôt. Between 1979 and 1987, Burundi, which has no elephants, but does border on Zaire and Tanzania—which have large elephant populations and corrupt officials— exported 1,450 tons of elephant tusks. Burundi joined CITES in 1988.

Most of the illegal ivory from these countries went to Japan. Japan was a CITES signatory, but the treaty does not require any documentation by an *importing* nation for an Appendix II species. Of course, Japan could have banned imports from these countries, since it was obvious that the ivory had come from poached elephants, but not until 1985 did Japan, under international pressure, require importers to have certificates stating that their shipment did not violate CITES.

Another major loophole in the treaty was that it applied only to raw ivory, and not to ivory that had been worked. Thus, a tusk that had been cut into pieces, or carved even slightly, was not covered by CITES regulations. A carving industry for illegal ivory sprang up in Dubai, in the United Arab Emirates. Tons of tusks arrived in Dubai on rickety wooden dhows that had sailed across the Indian Ocean from Tanzania; after being carved, the tusks were shipped to Hong Kong. Late in 1988 Hong Kong finally closed that loophole, banning the importation of worked ivory without a permit that declared the ivory to have originated from a legal source.

A major move to strengthen the CITES system was made in 1985, at the fifth biennial meeting of the signatories, in Buenos Aires. Concerned about the continuing illegal trade, and the depletion of the herds, the African nations that had elephants proposed what became widely known as the "quota system." It was something of a misnomer because no central authority decided what the total trade in ivory should be and then divided it among the various countries. Rather, under this system, each CITES country that wanted to sell ivory determined on its own how many tusks it would export each year and then simply informed the CITES secretariat. The "quota" was supposed to be based on a "sustainable off-take," that is, on how many elephants the country could eliminate without threatening the survival of roughly the current level of its elephant population. While it may appear to be Orwellian double-speak to talk about maintaining a population size while killing some elephants, it is in fact possible to do so—by killing older elephants that are beyond their reproductive years, and by killing fewer in number than are born to a population.

There were good grounds for skepticism about the quota system. Among other things, it provided no mechanism for preventing a country from setting a preposterous quota, which is precisely what happened. Somalia, for example, put its 1986 quota at 17,000 tusks. The country only had 6,000 elephants. It was obvious that Somalia intended to export tusks from elephants poached in neighboring Kenya.

In spite of the weaknesses of CITES and the abuses of the quota system, most conservationists felt in 1988 that more time was needed before concluding that it would not work. The United States chapter of WWF went along with this position, but reluctantly. The American public, incited by campaigns like AWF's, was beginning to demand some action to protect the African elephant, the head of the WWF-US delegation to the Lusaka meeting, Curtis Bohlen, warned the others. Supporting the quota system was, he said, essentially a "no action" policy, and he added, "We must be seen to be doing something." If not, the organization would lose members.

There was another conservation principle that allowed an ivory trade, and that was the doctrine of sustainable utilization, the essence of which is that it is permissible to use resources in a rational way. WWF endorses sustainable utilization as an essential element of conservation, and Charles de Haes, the head of WWF-International, said at Lusaka, "WWF should not sit on the fence but stand up for what it believes in." Bohlen replied that most WWF-US members did not understand the doctrine and would not agree with it if they did; therefore, he said, "we have no choice but to sit on the fence." It would not be long before Bohlen would get his organization off the fence and into the laps of the fund-raisers, who wanted an ivory ban.

THE BATTLE among conservationists over the utilization of resources is almost as old as the organized conservation movement. Though "conservation" has become an all-embracing generic term meaning all efforts to save the environment and resources, initially it meant the wise and planned use of resources—wise and planned, but use nonetheless. In the United States this was the foundation for the conservation movement and for the first conservation laws: save trees and water so that they will continue to be available for our use, and set aside land for parks to provide areas for recreation. This came to be known as the utilitarian approach to conservation. In another camp were individuals such as John Muir who argued that nature should be left undisturbed by man for aesthetic or ethical reasons. They were called the "preservationists." Early conservation battles were not about wild animals, but about resources like water and trees. Should rivers be dammed in order to provide hydroelectric power for cities, but at the expense of destroying deep valleys? Should forests be cut to supply the timber for houses and all sorts of other products, or should they be left pristine to provide places of solitude? And, more recently, should oil pipelines be built across Alaska?

Thirty years ago, Julian Huxley, in his seminal articles in *The Observer* about wildlife conservation in Africa, encouraged "proper utilisation" of wildlife for the benefit of local people. He described how the Waliangulu, a hunting tribe in Kenya, had been allowed to hunt elephants moving out from Tsavo National Park. Most of the proceeds from the sale of the elephant meat and the ivory were given to the tribal council. He suggested such practices might also need to be introduced *in* this and other African national parks. Huxley's ideas went nowhere. They were far too radical, particularly that of allowing Africans to continue shooting wildlife. If Huxley's vision had been adopted, if local people had been given some benefits from the wildlife, it is likely that poaching of elephants and rhino would never have reached the alarming levels that it did. Huxley thought it would be possible to implement utilization programs because "we have replaced the old essentially negative notion of preservation with the positive concept of conservation." Huxley himself may have been committed to "conservation" over "preservation," but it was not until twenty years later that sustainable utilization became a part of the conservation orthodoxy, and even then the battle was far from over.

In 1980, sustainable utilization was finally incorporated into the World Conservation Strategy, which is considered a landmark conservation manifesto and bears the imprimatur of WWF, IUCN and the United Nations Environment Programme. The scientists and conservationists who prepared the document concluded that one of the principal objectives of an effective conservation policy should be "to ensure the sustainable utilization of species and ecosystems." In adopting this principle, the conservationists were not acting out of any philosophical commitment to the use of resources. In fact, they probably would have preferred to remain preservationists, or to severely restrict resource use. But they faced the reality of the Third World. As the document puts it, "Hundreds of millions of rural people in developing countries, including 500 million malnourished and 800 million destitute, are compelled to destroy the resources necessary to free them from starvation and poverty." The conservationists understood that the poor of the world were going to use the resources around them in order to survive, notwithstanding philosophical and ethical appeals by wealthy Westerners. Therefore, people in the

Third World must be encouraged to use their resources in a sustainable way.

With few exceptions, African nations lack minerals, either for their own development or to sell to the rest of the world; the Europeans discovered that in the early days of the explorers, which is why so many companies that thought they would make a fortune in Africa went bankrupt. Kenya, for example, has virtually no minerals. It has land suitable for growing coffee and tea, but these products are not the basis on which to build a country, not given the instability of world prices. The most valuable resource in Kenya and most other African countries is wildlife. But if that cannot be used, it is not worth much.

One obvious way to "utilize" wildlife, to make money from it, is through tourism. This is not the only way, however, and not necessarily the most profitable or efficient one. Other forms of sustainable utilization mean that animals will be killed: crocodiles, leopards and zebra for their skins, for example; impala, eland, wildebeest for their meat; lions and buffalo for hunting trophies. Sustainable utilization also permits the killing of elephants for their ivory. It is not a very pleasant thought—killing animals for commercial reasons. But the reality of the impoverished continent—of children covered with flies and dying from malnutrition; of women stooped over in fields, struggling to grow enough food for their families' survival; of crippled men begging—is not a pleasant one either.

To argue that impoverished Africans should be allowed to utilize wildlife, including elephants for their ivory, does not mean that we should allow the cutting of more timber in the Pacific Northwest or dam more rivers. At this stage of development in the West, we are generally cutting down more trees and erecting more dams in order to raise an already very high standard of living, to build bigger houses or more furniture or generate more electricity so that we can have more air conditioners, larger refrigerators and more electronic gear. In the West opponents of environmental protection laws argue jobs—in the timber and whaling industries, for example. In Africa it is a matter of allowing the use of resources in order for people to survive, to have a dignified standard of living.

WWF is committed to the principle of sustainable utilization. Indeed, it even funds programs in Africa through which the concept is put into practice, so that communities make money from selling wild animal products and from the right to hunt them. But the organization does not want its members to know this. It fears that most people give money to conservation organizations because they want to see animals preserved, not utilized, and that people in the West do not see the connection between the two. "We're trying to bring our members along on utilization, but our development people, the fund-raisers, are very nervous because there is no question that the great majority of our membership are animal lovers and have difficulty in making the evolution to a more sophisticated understanding of conservation," Russell Train said in 1991.

The ivory ban debate intensified the conflict between good conservation and fund-raising, between the professional conservationists and the money people. Every conservationist at WWF-US who knew anything about Africa was opposed to a ban. Rick Weyerhaeuser, who had studied elephants in Uganda and Tanzania, and had set up the organization's Africa program, was against it. When Weyerhaeuser left Washington, in December 1988, to go to the International office as the deputy director of the Africa section, he was succeeded by Tom McShane. McShane had been a Peace Corps volunteer in Niger and had worked in Malawi. He argued against the ban. So did Michael Wright, a vice-president whose responsibility was the development of conservation policies that considered the needs of rural people (something WWF did not begin to do, it should be noted, until the mid-1980s). One of the community programs Wright worked most closely with was in Zambia. Weyerhaeuser, McShane and Wright, as well as other professional conservationists and scientists in the office, argued that a ban was bad conservation and bad for Africans. And they asked how WWF could endorse a ban and at the same time support the doctrine of sustainable utilization, calling this position inconsistent and hypocritical.

At the WWF-US offices in Washington, D.C., the organization's senior staff engaged in what to many seemed like a never-ending debate about the ban. They were "blood and guts" meetings, as one participant described them. Those people at WWF-US whose job it was to bring in the money and members argued that the organization had to support a ban. If it didn't, it would lose members, perhaps a large number. It was that simple. The fund-raisers and public relations people would eventually win, and the organization would, in June 1989, publicly call for a ban. It *was* inconsistent. It *was* hypocritical. But sustainable utilization wasn't the only conservation principle that WWF, and other conservationists, jettisoned in the ivory ban storm.

. . .

SOMETIMES there are simply too many elephants. Elephants spend sixteen hours a day eating, and an adult bull consumes three hundred pounds of trees and grass and fifty gallons of water every day. A herd of elephants goes through an area like a slow tornado, snapping off branches and uprooting trees, leaving devastation behind. The issue is whether man should leave nature alone, or intervene. Should we cull elephant herds? Most scientists and conservationists believe that culling is sometimes necessary for ecological reasons—to save trees and forests, to preserve other species, and, however daft it may sound, even to save elephants. But the general public, understanding little about the complexities of ecosystems, recoils at the idea of shooting elephants.

In the 1960s the wildlife authorities in Uganda's Murchison Falls National Park, one of the most popular with tourists until Idi Amin came along, decided they had to deal with the elephant population. There were 15,000 elephants in the 1,500-square-mile park, and they had destroyed the woodlands; as a result about half the park's birds, as well as the chimpanzee and forest hog, had lost their habitats. Two thousand elephants were culled. Something also had to be done about the hippopotamus population. Fourteen thousand hippos wallowed in the Nile, which flows through the middle of the park, and they were eating so much of the grass on both sides of the river that the buffalo, antelope and warthog were on the verge of extinction. The authorities culled 4,000 hippos, without any public outcry—and one wonders whether there would be any today, for the inelegant hippo hardly excites the same passion as the elephant. Yet is the hippo, with its own built-in aqua-tanks so large that it can remain submerged for four minutes, really any less important than the elephant?

One of the key figures in the Murchison culling was Ian Parker, a Kenyan resident who at various times in his life has been a hunter, game warden, ivory trader, writer and entrepreneur—and always an iconoclast, a thorn in the side of the mainstream conservation world. It was Parker who back in the 1950s had proposed letting the Waliangulu shoot elephants in Tsavo, the plan that Julian Huxley lauded. A bantamweight man, fond of wearing khaki shorts, he did not move on the cocktail circuit where the other expatriate conservationists in Nairobi were regulars. He was a long-time opponent of an ivory ban, and didn't change his views to fit public opinion, for which he became the victim of smear campaigns by pro-ban militants. As for culling in Murchison, "We were sickened by the work of slaughtering day after day, yes, we were," Parker writes in *Ivory Crisis*. "It was an unpleasant task. However, we acknowledged it in the same way that a rancher acknowledges the fate of all he rears but does not dwell on it. It is easy to become emotional about killing animals; it is less easy to be rational."

Parker participated in another culling operation in the 1970s, and this one, in the Central African republic of Rwanda, he found even more unpleasant. Rwanda is a tiny country, about the size of New Hampshire, with eight million people (New Hampshire has one million), which translates into nearly eight hundred people per square mile. The country did not have very many elephants, but too many for the space available. During two separate operations, one of six days, the other five, Parker and colleagues, using standard NATO .762 rifles, killed 106 elephants, including a few infants less than six months old, who were shot because they would not have survived after their mothers had already been killed. Virtually all of Rwanda's elephants were eliminated.

And who besides the Rwandan government wanted the cull? The African Wildlife Leadership Foundation. It was AWLF's executive director at the time, Robinson McIlvaine, who had approached Parker. Initially Parker said no. "Exterminating a bunch of elephants, I didn't want to have any part of that," Parker recalled years later. But McIlvaine, who had just completed a four-year tour as the U.S. ambassador in Kenya, was a good friend. "He really laid it on hard," Parker says. For AWLF, it was a question of elephants or gorillas. The gorillas lived inside Volcans National Park, where Dian Fossey was studying them. The government did not feel that it could keep so much land from its people for the sake of the gorillas and also have people losing crops to elephants trampling in their fields. AWLF sided with the gorillas.

While it is surely stunning today to think that AWLF was involved in killing elephants not that many years ago, there was nothing shocking about it at the time. Culling was a critical principle in AWLF's conservation policies. At the time of the Murchison Falls cull, AWLF had just launched a conservation program in the park, and Dietrich Schaaf, AWLF's education officer in Uganda, explained the reasons for the cull, not in complicated scientific jargon, but in language powerful in its simplicity and clarity. "Many people are wondering why elephants and hippos are being shot in Murchison Falls Park," he began. "Once they were told that the park was created because some of Uganda's animals must be preserved in a place where the visitors from other countries who come to see them and who bring a great deal of money to Uganda each year will be able to find the animals. . . . Then why do people now shoot elephants and hippos within the park?"

One reason was the increase in the human population. As Schaaf wrote:

> With the arrival of medicines and doctors in Uganda, people live longer, they no longer die from diseases which once killed many and new-born babies are no longer in danger of dying as they once were. All this means that the number of people has increased in Uganda, and they have come to use the land around the park which was once open country. This means that the animals which live within the park have less room than they once had, and as their numbers increase they find it more and more difficult to find new food supplies and room to live within the park. Even in a large area of land like the park, when the numbers of certain animals have become too large, they can damage the land and make it useless for other animals which may depend upon it.

The elephants were putting more pressure on the park because their numbers had increased inside it. Schaaf explained why: "In past times they were able to wander back and forth across Uganda in search of food, but now if they leave the park land, they come upon the people's land and damage their crops. The people become angry, and rightly so, and call upon the game department to shoot the elephants." To escape being shot, the elephants, highly intelligent animals, were remaining in the park, and Schaaf went on to describe the damage they were doing. "They kill trees by breaking them or pushing them over to get leaves and by peeling away the bark as food. Visitors often remark on the large number of dead trees within the park."

Park officials, Schaaf went on, decided they had to intervene. "They foresaw a day when most of the park trees would be destroyed and their broken branches and trunks would litter the ground, leaving all the land exposed to the hot sun. Elephants would not find the food they need from the trees, and other animals would not find the shelter they need. Visitors from other countries would no longer be interested in such a place, and Uganda would lose a great source of wealth and national fame." So, to prevent an outcome undesirable for people, for elephants, for other animals, for tourists and for Uganda, the park officials decided to cull.

Common sense and sound conservation principles haven't changed since then. What has changed is the popular and emotional appeal of elephants and wildlife, and the reluctance of conservation organizations such as AWF to stand up to public emotion and to come forward with honest explanations like Schaaf's.

The most intense debate about culling occurred in the late 1960s in Kenya's Tsavo National Park. The elephant population in and around the park had reached about 40,000, and virtually every scientist agreed that the range could not support that number. What they could not agree on was what to do. Some conservationists and wildlife officials wanted to cull 3,000 elephants. Others argued that man should do nothing, that nature should be allowed to take its course. It was another skirmish in the long war between those who believe in managing wildlife (in this case for the species' own good) and the laissez-faire, or preservationist, school of conservation. The latter prevailed. Then the area was hit by a severe drought. The elephants and the park suffered. Boyce Rensberger, a science writer for the *New York Times* (he is now with the Washington *Post*), visited the park in the early seventies and described the horror: "Much of Tsavo looks as if a war had just ended there. It is a ravaged land. The elephants shuffling about, scrounging bits of grass under fallen trees, are both the war's orphans, and its combatants."

At least 9,000 elephants died of starvation. (Parker and others put the toll at closer to 15,000.) Several hundred rhino also died, victims of the elephants—the elephants had destroyed not only their own vegetation, but the rhino's as well. In fact, the rhino suffered more because their diet is more limited than the elephants' and they do not range as far in search of food.

Though the drought was severe, most scientists say that if the elephant herds had been culled, far fewer elephants and rhino would have died, because there would not have been such a large population competing for the reduced grazing. In addition, Parker argues that the ivory and hides from the culled elephants could have been sold for $3 million. The money could have been used for conservation or for the benefit of the subsistence farmers living near the park, who were also suffering from the drought. Instead the elephant carcasses rotted in the sun, feasted on by hyenas and vultures, which fueled the resentment of the local people toward parks, wildlife and conservation laws.

In recent years, Zimbabwe has been the focus of arguments about culling and attacks from the ivory ban advocates for doing so. In the past two decades, the Zimbabwean wildlife department has culled at least 44,000 elephants. Without the culling, Zimbabwean wildlife officials say, their elephant population would exceed 134,000 (it is about 60,000). That would be roughly one elephant for every square mile, or the equivalent of 60,000 elephants in England and Wales.

The idea of culling is anathema to animal rights organizations, as their approach to conservation focuses on saving each and every animal, rather than on the larger question of saving a particular species or habitat, which may require sacrificing individual animals. In one of his many attacks on Zimbabwe, Allan Thornton, director of the London-based Environmental Investigation Agency and one of the most vocal and effective of the ivory ban advocates, wrote: "There is no scientific information that has ever been independently scrutinised which states that the 'cull' of elephants in Zimbabwe is necessary." He was guilty of innuendo and half-truths. If there was no "scientific evidence" that had been "independently scrutinised," obviously the Zimbabweans were guilty of flimflam and were hiding something. In point of fact, however, there were many scientists and reputable conservationists, inside and outside Zimbabwe, who thought that Zimbabwe's culls were ecologically justified. The biggest problem with Thornton's accusation, however, was the word "necessary." Necessary for what?

What if Zimbabwe decided to cull elephants for no scientific reason whatsoever, but simply because Zimbabweans were complaining that there were too many elephants? Can one imagine 50,000 black bears in California, which is about the size of Zimbabwe? The issue is not just numbers, but sovereignty: Does the international community have the right to tell a country what to do about its wildlife? Would New Yorkers tolerate Canadians or Frenchmen, let alone Africans or Asians, telling them how many bison there ought to be in Central Park? Many Americans do not even want their own government interfering. Recently the U.S. Fish and Wildlife Service has proposed reintroducing the gray wolf to Yellowstone and other areas in the West, where it once roamed in great numbers but had been hunted to near extinction. "The wolf is a symbol of the American wilderness and represents all we have lost in two hundred years of exploitation of nature in America," the president of Defenders of Wildlife, a conservation group, said in support of the plan. The director of the Wyoming Wool Growers Association countered, "A howling wolf inside the park may be romantic, but a howling wolf outside the park is a howl of death for a rancher." The executive vice-president of the Montana Stock Growers Association said that bringing the wolves back could result in the loss of up to a thousand head of cattle a year on ranches near the park. This view echoes the sentiments that many Africans have about elephants and other wild animals—they might be wonderful, and even worth conserving, but not near my farm.

Zimbabwe has decided that there should be 34,000 elephants in its parks and protected areas. This determination was based on a considered judgment about what other fauna and flora the country wanted to preserve in its parks. "Nobody's trying to bluff that it's a wholly scientific decision," said David Cumming, deputy director of Zimbabwe's Department of National Parks and Wildlife Management when the decision was made. "It's a value judgment—that the baobab have as much right to exist in those parks as elephants." The baobab is an eccentric-looking tree, with a huge girth, some thirty feet or more, and limbs shooting wildly out of the top; the Shona of Zimbabwe call it the upside-down tree, and indeed it does look as if the roots are at the top. The elephants love to eat it because the bark of the baobab is high in calcium and the tree also stores water; with their tusks, they rip the bark and then dig into the wood. I was delighted every time I saw a baobab, but when, in October 1991, I visited Tanzania's Tarangire National Park, I was overcome. The park is a baobab paradise, and I snapped as many photographs of the trees—silhouetted across the plains, propping up a fiery setting sun—as I did of the lions and elephants. And I saw the baobab hell that the park may become, with trees dead or dying because of the elephants.

Conservation inherently involves value judgments. Gorillas or elephants? AWLF had to decide. To set aside land for a national park requires a judgment that the land will not be used for farming or cattle grazing or housing. And then what will the park be for? Will there be cars and lodges in the park? Or will visitors be allowed only on foot and to camp? What species of animals do we want in our park? What trees and other plants?

The chief ecologist in the Zimbabwe wildlife department in the 1980s, Colin Craig, explained to me that "the elephant induces changes in the ecosystem, which basically means loss of trees." He said there was even some fear that the Zimbabwean elephant population might have to be reduced to below 25,000. "It sounds a bit wet, I know, to say that just because we're losing a few trees, we have to wipe out twenty-five thousand elephants. But there's no point in having a national park if you allow the entire ecosystem to be destroyed. Trees are a major part of the ecosystem. If you lose trees, you may lose a hell of a lot of species. What we're saying is that we can't take the risk that elephants will ultimately harm things in an irreversible way." He explained that in Sengwe, an area of western Zimbabwe where he had done research for a decade, aerial photographs from 1959 showed no perceptible damage by elephants to the woodlands, but that 50 percent of the trees in one area had been lost by the mid-1960s, and half of those remaining were gone by 1972. "So we're down to twenty-five percent of what we had," he said.

Zimbabwe says that it culls for ecological reasons, not economic or commercial ones, and this may be the primary objective, but the central treasury expects revenues from the ivory and hides. During the 1980s, Zimbabwe was earning about $2 million annually from the sale of the ivory taken during the culls; the real earnings to the country were far greater because there was a thriving domestic carving industry and carved ivory sells for about ten times as much as raw ivory. The money went into the general treasury, but some of it was returned to the country's parks and conservation departments.

Cynthia Moss abhors culling. "I'm against it for moral reasons," she says. "I'm opposed to undue cruelty to animals. Elephants know what's happening. They're terrorized by culling. They lead terrorized lives, afterwards. I hate it." Nevertheless, she accepts that Zimbabwe has the right to cull. "It's not for me to tell a country what to do," she says. "I'm not saying they [the Zimbabweans who cull] are horrible people. I just disagree with them."

SIX MONTHS AFTER WWF had convened the urgent meeting of the heads of major African wildlife departments and its own people in Lusaka in April 1988 to come up with a policy on the ivory ban and elephant conservation generally, it had still not done so. This was not surprising. The organization was trying to balance its commitment to sustainable utilization and its knowledge that culling was necessary for ecological reasons with its scramble for members and money. It might have been able to do both. It could have made an effort to explain sustainable utilization and culling. It might not have been easy, given the complexity of the issues—you can't explain sustainable utilization with catchy slogans like "Only Elephants Should Wear Ivory" and "Ivory Kills"—but WWF never tried. Instead its creative energy went into crafting a policy that wouldn't offend the public, even if that meant concealing from the public what it stood for.

In the fall of 1988, with the West becoming more emotional about the African elephant, WWF was under increasing pressure to come up with a policy. Memoranda and comments went back and forth, often by fax, between the International office and the national organizations. The policy wasn't intended to be made public, only to provide the national organizations with something so they could respond to a steadily expanding volume of letters from members and questions from journalists. At one point, it was proposed that WWF should say that it was opposed to killing elephants "solely for their ivory." That would have permitted culling in Zimbabwe, as well as South Africa, where a few hundred elephants are culled each year, and in Botswana, which wanted to begin culling. The U.S. chapter could not accept this statement.

Finally, it was decided that WWF's policy should be that it opposed the killing of elephants "except where absolutely necessary for the conservation of the species." Several national organizations found this policy acceptable—"excellent," responded WWF-Netherlands; "sensible," and they were "absolutely behind" it, said WWF-Finland; "OK with us," said WWF–New Zealand. Again, WWF-US balked. "We dare not go public" with that statement, Kathryn Fuller, a senior vice-president (and soon to become president), faxed the International. The president of WWF-US, William Reilly (soon to become head of the Environmental Protection Agency in the Bush administration), explained why. "Based on our survey research in this country, there is a major problem with any policy that condones killing elephants—when the elephant population is dwindling—in order to save them. It has too much of the flavor of what the U.S. military used to tell the American public about why they destroyed Vietnamese villages—to protect them," Reilly wrote Simon Lyster, an officer with WWF-UK who was coordinating the effort to develop a policy.

It was a catchy analogy, but the reality was that it might be necessary to destroy elephants in order to save them, as the experience in Tsavo had shown. In his letter to Lyster, Reilly revealed what was really bothering the organization: "I know that U.S. animal rights groups—which have already directed considerable criticism at us for our position on the legal ivory trade—will misrepresent our stance and cloud our efforts to advise WWF members about our position."

WWF had not made a serious effort to explain to its members and the public why a ban was not a good idea or why culling was necessary. But Reilly was right that the animal rights organizations lay in wait to attack.

ORGANIZED concerns in America about humane treatment of animals go back more than a century—the American Society for the Prevention of Cruelty to Animals (ASPCA) was founded in 1866—but the modern animal rights movement, or certainly its meteoric growth, can be dated from the publication in 1975 of *Animal Liberation*. Written by an Australian philosophy professor, Peter Singer, the book is a well-reasoned and persuasive treatise against cruelty toward animals on ethical and moral grounds. Singer's argument is based on the capacity of animals to experience pain and suffering. To accept that idea one only needs to think about how every animal, from a mouse or a dog to a cow or an elephant, reacts to avoid the infliction of physical harm. Singer does not say that animals and humans are equal, for that would lead to obvious absurdities. Rather, Singer argues that because animals share with humans the desire to avoid pain, they deserve "equal consideration" with humans. Such consideration means that animals, like humans, should not be subjected to unnecessary pain and suffering. "If a being suffers, there can be no moral justification for refusing to take that suffering into consideration," he writes.

Singer was concerned primarily about the use of animals in laboratory experiments and with how farm animals are treated, and he said very little about wild animals. He allows that it might be permissible to kill some animals—for instance, for food if absolutely necessary, or to protect one's own life or property. He would almost certainly be opposed to killing elephants for their ivory; there seems to be nothing in his argument, however, that would preclude the sale of ivory from elephants that die from natural causes. For Singer, however, it is permissible for man to reduce the size of animal populations when it is necessary to do so for their own good or because they threaten the survival of other animals, but he would prefer it be done by population control measures that affect fertility and not by hunting. He does not address what to do in cases where no contraceptive method has been developed, as it has not yet been for elephants.

Not all of Singer's premises were new. Two centuries earlier, the English liberal philosopher Jeremy Bentham had argued that the question to be asked in deciding whether humans and nonhumans were deserving of the same ethical considerations was not whether they can reason or talk, but "Can they suffer?" And in 1891, another Englishman, Henry Salt, wrote *Animals' Rights Considered in Relation to Social Progress*, which greatly presaged today's environmental movement. But Singer drew the past thinking together and added his own, and it may have been that he found a more favorable intellectual climate—that by the 1970s people were willing to listen to arguments about the rights of animals as they had once listened to arguments about the rights of slaves and women. In any case, more has been written about animal rights in the eighteen years since the appearance of *Animal Liberation* than in the eighty preceding it, and the movement is stronger than it has ever been. A *Newsweek* cover story in December 1988 on the animal rights movement estimated that there were ten million members in the United States; they belonged to organizations that had $50 million in their coffers. During congressional hearings in the summer of 1988 on legislation that would have barred ivory imports into the United States, Curtis Bohlen, representing WWF-US, prefaced his remarks by noting that his organization had 400,000 members. When it was the Humane Society's turn to testify, its representative, Susan Lieberman, pointedly noted that her organization had nearly a million members.

Though the mainstream conservation organizations derisively refer to them as "humaniacs," the animal rights advocates have a critical role to play in conservation. There are moral and ethical questions that need to be addressed, which the traditional conservation organizations avoid. If culling is ethical, how can it be done to minimize the suffering of both the elephants that are killed and of those that survive and have watched a relative die? If animals have the right not to be killed by humans, how do we balance that right against the right of people not to be killed by a lion or a leopard, or to protect their crops from elephants?

Singer could honestly claim to have made his case for the rights of animals by "appealing to reason, not to emotion or sentiment." The animal rights groups cannot. In the debate over the ivory ban, they accorded rights to elephants, but ignored the rights of people. And instead of raising philosophical questions, they indulged in hyperbole, incited passions with horror stories and leveled ad hominem attacks on anyone who disagreed with them. It was not possible to have intellectual

disagreements over the merits of a ban with the animal rights activists—
you were either on their side or you were an "elephant killer."

In addition to their zealotry, the animal rights groups involved in the
ivory ban issue had other things in common. They wanted to save each
and every animal, but they did not possess the scientific knowledge to
understand what this meant for the ecosystem. They also lacked any
experience in Africa. Susan Lieberman, who handled wildlife and environmental matters for the Humane Society and lobbied hard for a ban
on ivory trading, had never been to Africa or seen an elephant in the
wild. Another organizational advocate for a ban was the Animal Welfare
Institute, headed by Christine Stevens, whose only trip to Africa had
been to Egypt. Her organization had fewer than 10,000 members but
disproportionate influence, because Mrs. Stevens was part of the George-
town social-political scene. She was the wife of Roger Stevens, who had
made a fortune, first in New York real estate and then as a Broadway
producer (*Cat on a Hot Tin Roof, West Side Story*), before moving to
Washington, where he served as a special assistant to President Johnson
and was awarded the Presidential Medal of Freedom by President
Reagan. Mrs. Stevens used her connections to lobby the White House
for support of a ban, and she used her organization's money to campaign
publicly for the cause.

Some of the most vicious attacks during the ivory ban war were the
work of an organization called Friends of Animals (FoA), which defines
its purpose as working "to reduce and eliminate the suffering inflicted
by humans upon non-human animals." Founded in 1957, it has its headquarters in Norwalk, Connecticut, and in 1988 had about 100,000 members. The president was Priscilla Feral, whose only visit to Africa had
been to an animal orphanage supported by the organization in Liberia.
After graduating from Centenary College in New Jersey, Feral worked
as a secretary at Pepperidge Farms before joining Friends of Animals in
1974 as public information director, and she let her name speak for her
commitment. She was born Priscilla Brockway in 1949, became Priscilla
Brennan when she married in the early seventies, and then Priscilla
Seymour in 1978, after a divorce and remarriage. But sometime in the
seventies she began using the name Feral, and she had the change
made legal in 1990. (The word "feral" refers to a wild animal, or to a
domesticated animal that has returned to the wild state.) During a lawsuit
that Friends of Animals brought to block United States Surgical from
using dogs for testing surgical staples, a federal magistrate criticized

Feral and FoA's attorney for "obstreperous, obstructive, and obnoxious" behavior. It was a description that many in WWF and on the front lines of the ivory wars would have found apt for Priscilla Feral.

In the April/May 1988 issue of the magazine for its members, *Act'ionLine*, FoA rebuked WWF for its adherence to the principle of sustainable utilization, and it also chastised WWF for "feverishly lobbying to PREVENT the total ban on ivory products that even the world's foremost experts on elephants say is needed to save the species." At the time, Congress was considering legislation that would have banned all ivory imports into the United States, and FoA urged its members, *"Tell your Congressman the World Wildlife Fund does not speak for you."*

The world's wildlife experts were, of course, far from unanimous about a ban, and if anything the vast majority were against one, which is one of the reasons that in the spring and summer of 1988 WWF-US was indeed lobbying against legislation that would have banned all ivory imports.

Friends of Animals also exhorted its members to write WWF. Many did, often parroting FoA's language. Thus, one woman wrote that she had read—she did not say where—that "WWF is feverishly lobbying to prevent the total ban on ivory products that even the world's foremost experts on elephants say is needed to save the species and instead lobbying against a full ban." She added: "Much to my dismay, I am going to have to cancel my membership in your organization and will encourage all my friends to do the same."

WWF-US received thousands of letters about the ivory ban, more than it had ever received on any other issue, and the overwhelming majority of those who wrote wanted a ban.

THIS, THEN, was the conflict WWF found itself confronted with at the end of 1988, and indeed during the entire ivory ban controversy: its members and the general public, their sentimental feelings about elephants aroused by misleading appeals like those of AWF and shrill language from Friends of Animals, wanted a ban on ivory trading, whereas science and good conservation dictated against one. An internal WWF-US memorandum written in May 1988 captures the predicament. "Although we support sustainable wildlife utilization projects following the philosophy of the *World Conservation Strategy*, and are committed to an all-out effort to make the CITES quota system work," the authors wrote, "these concepts are not understood by the vast majority of the 450,000 WWF-US members." They went on, "Most of these members are more traditionally oriented towards species 'preservation,' and there is little understanding of the complexities of conservation in Africa in the 1980s, particularly where wildlife utilization programs are concerned."

The same battles between money and science haunted leading British conservationists, with the same outcome. "It's a dilemma," says David Jones, a trustee of WWF-UK and former director of the London Zoo. "Do you go the professional route or do you compromise?" The scientists and conservationists at WWF-UK supported sustainable utilization and culling, but there were fears that the organization might lose 20 percent of its members if they were aware that their money went for such activities. The organization would compromise.

CYNICS SAY that the conservation organizations got on the ivory ban issue in order to perpetuate their existence. But there are legitimate reasons for an organization's putting a premium on recruiting members and raising money. After all, an organization has to raise money to stay in business, to carry out its good works even beyond the immediate cause that brings in money. Thus, WWF might use the money that "saving the elephants" raises to support working with a small community in Costa Rica to save its forests or for a park in Tibet—neither of these projects alone could bring in enough public support to pay for it.

There was money in elephants. Big money. More than in saving whales, or dolphins, or gorillas, or any other species. And, granted, conservation principles like sustainable utilization and culling are not easy ones to sell to the public. Surely, however, given the brainpower and imagination of direct mail fund-raisers and Madison Avenue advertising executives, the means could be found. It would take moral courage as well, to come up with, for example, a slogan like "Buy Ivory, Save Elephants," which is what sustainable utilization is all about.

In the end, maybe the public would not understand the complexities of conservation; maybe WWF and AWF would lose members if the organizations said they supported culling and sustainable utilization. But if so, if explaining these concepts meant losing members, at least the organizations would be true to their conservation principles. Instead they sacrificed their principles—and abandoned most Africans as well.

AFRICA BESIEGED

|||| NINETEEN EIGHTY-NINE was the year of the environment. On January 2, *Time* magazine's "Man of the Year" was the planet—"Endangered Earth." There were fears about global warming, the greenhouse effect and a hole in the ozone, appeals to save Brazil's rain forests, outrage at an oil spill off the coast of Alaska, and questions about what to do with the world's hazardous wastes. But no issue reached the public—in their hearts and pocketbooks—as deeply as the African elephant. Western passions rose, as did the sums of money pouring into organizations that catered to them.

At the beginning of 1989, not one African country was in favor of a ban on ivory trading. Nor had a single Western country called for one. Nor even had any of the major conservation organizations. At IUCN, the most scientifically solid of the world's conservation groups, there was virtually no debate—opposition to a ban was unanimous. At WWF-US, the conservationists and scientists were still prevailing in their fights with the fund-raisers and Bohlen, and this pleased the International, where the sentiment was strongly against a ban. The African Wildlife Foundation's position was still that people should voluntarily refrain from buying ivory, but the organization was not calling for a total ban.

The denouement, the shifts of positions, came fast, amidst heavy lobbying and behind-the-scenes maneuvering. In the West, the outcome might be viewed as the result of democracy at work, with governments responding to public pressure. Many of the Africans involved had never seen anything quite like the way in which the pro-ban advocates got their news into the press and lobbied, and they felt powerless to counter it. They did not have the money or the political experience to engage in public relations campaigns. To them it also looked like colonialism, the will of the West being imposed.

In November 1988, wildlife officials from a dozen African countries, those which had nearly all of the elephants, had met in Nairobi in a new effort to find a solution to the poaching. The stolid and judicious Perez Olindo, director of Kenya's wildlife department, was elected to chair, but he had barely settled into his seat on the dais in the front of the spacious U.N. amphitheater when he had to leave. Word arrived that six white rhino had been killed by poachers in Meru National Park, about an hour north of Nairobi by single-engine plane. The rhino had been under special protection, kept behind an electric fence and guarded by armed rangers. The poaching gang broke in shortly after dark, fired a few shots at the warden's house, killed the rhino, cut off their horns with chain saws, and vanished. It was the most brazen poaching incident to date, but it underscored the obvious: poaching was out of control.

Held at the modern United Nations Environment complex on rolling hills twenty minutes from the center of Nairobi, the meeting was attended by virtually all the expatriate elephant experts and wildlife conservationists—Iain Douglas-Hamilton, Ian Parker, David Western and Esmond Bradley Martin, who knew more about the rhino horn and ivory trade than any single individual. AWF was represented by Cynthia Moss and Mark Stanley Price, WWF-US by Curtis Bohlen.

"The large number of participants and the intensity of their sometimes conflicting views made it difficult to get meaningful discussion of solutions," observed Marshall Jones, who attended as a representative of the U.S. Fish and Wildlife Service. "This was particularly true because European and North American 'experts' tended to dominate the meeting, whereas African governmental representatives seemed inhibited from speaking frankly about the situation." That was a fitting characterization of the entire ivory ban debate—it was dominated by Western "experts," to whom Africans deferred. It might seem chauvinistic or, worse, racist to suggest that Africans meekly submit to Westerners. But during my four years in Africa, I continually witnessed the deference that Africans displayed toward whites. If you have a white face, you probably will be waved through airport customs in Kenya and Zimbabwe; but observe what Africans have to endure, as customs officials paw through their luggage. Walk into a bank in Nairobi, an airline ticket office in Lusaka, and if you're white, you'll likely be motioned to the front of the line by an African clerk. I was never able to comprehend this subservience. Maybe the colonial experience took a greater toll on the African character than I can ever grasp. Maybe after four generations of being told that you are inferior to whites, and brutally treated accordingly, you begin to believe it; maybe this inferiority complex becomes so embedded that it cannot be erased after only one generation of freedom. Whatever the reasons, the deference is a reality, at least for many Africans in many parts of the continent. It may explain why the officers of the East African Wildlife Society, the only African-run conservation organization in Kenya, showed up at conferences dressed in well-tailored dark suits, looking like bankers, not outdoorsmen, and rarely spoke. It might also partially explain, I believe, why Olindo would never openly accuse the conservation organizations of discrimination in not hiring Africans, using the clumsy euphemism "partiality of appointment" instead, and why even though he thought a ban was a bad idea, he never openly and directly took on the Western conservation organizations once they called for one.

For three days in Nairobi, the African wildlife officials and white conservationists listened to ominous reports about the future of the African elephant. One animal population biologist, Graeme Caughley, an Australian, using computer modeling, predicted the "commercial" end of the elephant in East Africa within seven years, and in all of Africa by 2010. Once again, however, the sentiment was against a ban on ivory trading. Not just from the African governments, but from nearly all of the Western conservationists present.

"A proposition for an all-embracing moratorium would ignore the fact that sustainable yield is a reality in parts of Southern Africa, on which a whole policy of conservation and development is based," said Iain Douglas-Hamilton, who was attending the meeting as a consultant to the European Economic Community and WWF. He was referring to Botswana, South Africa and Zimbabwe, where, he noted, elephant populations were "well managed and well protected," and the countries made money from the sale of ivory. Therefore, he said, a ban on ivory trading, even a moratorium of five to ten years, might be argued to endanger elephants.

This was one of the most reasonable statements made during the entire ivory ban ruckus—Douglas-Hamilton recognized that something needed to be done, but that a blanket ban would not be fair to the southern African countries. Other people said the same thing, of course. But no one with the prestige and following that Douglas-Hamilton had.

Iain Douglas-Hamilton is widely thought of as "Mr. Elephant." In the 1960s, having come to East Africa from Scotland, he pioneered research in elephant behavior, beginning in Tanzania's Lake Manyara National

Park, and in the 1970s, he wrote a book, *Among the Elephants*, that became a best-seller in several countries. He has a doctorate in zoology from Oxford, and has been the mentor for just about everyone who has studied elephants in Africa, including Cynthia Moss. Douglas-Hamilton is charming and dashing, a celebrity from London to Los Angeles, a favorite of *National Geographic* and documentry filmmakers. Over the years he has been accompanied in what he has described as the *Battle for the Elephants*—the title of his 1992 book—by his wife, Oria. A vivacious Italian raised in Kenya, the mother of their two teenage daughters, fond of pushing sunglasses back on her long blond hair, she has been an *apasionada* for the elephants, able to cry or curse for the cause. "You bastard," she once sputtered when a reporter, in the course of asking a question, suggested that a ban might not be a good idea.

If Douglas-Hamilton had ever said publicly, to a television camera, or to an audience in the United States or Europe, what he said at that meeting in Nairobi, the outcome of the ivory ban debate would have been different. He never did. And as many times as I talked to him about the ivory ban, I could never figure out what he really believed. One time he told me that he had always favored allowing the southern African countries to keep their elephants on Appendix II, while another time he said that he had always been in favor of a complete ban, but never thought it was politically possible to get. One of his colleagues and admirers said that intellectually Douglas-Hamilton knew that a ban was not the best solution to poaching, but that he was influenced by his wife. She was certainly more uncompromising on the issue than he. While he, for example, recognized that there might be a need for culling, she once said, "The African elephant needs management by man like it needs a hole in the head." Whatever the reasons, Douglas-Hamilton became one of the principal and most influential lobbyists for a complete ban. And the public juggernaut, which his wife fueled, flattened the kind of wisdom and moderation he had expressed in Nairobi.

AWF ESCALATED its "Year of the Elephant" and "Don't Buy Ivory" campaign on February 12, 1989, with a full-page ad in the Sunday *New York Times*. As the ad appeared two days before Valentine's Day, it was hoped that men would be deterred from buying their wives and girlfriends ivory bracelets, necklaces and so on.

"TODAY, IN AMERICA, SOMEONE WILL SLAUGHTER AN ELEPHANT FOR

A BRACELET," the ad declared, over a picture of an elephant with its face hacked off. The organization claimed that in the past ten years Africa's elephant population had been "sliced" from 1,300,000 to fewer than 750,000 and that 70,000 elephants were killed each year to meet the demand for ivory. At that rate, there would be no elephants left in Africa by 1999, the organization asserted, and it went on: "It's a sickening thought. In ten short years we could have to explain to children why there are no more elephants." The ad had been prepared free of charge by Saatchi & Saatchi, the international advertising conglomerate, and it appeared frequently, in a smaller size, in the *International Herald Tribune*, which donated space.

AWF placed appeals in consumer magazines. In one ad, a woman wore an ivory necklace over bare shoulders. "Dressed to Kill," it said. In another a woman was wearing three ivory bracelets—"Accessories to Murder." And the organization received a phenomenal amount of free publicity. The actor James Stewart made a public service announcement, which was used by several hundred radio stations around the country. "Good Morning America" and "CBS This Morning" interviewed Stewart. ABC's afternoon soap opera "General Hospital" managed to make a pitch against buying ivory. Articles about AWF's campaign appeared in the *New York Times*, *Time* and *Newsweek*. Television stations and newspapers in Canada, Germany, France and Holland contacted AWF; one of Rome's largest newspapers wanted to collect funds and send them to AWF for the elephant campaign.

Four days after the AWF ad appeared in the *Times*, a coalition of animal rights groups, including the Humane Society, Friends of Animals, and the Animal Welfare Institute, held a press conference in Washington, D.C. They announced that they were filing a legal petition with the Interior Department, which has jurisdiction over the introduction of wildlife products into the United States, to have the elephant declared an endangered species under United States law. The elephant had been on the "threatened" list since 1977, which meant that ivory could not come in without a permit; raising it to the status of "endangered" would have stopped all ivory imports.

Meanwhile, the members of Defenders of Wildlife were reading a somewhat surprising and feverish article about poaching of elephants. It was surprising because the organization was founded in 1947 to protect species and habitats in the United States, and that had remained its focus; in 1989, it took up the cause of the African elephant. The article, in the

March issue of *Defenders*, was written by Janet Trowbridge Bohlen, who had once been the head of public relations for WWF-US, and who was the wife of WWF's Curtis Bohlen. She characterized the poaching of the African elephant as "genocide," not only overstating what was happening, but cheapening the word.

In April, an organization called the International Wildlife Coalition got into what seemed to be degenerating into a contest to see who could come up with the most excessive language. "AFRICAN CHAINSAW MASSA-CRE" was the headline on the half-page ad that it placed in the *New York Times*. The organization was another of those born in the early 1980s at the time of rising enthusiasm for animal rights; the organization's purpose is to "protect wild animals from cruelty and needless killing." The ad juxtaposed a picture of a happy elephant family with one of elephant carcasses. "MURDERED FOR THEIR IVORY" was the caption. This organiza-tion claimed the elephant would be extinct by 1997, and it went on: "The last elephant to die will likely be a baby. . . . The last thing this baby will see before it dies, will be its mother being killed and mutilated with a chainsaw."

Three days later, it was time for Friends of Animals. Their immediate target was Sotheby's, which was planning to auction two large pairs of elephant tusks, worth at least $16,000 a pair. "WHY AUCTION ELEPHANT TUSKS IN THE MIDST OF AN ELEPHANT HOLOCAUST?" the organization demanded in a half-page ad in the *New York Times*. "Hyperbole? Judge for yourself. Since 1979 alone, nearly ONE MILLION elephants—three quarters of Africa's wild elephant population—have been wiped out." Sotheby's canceled the auction and declared it would not sell any tusks or "any ivory or work of ivory" post 1940. Reflecting the competition among these organizations for glory, Priscilla Feral, FoA's president, told me that Sotheby's had backed off because of the ad and because the organization was threatening to picket Sotheby's. According to Diana McMeekin, the AWF vice-president, her organization had been having ongoing discussions with Sotheby's and that, she claims, explains why the auction house did not go ahead.

THERE WAS SOMETHING ELSE about these appeals in behalf of the African elephants, something other than the shrill, exaggerated and hyperbolic language employed—they were phenomenally successful in raising money. Elephants had become *the* environmental fad. The article in *Defenders* asked readers for a tax-deductible donation to help the elephant campaign. The organization had fewer than 80,000 members, but the appeal brought in $40,000, making it the most successful fund-raising effort of its kind in that organization's history.

When AWF launched its elephant campaign in 1988 with the Urgent Memorandum and press conference, it was a small organization with 24,000 members, not well known outside a small circle of African wildlife aficionados, and struggling financially. Within a year, its membership had nearly doubled, and AWF had become a major player in the African conservation game. In its full-page ad in the *New York Times*, AWF asked readers to help stop "the slaughter" of African elephants by sending in a tax-deductible donation of $25, $50, $100 or more. It provided a coupon for the reader to clip or a toll-free number to call. The response was beyond anything that AWF or Saatchi & Saatchi had anticipated. It is unusual that an ad raises enough money to pay its costs. (Organizations place them anyway, to get their messages across and their names before the public, and in the hope of expanding their mailing lists with the names of people who write in.) The *Times* ad cost $40,000. Twelve hundred people responded, and the organization received $42,526. Later the ad appeared twice in *USA Today*, at a cost of $26,000; virtually that much was donated.

If any evidence were still needed that organizations couldn't afford to pass up using the elephant for their own benefit, and that grisliness paid, it was provided by the International Wildlife Coalition and its "chainsaw massacre" ad in the *Times*. The organization had concentrated on saving whales, spending more than $1.3 million on that cause and $52,000 on elephants in the fiscal year of the elephant ad, according to the organization's audited financial statement; it had spent more on kangaroos and sea turtles—combined, $75,000—than on elephants. The elephant ad cost $22,000; it raised $25,000.

It was not only in the United States that the elephant was loved. In Britain the local WWF sent out a four-page letter in behalf of the elephant. The letter was bland (reflecting characteristic British reserve) when read alongside the appeals from AWF and other U.S. organizations. It noted the alarming decline of elephants in Kenya, Tanzania and Zambia, but it used the word "slaughter" only once. The mailing went to 50,000 people. It raised £300,000 (more than $500,000). In July 1989, WWF-UK sent out another elephant appeal. An additional £200,000

came in. That was twice as much as people sent to WWF-UK in response
to pleas for sea turtles and gorillas.

In South Africa, the Endangered Wildlife Trust, the organization that
supports Garth Owen-Smith's community game guard program in Namibia, raised nearly $150,000 from selling original prints of the Kaokoveld's
desert elephant, drawn and signed by the well-known wildlife artist
David Shepherd. That made it one of the most successful conservation
appeals in South Africa, which has a strong and active environmental
movement and consciousness. "We rode on the backs of elephants, and
rhinos, for years," says the organization's director, John Ledger.

WITH ADS in the *Times*, press conferences, articles in magazines and newspapers, and appeals by celebrities, the rumblings that
began in early 1988 were becoming a stampede. African points of view
would be buried. WWF feared it would be, too.

"You cannot believe all the film crews that are here right now doing
elephants," the besieged director of the WWF office in Kenya, Ed Wilson, notified a colleague at WWF-US by fax a week after AWF's ad in
the *Times*. "BBC was here last week with David Attenborough . . .
Italian, French and German national televisions are here. . . . An Italian
newspaper journalist is here. . . . The Kenyan authorities are getting
quite confused and so am I."

On the same day, in Washington, D.C., the chief fund-raiser for
WWF-US was venting her consternation. The AWF ad in the *Times* "has
everyone agitating and since then they have been on network news," Jan
Stout, vice-president for development for WWF-US, faxed the International office; she added that "the humaniacs have held a press conference"—meaning the organizations that had filed the petition with the
Interior Department. It was bad enough that these groups were receiving
media attention, but, Stout noted, an article in *Time* magazine about the
African elephant did not even mention WWF. "We are in danger of
losing our position with elephants," she said. Stout's fears were not that
elephants were threatened by this hyperactivity, but that WWF was.

Stout's memorandum also reveals something that the conservation
organizations would just as soon not have exposed in public—the internecine friction between them. It is not just conservation organizations, of
course, which suffer from this debilitating ailment. In spite of their

common objective of ending torture and cruelty, human rights groups have fought with each other as well as with foreign governments, and it is not uncommon to hear humanitarian organizations delivering food aid to famine victims in Africa belittle the work of other groups. Part of the reason for the strife is ego—individuals and organizations want recognition and acclaim. And they need money in order to carry out their good works. To raise money, an organization has to show itself to be better than the others, to be doing more, which often means taking credit that is not their due and denigrating the work of others. "There is serious competition in the marketplace for funds and attention," says John Ledger. "We're all out there rattling the can. The more the better in conservation, perhaps, but there is petty competition."

The rivalry is palpable—and often very petty—in Nairobi, where the big names in the African conservation game are concentrated: among them, Iain Douglas-Hamilton, Mark Stanley Price, Cynthia Moss, Joyce Poole, David Western and Esmond Bradley Martin. "Prima bwanas" someone once called the Nairobi crowd of conservationists, and their double-barreled names reinforced the colonial nature of the conservation movement. There can be no gainsaying their academic credentials and their commitment to saving Africa's wild animals; there are serious questions, however, about how much some of them care about African people. All the Nairobi conservationists combined do not spend as much time in the field as Garth Owen-Smith does with his community game guards, and when they do they are studying animals, not talking to humans. Nor, with the exception of Western, have they done much to bring Africans into conservation.

The "prima bwanas" live in large houses on vast well-landscaped properties in fashionable areas of Nairobi, and they are well paid for their conservation work. A few years ago, Douglas-Hamilton had a sixteen-month contract with WWF-International worth at least $60,000, including salary, insurance, and education allowance. As the director of AWF's office, Stanley Price earned about $60,000. (With a string of degrees and successful field projects behind him, he wasn't overpaid by the standards of the desk conservationists in faraway Washington. The president of AWF, Paul Schindler, earned $122,000 in 1990; vice-president Diana McMeekin made $86,000—for running an office with half a dozen employees.) In contrast, the director of Kenya's Wildlife Conservation and Management Department, Perez Olindo, who was in charge of several thousand employees and was responsible for conserving the wildlife and maintaining the parks that brought Kenya millions of dollars of foreign exchange every year, earned about $10,000 in 1989, his last year there. When Olindo went to AWF as a senior associate, he was paid $30,000, or half what Stanley Price received.

The Nairobi conservationists are opinionated individualists with strong egos, friendly to each other at cocktail parties and conferences, but in private they can be biting in their remarks. One day in March 1989, for example, when the ivory ban controversy was raging, Stanley Price called on an American diplomat. He complained that WWF was belittling AWF's "Don't Buy Ivory" campaign (which it was), and then he criticized WWF for putting too much faith in lobbying in Washington. The friction between AWF and WWF was senseless, Stanley Price said, but he was quick to add that it was WWF's fault. Within an hour after Stanley Price left, Esmond Bradley Martin went through the same security screening at the embassy, on a busy corner in downtown Nairobi, then took the elevator up a few floors to visit the same diplomat. Bradley Martin received funding from WWF, and he did indeed criticize AWF for its campaign to persuade people not to buy ivory, which he felt was not the solution to the poaching.

The jealousies and backbiting could be overlooked if they did not interfere with effective conservation, but they do. The conservation nerve center is Embassy House, a nondescript five-story office building in downtown Nairobi, by chance a few blocks from the American embassy. AWF and WWF had their offices at the same end of the corridor on the same floor (until 1992, when AWF moved to another building). One floor below were Western and Wildlife Conservation International. Tucked away in another part of the building, Douglas-Hamilton had an office, shared with Friends of Conservation, a Connecticut-based organization funded by Jorie Butler Kent, of Abercrombie & Kent, the travel conglomerate. "Look at this building," Olindo once said, sitting in his AWF office. "We are all paying for office space, we are paying for power, we are paying for electricity, for water. And look at the machines we are buying. It is definitely not the best way to do the job. We could do much more conservation in the field if we had one management. Once we identify a project, then everyone would chip in." Asked how well the organizations did work together, he reached over to a desk and picked up a piece of paper, then slowly placed it tight against his chest. "On rhino and the elephant, we meet and we talk," he said, "then every organization goes behind its closed doors."

AT LEAST the expatriate conservationists talked to each other before going their own way. That was more respect than they showed for the Africans.

The first major wildlife conservation organization to call for a total ban on ivory trading was AWF, on May 5, 1989. When AWF had started its campaign just over a year earlier, it had consciously refrained from suggesting an end to all ivory trading because it thought that would be "arrogant." So what did it feel when it reversed its position? "We still thought it was arrogant," says vice-president McMeekin. She said the organization made the decision to urge a ban only after a lot of "soul searching." But not much consultation with Africans.

It was true that AWF had just hired Olindo—he had been dismissed by Moi as head of the wildlife department—and in its press release on May 5 the organization said, "For the first time in the history of conservation, the voice of the nations of Africa will be heard and respected as a clear expression of the will of the continent." It is almost certain that AWF didn't realize what it was admitting—that in the history of conservation, Africans had been ignored—and even now it wasn't really prepared to listen to Africans. At the time AWF called for a ban, no African government had done so, and never would there be a "will of the continent," which remained split over the issue; moreover, when Olindo expressed views at odds with AWF, the organization would ignore him as well.

Across town, WWF also wanted to convey the image that it wasn't acting like some latter-day colonial power, but it was not easy to make the image conform to the reality. "A lot of behind-the-scenes work went into making sure that Africans got out front," Curtis Bohlen, the vice-president of WWF-US, told me. He was unwilling to be more specific. A massive behind-the-scenes effort was necessary not only to make it look as if the Africans were out front, however. It was also needed in order to get WWF-US and then the International to endorse a ban. And E. U. Curtis Bohlen, whom just about everybody calls "Buff," was behind it all, playing a role for which he was well suited.

Bohlen was born to a family in which commitment to public service was ingrained. His own career has been overshadowed by that of his uncle Charles E. "Chip" Bohlen, one of the "Wise Men" of the American foreign policy establishment, who was probably best known for his stint as ambassador to the Soviet Union. After graduating from Harvard and fulfilling his military obligation in the army during the Korean War, "Buff" Bohlen also went to work for the State Department. At least his official biography says he worked for the State Department, from 1955 to 1969. But in fact he was working for the CIA, with the State Department as his cover; from 1955 to 1958 he was in Kabul, and after a time back in Washington, he was sent to Cairo in 1960, where he remained until 1963, according to the *Biographic Register*, the State Department's annual publication listing its employees. (The department ceased making the *Register* public in the mid-seventies, after journalists and others discovered how easy it was to use it in order to determine who was working for CIA.) What Bohlen did for the Agency between 1963 and 1969 is an even deeper, more highly classified secret, for his name disappears from the *Register* after 1963; nor does it appear in the State Department directories for those years, even though his public résumé says he remained at the department until 1969. Bohlen's conservation career began in 1969, when Russell Train, the AWF founder who had become Nixon's Under Secretary of the Interior, asked Bohlen to join him. (Whether or not he had left the Agency is not known.) While at Interior, Bohlen assisted in drafting the Convention on International Trade in Endangered Species.

Bohlen joined WWF-US in 1981, as the director of government affairs, a newly created position, which reflected the organization's transition from one that did research and public education to one that thought it was also necessary to lobby the government for environmental causes. Some of the WWF staff objected to Bohlen's being hired, because of his CIA background. Many in the Third World have long been convinced that WWF, both the International and the U.S. chapter, has links to the CIA and Britain's MI-6. It would be reasonable for the intelligence agencies to try to use the conservation organization—after all, their people get out into remote rural areas—and at least one WWF staff officer was approached by the agency in the 1980s to provide regular briefings. He declined. (In the major books about the Agency, nothing has surfaced linking it to WWF, nor in my own research did I find any connections other than the overture just noted.)

Bohlen was hired at WWF by Russell Train, who was its president. The men were friends and "class" mates, good Republicans who had their vacation homes on Maryland's Eastern Shore (along with other wealthy and powerful folks from Washington, D.C.). At WWF, Bohlen operated as the consummate inside politician; his door was closed most of the time, and colleagues say he did everything by phone, careful to put almost nothing in writing. He was a somewhat mysterious figure around WWF, where colleagues would jokingly ask, "Has anyone seen Buff?" or "Where's Buff?" He was a diplomat of sorts, steeped in intrigue, but he knew virtually nothing about animals and less about Africa. "He's like most of our members, I suppose," a WWF-US conservation officer observed ruefully.

If Bohlen had not decided that a ban was an appropriate response to the poaching, WWF-US would almost certainly not have endorsed it. And if the U.S. chapter had not, then the International would not have. As critical as his role was, why Bohlen came to support a ban is not clear. He is a cordial and gracious man, easy to like, but he is not an individual who by personality or training is going to reveal the true reasons for his thinking, particularly if they are likely to be controversial. He says he supported a ban because of the weight of the scientific evidence—that is, that without a ban, poaching would continue until the elephants disappeared. But that is hard to accept, given that the overwhelming majority of scientists and professional conservationists, including those in his own organization, didn't reach that conclusion. Bohlen wasn't an animal rights zealot; in fact, he believed in hunting and in sustainable utilization, and while at the Interior Department he had opposed a moratorium on commercial whaling and supported sport hunting of Montana's grizzly bears, for which he was denounced by animal rights militants. Nor did he always side with the fund-raisers at WWF, as, for example, when he supported the right of Eskimos to continue hunting fur seals. Even Bohlen's colleagues at WWF say they could not fathom what was behind his position on the ivory ban. "Did he want to destabilize Africa?" one asks, then quickly rejects the idea as "farfetched." "Was it a favor to Janet?" the same colleague goes on. Bohlen's wife, Janet, is the former public relations director at WWF-US who referred to the elephant poaching as "genocide."

WHATEVER BOHLEN'S REASONS, he had come down on the side of the fund-raisers well before WWF-US had decided what its organizational position would be—the conservationists and fund-raisers were still slugging it out—and he secretly began assisting the pro-ban forces outside the organization. It was a loose operation that involved Jorgen Thomsen, a senior program officer at WWF-US who reported to Bohlen, Christine Stevens of the Animal Welfare Institute and Allan Thornton of the London-based Environmental Investigation Agency.

Thornton, a lanky Canadian, had been fighting in environmental wars since the mid-seventies; as a member of Greenpeace, he had once gone into the cold, choppy seas to block the killing of seals. In 1985, Thornton founded the Environmental Investigation Agency (EIA). "We're not fund-raisers, we're not scientists. We're campaigners, first and foremost," Thornton says. It is a small outfit of militant environmentalists—Thornton's salary in 1989 was only £12,000. Because it was small and had no membership base, EIA needed money for its elephant campaign. This is where Christine Stevens came in. She gave EIA $165,000 in 1989 and 1990, a substantial portion of EIA's total budget. In effect, Thornton and EIA were the alter egos of Stevens and the Animal Welfare Institute.

In late 1988, Thornton went to Africa to film dead elephants and ivory stockpiles. He quickly became "public enemy number one," as a wildlife department official in Zimbabwe scribbled on a copy of an article Thornton wrote. Thornton's manner of operating offended many. To get into the meeting in Nairobi in November 1988, he says, he intentionally misled the chairman, Olindo, as to whom he represented, and during another meeting he warned African officials that if they did not go along with a ban, he would step up the public relations assaults on their countries abroad, a threat that many of the conservationists who worked in Africa, such as AWF's Stanley Price, felt went too far. For Thornton, almost anything was justified to stop the ivory trade.

Thornton approached Thomsen of WWF-US to write a proposal that would put the elephant on CITES Appendix I—that is, have it declared an endangered species. At first, this would seem a strange choice. It was Thomsen who had written the memorandum, in May 1988, saying that the elephant was not endangered, and he had long argued against a ban. By early 1989, he had changed his position, though it is unclear why. He says it was because of the evidence that came to light about the extent of the poaching. Many of his colleagues don't believe it. They think Thomsen's change of heart came after he spent time working with Joyce Poole in Amboseli, and, even less charitably, they say Thomsen felt that the glamour was in being on the side of the ivory ban; among other things, Thomsen and Poole worked together on a documentary,

Ivory Wars, which was narrated by James Earl Jones. Whatever the reasons, having become a convert, Thomsen signed on with Thornton and in March 1989 he began working on a proposal to put the elephant on CITES Appendix I. In recruiting Thomsen, Thornton hoped he would be getting access to WWF's valuable files and data. Thomsen did indeed use them. The problem, however, was that WWF was still opposed to a ban.

No one at WWF knew what Thomsen was up to, except, of course, Bohlen. When the WWF-US president, Kathryn Fuller, eventually learned about Thomsen's activities, she was not pleased. In a book Thornton wrote acclaiming the role that he and EIA played in getting an ivory ban put in place, he stated that Thomsen had taken an unpaid leave of absence from WWF while working on the Appendix I proposal; among other things, Thomsen traveled to Kenya and Tanzania. In fact, Thomsen had not taken leave. While being paid by WWF and using WWF's files, Thomsen worked on the proposal with Poole, and the document they eventually drafted came to 149 pages. It had the authority of a scientific paper and the persuasiveness of a Supreme Court brief.

That was not, however, the end of the battle by Westerners to stop the ivory trade, and to make it look as if it were something the Africans wanted. An Appendix I proposal had been written, but it was necessary for a country to submit it to CITES. Any country that was a member of CITES could put the proposal on the agenda, but if it was done by the United States or a European country, it would look to Africans like another case of colonialism, and most African countries and their Third World allies would probably vote against it. Thus Thornton set about trying to find an African country to propose an Appendix I listing for the elephant. Since Olindo and Kenya were opposed to a ban, Thornton looked to Tanzania.

He wrote letters that the Conservation Society of Tanzania sent to conservation organizations around the world asking for their support; soon letters were coming back to Tanzania urging the government to call for a ban on the ivory trade. Ultimately, Thornton drafted a letter that the society sent to the minister of tourism officially asking the government to file an Appendix I proposal, and then Thornton wrote a memorandum for the Tanzanian president, Ali Hassan Mwyini, explaining why a ban was needed.

When John Hanks, the director of Africa programs at WWF-International, got wind of what Thornton was up to, he hurriedly flew to Dar es Salaam and met with conservationists and government officials in an effort to dissuade them from calling for a ban. Hanks, who had a doctorate in zoology from Cambridge—his thesis was on elephant reproduction—and who had more than two decades' experience in Africa, thought the ban was bad for the elephant and for Africans. Those at the top of the International agreed with Hanks, though not for the same reasons. "The 'ban' is a typical 'knee-jerk' reaction by the 'greens' and it is not going to be easy to get rational measures adopted for the control of poaching and for limiting demand to sustainable supply," Prince Philip once said. Philip's opposition to a ban on ivory trading didn't arise from any sympathy for poor Africans who needed the income from ivory, but from his belief that a laissez-faire economic system was the cure for all ills.

In early May, Thornton and the other ivory ban advocates were not only struggling to overcome the influence of Hanks and the International, but they were now also racing against the clock. If the elephant was to be declared an endangered species at the CITES meeting in October, a proposed resolution had to be filed by May 12, 1989. A week before the deadline, Tanzania formally submitted an Appendix I proposal, supporting it with the document that Thomsen and Poole had written, though of course their names were nowhere on it.

On May 11 the ivory ban forces received a major boost when Kenya announced that it, too, would ask to have the elephant placed on Appendix I. Though Kenya is generally credited with being the leader in pushing for the ivory ban, not only had it followed Tanzania, but the move had come as a shock to most Kenyans, and indeed to just about everyone who had been monitoring the issue. WWF-International had been lobbying the Kenyan wildlife officials not to call for a ban, and seemingly with success until the final days. Kenya's call for a ban "represents a quick turnabout in GOK [Government of Kenya] thinking," the U.S. ambassador in Kenya, Eleanor Constable, a wildlife enthusiast, cabled Washington. She noted that the director of Kenya's wildlife department, Olindo, had been opposed to a ban on the ivory trade, as, she reported, were many of the conservationists in Nairobi. In particular, Constable singled out Esmond Bradley Martin—"the leading local expert on ivory demand"—as being against the ban.

A great-grandchild of Henry Phipps, the nineteenth-century industrialist, whose estate paid Bradley Martin's father some $500,000 annually, he came to Kenya in the 1960s to study the dhow trade in the Indian Ocean for a doctorate in geography at the University of Liverpool. Those studies and travels led to an ardent pursuit of the trade in rhino horn, and eventually to an interest in the ivory trade. It was largely because of Bradley Martin, whose shock of unruly and prematurely white hair makes him instantly noticeable in any crowd, that the rhino had been declared an endangered species under CITES, and international trading in rhino horn became illegal in 1973. Asked how he could square support for ivory trading with his adamant opposition to trading in rhino horn, Bradley Martin said it was because the elephant wasn't endangered, and that indeed there was a "surplus" in some countries—Zimbabwe, Botswana and South Africa. If elephants did not have an economic value, he went on, they would not be protected. To make the point, his wife, Chryssee MacCasler Bradley Martin (as her calling card reads), who seeks to play a conservationist role in her own right, interjected, "They say you're killing elephants if you buy ivory. I say you're killing elephants if you *don't* buy ivory." Once Kenya announced that it wanted a ban, however, neither of the Bradley Martins spoke out against it. It was not that they had changed their views; indeed, they had not. But they were not about to challenge what had become the popular position. They were not alone. None of the other conservationists in Kenya who believed the ban was a bad idea—and most felt that way—had the courage of their convictions.

The change in Kenya's position on the ban came after a shake-up at the very top of the wildlife department. Three weeks before the May 12 deadline to file the necessary resolutions with the CITES secretariat, Olindo had been ousted. His replacement was Richard Leakey, the well-known paleontologist, who had been calling for a ban for several months. Both Olindo's ouster and the choice of Leakey caught nearly everyone in Kenya by surprise. No reason was given, but it may not only have been their different views on an ivory ban that led President Moi to make the substitution. Olindo was also under attack from other quarters, including—though he did not know it—the white conservation community. A few weeks before Olindo was moved out, Ambassador Constable had notified Washington that the Nairobi-based conservationists were "alarmed by the GOK's [Government of Kenya's] inaction and the extent to which political infighting is paralyzing wildlife conservation efforts." She went on to say that Stanley Price, the AWF director, was heading to Washington for his organization's board meeting, and he was "in a quandary." "He is tempted to tell the board that Kenya's leaders simply lack the political will to end the poaching problem and he is worried that this may result in a decline in members' contributions to Kenya." Stanley Price also told the embassy that Olindo was an "excellent field man, but a poor administrator and should not be given too much authority."

Kenya's wildlife management and conservation programs did seem to be in bad shape, and Kenya's reputation as the place to see wildlife had been badly tarnished recently, not only by the killing of elephants: in early 1989 there had been several attacks by bandits on tourists while they were on game drives. It may have been true that Olindo was better in the field than behind a desk (how many lieutenants fail as generals, reporters as editors?), but still it was unfair to blame him for the deplorable state of the parks and the conservation programs. Indeed, he had an exceptional management record. He had been the head of Kenya's National Parks between 1966 and 1976, and during that period the parks were well managed, with very little corruption. Then the parks department was merged into the game department, which was riven with corruption, and Olindo was demoted to a deputy director slot; after a few months he left. Corruption in the new Wildlife Conservation and Management Department flourished, with money from ivory sales and park entrance fees going into the pockets of government officials at all levels, from wardens to ministers.

The responsibility for the sad state of conservation in Kenya lay above Olindo, in the office of President Moi himself. When Olindo was brought back as head of the wildlife department, in February 1987, he set out to tackle the corruption. Almost immediately he notified sixty-seven people in the department—rangers, wardens and deputy directors— that they were finished. Olindo had evidence of their involvement in poaching and skimming of park entrance fees. But just about every one of the individuals Olindo wanted to dismiss had a protector somewhere in the government. After months of effort, Olindo was able to get rid of only sixteen of the sixty-seven; five senior people were allowed to retire with full benefits; no one was prosecuted. In spite of threats against his family, Olindo persisted in trying to eliminate the corruption and make the department more professional. He was so thwarted by high-level government officials that he could not even transfer—not fire, just transfer to another park—a warden at Amboseli. Among other things, the warden routinely demanded 600 Kenyan shillings from drivers of tourist vans, under the threat of keeping them out of the park if they did not pay; that earned him the sobriquet "Mr. Six Hundred." Every time Olindo thought he had succeeded in transferring "Mr. Six Hundred," the man would hurry to Nairobi and then return to Amboseli with his job secure.

Olindo probably would have succeeded if he had had the backing of the president, but in two years he was never even able to get in to see Moi. When Leakey took over, he demanded access to the president, and he got it, largely because Moi knew that Leakey had a following in the international community, and that he would not hesitate to play that card if he had to.

Leakey did not, however, have Olindo's experience in conservation or with wildlife. Like his parents, Louis and Mary Leakey, Richard had made his reputation digging for fossils, and at the time of his appointment he was director of Kenya's museums. But the hefty, forty-four-year-old Leakey possessed what was needed to salvage Kenya's damaged image: he was an international figure, noted for his books and innumerable documentaries about the history of mankind, and it was lost on no one that he was white. He appeared on American television more often during the first days after his appointment than Olindo had during his entire two years as director of the department.

And contributions rolled in, in money and in kind, as individuals, corporations and governments fell over one another to give to Leakey's wildlife department—eighty vehicles and seven airplanes donated within three years, which was more than the total of what most African countries had for their conservation work. Energetic and self-assured, Leakey went to the World Bank and national governments, including those of the United States, Britain, Germany, Italy and Japan, and came away with $150 million for a five-year conservation program and an understanding that another $150 million would be available if needed. It was a staggering sum of money, more than was going to all of the rest of Africa for conservation. And Kenya was not the most important ecological investment. There is, for example, more biodiversity in Madagascar, and preserving the Serengeti and Ngorongoro in Tanzania or the Okavanga Delta in Botswana is a higher environmental priority for most conservationists. But donors and tourists love Kenya. And Leakey, a good speaker and an amiable person, excels at public relations.

Though often referred to as "Dr. Leakey"—which is how his office staff answers his phone—he does not have even an undergraduate university degree. He has honorary doctorates from Rockford College in Illinois and Wooster College in Ohio, but he could teach a post-doctoral seminar on media relations. Leakey rarely gets bad press, in part because he makes himself available to reporters, usually talks on the record, and gives the impression that he is speaking candidly. He has a comfortable sense of humor. During a meeting with American officials, soon after becoming head of the department, he declared confidently that his department would receive substantial private and government contributions from the United States because for "fad-conscious America," the elephant had become "a good fad." Then he joked, "Better than cocaine."

Wildlife and conservation for many Kenyans, particularly the whites who have been involved one way or another for so many years, is what basketball is to Hoosiers or politics to New Yorkers, and Leakey was as surely the subject of dinner table conversation and of intense feelings as Bobby Knight or Mayor Koch.

"My criticism of Richard is that he's so egotistical," said the host of one dinner party, expressing a view that Leakey's friends and foes share. "But I still think he's done a bloody good job," the host continued; Leakey had been in office about three years.

The man sitting across the table, a white amateur conservationist like his host, strenuously disagreed: "He doesn't know anything about animals. He only knows about dead humans, not living animals. And he won't listen to anybody. He wants all the credit. He's surrounded himself with 'yes men.' If he thinks somebody is getting too much attention, he gets rid of him. He won't take advice."

Asked who Leakey should be listening to that he doesn't, this man said sharply, "Perez Olindo and David Western." He went on, "If someone gives him a paper on something and he agrees with it, he puts his name on it; if he doesn't like it, he throws it in the wastebasket. He won't have anybody who will upstage him."

"Having said all that, he's still done a bloody good job," said the woman at the end of the table, who through her husband and in her own right had been involved with wildlife in East Africa for more than three decades.

The debate continued.

Leakey's role in the ivory ban movement was overstated—he did not lead it, as was routinely reported in the West—though the exaggeration probably reflects as much the Western desire for a white hero as it does Leakey's quest for recognition. Still, he lobbied hard to have the elephant declared an endangered species, and if he had not, it might not have come to pass.

Leakey's desire for a ban undoubtedly reflected his acute sensitivity to

Western public opinion. At the same time, however, a ban was probably needed in Kenya, as well as in Tanzania. It was needed because wealthy Western nations generally would not come up with the money for anti-poaching, because CITES was underfunded, understaffed and lacking in power, and because governments like Japan's and Hong Kong's would not take the measures they could have to halt the flow of *illegal* ivory into their countries. And the ban was needed to halt the poaching in Kenya and Tanzania, as well as Zambia and Zaire, because the governments of these countries, and the conservation community, refused to tackle the root causes of the problem: corruption and mismanagement.

The advocates of a ban focused on the demand for ivory—in Japan, Hong Kong, the United States—and they wanted to shut off the illegal supply by stopping all trade. But whatever the demand, without the involvement of corrupt African officials, poaching could not have gone on at the levels that it did. Not long after he became the head of the Tanzanian wildlife department, in February 1989, Costa Mlay launched a serious anti-poaching campaign—poachers were captured in the act and wardens were caught with ivory in their possession. When asked why this had not happened before, he answered, "The department wouldn't capture any poachers since the department was actively involved." Rarely was any official so candid, but everyone knew this was the case, in Tanzania, in Kenya, in Zaire, in Zambia, in every country where poaching was a serious problem. In these countries, many government officials at the highest levels, including cabinet ministers, and in some cases relatives of the president, were engaged in the illegal ivory trade. They were simply greedy.

Rangers, on the other hand, poached out of need, out of desperation. "If I was paid what my rangers are paid, and if I loved my children as much as I do, and wanted to send them to school, I would be out poaching elephants," Leakey once said publicly. By some accounts, over a third of the rhino that were poached in Kenya in the 1970s, when the population crashed from 20,000 to fewer than 1,000, were killed by members of the game department.

In July 1990, after he had been in his position a little more than a year, Leakey released a comprehensive report about conservation in Kenya. The study was paid for by the World Bank, and prepared by white conservationists from abroad (which did not please many of the young African conservationists trying to get ahead in Kenya). It looked at the past and laid out the needs for the future. In the space of fifteen years, the report noted, Kenya's elephant population had declined by 85 percent and its rhino population by 97 percent. Then came the explanation:

> In the late 1970s corruption increased in Kenya and the wildlife sector was particularly prone to it, because of the high values of ivory and rhino horn and the difficulty of accounting for Park gate revenues. Poaching for ivory became big business. A few senior wildlife officials took an active part in poaching and also the embezzlement of funds. Rangers were often required to carry out illegal activities for their superiors, in addition to misdemeanors of their own. Honest officers attempting to resist corruption risked victimisation. This contributed to the rapid growth of poaching, which became practically uncontrolled by the end of 1988.

This statement is more revealing than intended. It was corruption that was a major cause of the poaching. Yes, there was a demand, but it couldn't have been met if it hadn't been for the corruption.

THE NAIROBI CONSERVATIONISTS who read Leakey's report weren't surprised; in fact, their collective reaction could be described as "So what's new?" They had known all along about the massive corruption. But they had done nothing. Where were AWF and WWF and the individual conservationists when corruption was fueling the destruction of wildlife in Kenya, Tanzania and other countries? Why didn't they blow the whistle? Worse, why did they keep funding projects when they knew that much of the money they were providing was going into the pockets of corrupt politicians?

Even Leakey pulled his punches in his report. He talked about "the difficulty of accounting for Park gate revenues." That was a politically cautious way of saying that millions of dollars of gate receipts were being stolen. The Maasai Mara, one of Kenya's most popular parks, has been visited by more than 100,000 tourists annually since the mid-eighties. About 40 percent of the entrance fees they pay have been siphoned off by officials at the Narok County Council, which manages the park, according to one prominent Kenyan conservationist. Gate fees were skimmed at other parks as well, he said. More serious from an environmental perspective, conservationists recommended a decade ago that no more lodges be built in the Mara. It is a relatively small park and it was feared that more vans driving over the dirt roads chasing after wildlife would damage the ecosystem, and that more people would also change the whole tourist experience, from a feeling of being in the wilds of Africa to a feeling of being in crowds of humans. In spite of the warnings, more lodges were built—after appropriate officials were paid off. Some of the large lodges also routinely underreported the number of guests, by about 20 percent, according to one Kenyan who has looked closely at the situation. This reduces the "bed-night" tax they pay.

The corruption in the Mara is "still being swept under the carpet," said one conservationist in 1991, giving voice to what all her colleagues knew. But the conservationists were afraid to lift the carpet. WWF and AWF have been funding projects in the Mara for many years, without saying anything about the corruption. In 1988, Douglas-Hamilton was asked by the Kenya wildlife department and the European Community's Economic Development Fund to conduct a study of the Mara, and he did. But he managed to write a 185-page report without ever using the word corruption, even though he noted that revenues generated by tourism "do not find their way back to the Mara Area in any substantial form as better services or infrastructure." One Nairobi-based Western conservationist got very nervous when, during a lengthy interview, the matter of corruption in the Mara was raised; she would talk about it only in general terms, and insisted that her name not be used. "I want to live here," she said.

That explains generally why conservationists have refrained from speaking out publicly about the corruption in Kenyan conservation. They have a good life in Nairobi, probably the most modern, comfortable city in sub-Saharan Africa outside of South Africa. It is not irritatingly congested like Lagos, not sweltering like Dar es Salaam, not run-down like Kampala. It is a pleasant, mile-high city, never too hot or too humid, and there is no malaria. Because they work for nonprofit organizations, the conservationists enjoy special privileges. Their salaries are not taxed—they are often paid in dollars or pounds abroad—and they can bring in their equipment without paying duty, which in Kenya can save $40,000 on a Land Rover and $5,000 on a laptop computer.

A more fundamental reason for the silence is the belief that conservation and politics don't mix, and that there is nothing wrong in associating with corrupt, repressive governments; all that matters is saving animals. One of the most exalted European conservationists ever to work in Africa, Bernhard Grzimek, whose books *No Room for Wild Animals* and *Serengeti Shall Not Die* were best-sellers in the 1950s and 1960s, once said that he would sit down with Hitler or Stalin if it would help his animals, and he actually found good reasons for dealing with Uganda's Idi Amin. "It can be easier to work with a dictatorship on these matters of conservation than with a democracy—you don't have to deal with parliaments," Grzimek said. Today's conservationists are more politically sensitive and would never make a statement like that publicly. But they have not blanched at dealing with the continent's dictators.

"We don't criticize governments," says AWF's vice-president McMeekin. And the organization doesn't like it when someone suggests that it does. In September 1990, with the environment the rage, *Outside* magazine sketched twenty-five major conservation organizations. The article had some lighthearted and humorous touches—it described the typical AWF member, for example, as an "ex–Peace Corps volunteer who composts the greeting cards sent to him by other environmental groups"— but it also advised readers where to put their money if they wanted their conservation contribution to be effective. AWF was ranked at the very top, along with only two other organizations (the Sierra Club Legal Defense Fund and Citizens Clearinghouse for Hazardous Wastes). That understandably delighted AWF. But *Outside* also said that AWF was "a longtime critic of African governments." That comment bothered the organization, so much so that AWF president Paul Schindler sent a letter to the magazine. "You got it wrong when you characterized AWF" as being a critic of African governments, he wrote; on the contrary, he said, AWF had "great respect for the sovereign governments of Africa." Too much respect for good conservation.

In the spring of 1989, Schindler praised President Moi for having "committed himself wholeheartedly to the preservation of Kenya's wild game." If Moi had been truly committed to the preservation of Kenya's wildlife, he would have done something about the corruption, and Schindler's remark echoes the praise that Western governments have heaped on dictators, from Somoza to Marcos to the Shah of Iran, men who were looting their countries but whom Washington or London or Paris did not want to offend for Cold War or cold business reasons. Just as that policy was often shortsighted, so is the willingness of conservationists to overlook corruption.

There is a connection between good government and good conservation. The CITES quota system, for example, worked in those countries with effective law enforcement. More compelling evidence of the relationship between honest, democratic government and effective conservation can be found by contrasting the countries where poaching was the most severe—Zambia, Zaire, Tanzania and Kenya—with the countries where it was not a serious problem—Botswana, Zimbabwe and South Africa. The former were one-party states (until changes in 1991) and senior officials up to the president used their office to amass personal wealth. By contrast, Botswana has been one of Africa's few democracies. In Zimbabwe, even though he has tried, President Robert Mugabe has been unable to impose a one-party state; the rule of law has generally prevailed, and corruption has been relatively slight. Moreover, Zimbabwe paid its rangers considerably more than their counterparts elsewhere received, and David Western has described Zimbabwe's elephant conservation as "excellent" and "its culling and utilization programs beyond contention." In terms of professionalism and financial integrity, South Africa's conservation and wildlife management programs are on a par with those in Europe and the United States. It was shortsighted, and hypocritical, for those who wanted an ivory ban to ignore South Africa's conservation successes because of apartheid, while they remained on friendly terms with repressive and corrupt black governments.

The myopia and zeal of the ivory ban advocates led them to portray Kenya and Tanzania as the good guys simply because the governments endorsed a ban, while they vilified Zimbabwe and South Africa because they were opposed to one.

EVEN AFTER Tanzania and Kenya had filed their formal documents to have the elephant declared an endangered species, WWF proceeded with caution. There was still a feeling among many of their key people that the organization should listen carefully to what Africans wanted, and not dictate to them. Before committing to an Appendix I listing for the elephant, WWF should assess how widespread African support for it was, Simon Lyster, of WWF-UK, noted a few days after the two countries had filed their proposals.

African support for an Appendix I listing as proposed by Tanzania and Kenya would turn out to be quite tenuous, with only a handful of the continent's governments endorsing it, but WWF did not wait to assess that support as Lyster proposed. Public emotion in the West was too inflamed. "All of us were under incredible pressure to make hard-line statements," recalled David Western, who as director of Wildlife Conservation International was advising the organization's parent, the New York Zoological Society, on what position to take regarding a ban. And Buff

Bohlen was stepping up the pace of his activities. "It was Buff's CIA days coming back to haunt us," says a senior WWF-US official who was opposed to the ban. "He really manipulated the system." Among other things, Bohlen was telling the staff at WWF-US that the International and other WWF national organizations favored a ban, which wasn't true, while he didn't tell the International that there was a vigorous debate going on within WWF-US about a ban. De Haes, the director-general of the International, was "astonished" when he learned of the division within WWF-US, says a WWF-US officer, adding that de Haes only found out during a casual conversation with someone from the American chapter several months later. It is difficult to fathom how Bohlen could get away with this. It might have been that because of the friction between Gland and Washington there was little communication between the two, or perhaps it was because no one had any reason to suspect Bohlen of duplicity.

June 1, 1989, was victory day for Bohlen and the fund-raisers at WWF-US. At a press conference in Washington, D.C., the organization announced that it "strongly endorsed" the proposals to put the elephant on Appendix I. The International went along, with de Haes holding a press conference in Geneva. It also faxed a memorandum to all WWF national organizations instructing them to "follow the line we are taking as closely as possible in order to avoid any further stories of splits in the WWF Family over the ivory issue." But split WWF certainly was, with the majority against a ban.

"We caved," WWF-International spokesman Robert SanGeorge says simply, explaining why the International endorsed a ban. A few days before WWF-US was to hold its press conference, Bohlen had called de Haes. Bohlen was not interested in a further debate about the issue. His call was to inform de Haes what WWF-US was going to do. The message did not have to be spelled out: Go along or be embarrassed. De Haes in turned notified the head of IUCN, whose offices were in the same building. IUCN also went along. "Buff railroaded us into supporting an ivory ban by threatening to upstage us publicly if we didn't go along," says an IUCN official. Bohlen's conduct might have been offensive, but it hardly speaks well for the leadership of WWF-International and IUCN that they did not have the courage to stick with what they considered good conservation.

Then, on June 5, 1989, President Bush announced that ivory could no longer be imported into the United States. June 5 was World Environment Day, and the Bush administration desperately needed to offer something to the environmentalists, particularly since it was under severe criticism because of the disastrous oil spill from the *Exxon Valdez* tanker off the coast of Alaska, one of the worst oil spills in history. The ban was also a "low cost" environmental action, as one administration official put it. It would not cost the federal government anything to enforce it, and it meant no significant costs for American business. It was, however, probably without legal foundation. The African Elephant Conservation Act, which had been passed by Congress the previous September, gave the president the authority to ban imports of ivory from countries that were not complying with CITES or were dealing in illegal ivory. Now, Bush simply barred all ivory from every country.

WWF-US gave Bush a giant stuffed elephant, with which the president posed, and the organization immediately issued a press release heralding his action as "the most sweeping and dramatic move yet in the all-out battle to help African nations protect their elephants from rampant poaching." Bohlen said, "The fact that this Administration was able to act within four days of WWF's request for an immediate ban is truly remarkable."

It was slippery to talk about "African nations" being helped since most of them were against the ban and many were angry that the United States was unilaterally banning imports. That aside, it must have taxed Bohlen's CIA training to have kept a straight face when he said it was "truly remarkable" that the administration had acted so swiftly, because WWF and the administration were working in tandem, and Bohlen was coordinating it all. The State Department is only a few blocks from WWF, and Bohlen was a de facto member of the administration on the ivory ban issue. Before Secretary of State James Baker met with Christine Stevens of the Animal Welfare Institute, for example, it was Bohlen who briefed the secretary, and Bohlen was routinely given access to confidential cables about the poaching situation which came into the State Department from embassies in Africa. (Soon after the international ban went into effect, Bohlen became the assistant secretary of state for oceans and international environmental and scientific affairs.)

A few days after Bush announced the unilateral ban on ivory imports into the United States, Prime Minister Margaret Thatcher followed for her country. In Britain there had been a public campaign as intense and emotional as in the United States—maybe more so. The British press

paid more attention to the poaching story than had the American, reflecting the country's colonial ties to Africa, as well as the fact that
nature and animals are serious issues in Britain—as a percentage of the
population, WWF-UK has four times as many members as WWF-US.
And elephant poaching was the stuff of British tabloids. The *Daily Mail*
ran tear-jerking stories about baby elephants orphaned when their mothers were killed by poachers. The newspaper provided coupons for readers
to cut out and send to WWF-UK, which urged the organization to call
for a ban on ivory imports. No fewer than 40,000 readers inundated
WWF-UK's red-brick offices outside London with letters and telephone
calls—and £7,000 in donations.

WWF-UK had been against a ban, but it too reversed its position, in
early June. Privately, senior officers in the organization said that the
about-face had come because of public pressure and the media's interest.
Publicly, when asked why it endorsed a ban, WWF-UK said it was
because of the findings of something called the Ivory Trade Review
Group.

THE IVORY TRADE REVIEW GROUP, or ITRG, and the study
it produced acquired an almost mythical significance in the ivory ban
war. In its statement on June 1 endorsing a ban, WWF-US said it was
doing so "based on new scientific findings released today." Indeed these
were the very first words of the organization's press release. The new
findings had come from ITRG. David Western of Wildlife Conservation
International, who at the time of AWF's press conference, in May 1988,
told the *New York Times* that a ban "would exaggerate the problems with
wildlife in Africa," said that he changed his position because of ITRG.
Over and over again, when I asked conservationists who had been opposed to the ban why they had come to endorse it, they answered simply,
"the Ivory Trade Review Group," or "the ITRG report." There were
certainly data and statements in the ITRG report to justify a ban. But on
closer examination, it was apparent that the report was flawed, if not in
its findings, then certainly in its preparation. And the release of a portion
of the report on June 1, 1989, was politically motivated.

The ITRG was yet another effort by conservationists to grapple with
the African elephant issue. There were already the African Elephant and

Rhino Specialist Group, the African Elephant Working Group and the African Elephant Conservation Coordination Group. In mid-1988, IUCN, WWF and Wildlife Conservation International established the Ivory Trade Review Group "to investigate the ivory trade and determine what effect it had on the declining elephant populations." Less prosaic and more revealing was a remark by Bohlen that its "primary purpose was to get all those prima donnas in the field to come up with a solid scientific report."

The full Review Group report was 700 pages. But that was not completed until October, more than three months after WWF had called for a ban. On June 1, only a nine-page summary was released. And it was released because WWF wanted to call for a ban at that time in order to put pressure on, and allow for, the Bush administration to do so on World Environment Day, June 5.

The brief summary made public in June included a recommendation that the elephant be placed on Appendix I, which meant, of course, a ban on all trade in elephant products. This did not, however, accurately reflect the views of all members of the group. Indeed, four days before the summary was released, a member of the group, David Pearce, sent a memorandum to the ITRG coordinator, Stephen Cobb, on behalf of the Review Group economists. The economists were opposed to an unconditional ban on all ivory trading. Pearce, a professor of economics and director of the Environmental Economics Centre at the University of London, said that by depriving countries of ivory sales, the ban was the equivalent of a $50 million tax on African governments; in addition, domestic carving industries in African countries would be severely hurt. Therefore, Pearce said, if there was going to be a ban, affected African countries should be compensated by the West with $100 million a year. None of this appeared in the ITRG's public statement (and, needless to say, no one ever came up with this kind of money).

When the full ITRG study was submitted at the CITES meeting in Lausanne in October 1989, it contained academic papers by scientists and economists on the overall numbers and trends of African elephant populations, on ivory exports from African countries, on imports to Japan and Hong Kong, on the economics of the trade. It was a weighty document in the debate (indeed, five pounds), but in the view of many scientists, it was deficient.

The most thorough analysis of the report was coordinated by David Cumming, who had been deputy director of Zimbabwe's Department of

National Parks and Wildlife Management before becoming, in 1988, the director of WWF's office in Harare. Cumming, who has a doctorate in ecology, asked other scientists and conservationists to review the report section by section. Several did, and one of the conclusions was that the question of the number of elephants remaining in Africa and the trends could not be answered with certainty; the population numbers being used were largely based on "guesswork" and extrapolations, according to Cumming. Cumming also concluded that the CITES quota system was in fact beginning to work and therefore should be given more time before resorting to the more drastic measure of a complete ban.

Cumming had been forced to analyze the ITRG report from the outside because he had not been asked to contribute to the study. He was excluded even though Zimbabwe had more elephants than Kenya and a far better conservation program, and although he was vice-chairman for southern Africa of IUCN's African Elephant and Rhino Specialist Group. Cumming's absence from the ITRG underscores the conclusion that the Review Group was not a neutral body searching for the scientific truth. To begin with, it was clearly biased against the southern African views. South Africa's Anthony Hall-Martin, director of research in South Africa's parks department and a foremost authority on elephants—he has as much right to be called "Mr. Elephant" as Iain Douglas-Hamilton—was not invited to participate in the study. Nor was anyone from Botswana.

But the absence of anyone from southern Africa is not what gives rise to the most serious reservation about the ITRG findings. Rather, it is the exclusion of all Africans. Twenty-five contributors and two co-chairmen were listed when the group released its statement on June 1. Four were associated with the Imperial College of Science and Technology in London, four with the University of London, three with Oxford and three with Cambridge. All twenty-seven were white. Only one person who participated was even a citizen of an African country, David Western of Kenya. When the final ITRG report was issued in October, the list of contributors had been expanded to thirty-eight, and now four of the individuals were Africans; none of these four, however, had his name on any of the papers in the report.

The fate of Africa's resources was being decided, once again, by foreign powers. By the end of June 1989, WWF and AWF had called for a ban on ivory trading, and the United States, the European Community, Switzerland, Australia and Canada had unilaterally banned ivory imports. Contrary to statements by AWF and WWF that this was what Africans wanted, there was hardly unanimity on the continent, and the prevailing sentiment was still against a ban.

SEVENTEEN AFRICAN countries convened in Gaborone, Botswana, in July 1989, hoping to come up with an elephant policy all could agree on. Once again, the affair was dominated by American and European conservationists and representatives from ten developed nations. "Expatriate influence over the issue is both strong and ego-driven," a member of the U.S. government delegation observed in a post-meeting analysis. For five days of morning and afternoon sessions the delegates and "observers"—as the representatives from conservation organizations were officially categorized, though they hardly observed—argued, threatened and snarled. "The most fractious group of men and women I've ever dealt with," said Richard Leakey, who chaired the meetings and received praise from all sides for maintaining order.

The meeting, at the Gaborone Sun (the only hotel with more than fifty rooms, as well as a casino and disco, in a city that resembles a small town in the American Southwest), was closed to the press, even though the conference hall was packed with the very organizations and individuals who churned out press releases and assiduously courted journalists in behalf of their cause or ego. Ban campaigners, such as Allan Thornton, were allowed inside and indeed to speak, as were ivory traders from Hong Kong and Japan. Even Douglas-Hamilton's teenage daughter and her girlfriend were allowed to sit in on the meetings. But no journalists. The people on both sides of the ivory ban debate wanted public support; they just didn't want public scrutiny. Perhaps understandably.

Gaborone was not a forum for a vigorous and open debate on the issue of an ivory ban. The summit was stacked in favor of East Africa and the proponents of a ban. That became immediately apparent on opening day when David Cumming and John Hanks were nowhere to be seen. Their scientific credentials, commitment to conservation and experience in Africa could be matched by few of those in attendance, but they were opposed to a ban. And it was because of this opposition that they were not present. Cumming's presence should have been axiomatic by virtue of his being the vice-chairman of the African Elephant and Rhino Specialist Group, and he had more than twenty years of conservation experience in Africa. Hanks was the head of the Africa programs at WWF-International, which meant that he should have been the head of the WWF delegation at Gaborone. But he had run afoul of de Haes.

Hanks had fought against a ban at every opportunity; when, for example, the ITRG report had come across his desk, he rejected it with a trenchant comment in the margin that it was biased in favor of East Africa, which, of course, it was. Undoubtedly, his opposition to a ban reflected his bias toward southern Africa, where he'd spent most of his conservation career, but that did not make it bad conservation. Once the International reversed its position and came out for a ban, Hanks began to pay for his views. First, while on vacation shortly after WWF had publicly called for a ban, he received a phone call from de Haes abruptly informing him that he would not be going to Gaborone as the head of the delegation. Eventually, he lost his job altogether, dismissed by de Haes as the head of Africa programs and sent into gilded exile in South Africa. De Haes and Prince Philip both insisted later that Hanks's dismissal was not directly related to the ivory trade issue, but had occurred because, as Philip wrote to a Zimbabwean conservationist, "it gradually became obvious that his talents did not lie in organised office work." No one at WWF in Switzerland believed that.

Hanks did not always exercise good judgment—Operation Lock, the undercover operation using the British mercenaries operating out of South Africa was a good example—but he understood Africa, far better than most of those involved in the debate. From a middle-class English family, his father a pilot in the Royal Air Force, Hanks set out for Africa after obtaining a bachelor's degree in zoology from Cambridge in 1965; he later earned a master's and a doctorate. He worked as a biologist in Kafue and Luangwa Valley national parks in Zambia, taught tropical resource ecology at the University of Rhodesia, was director of research for the parks in Natal, South Africa, and then head of the biology department there. Hanks knew conservation and Africa's problems, and the link between them.

To the Wildlife Conservation Society of Zambia, during WWF's conference there in 1988, he delivered one of the most alarming, but at the same time most sensible, environmental speeches I have ever read. The subject was "The Decline of Rhinos and Elephant in Africa: What Is the Lesson for Conservationists?" Hanks's answer, in brief, was that conservationists had to be more concerned about people. That, he noted, was a far cry from their traditional role of being concerned about pro-

tecting species in parks isolated from people. WWF and other conservation organizations must promote "conservation for human survival,"
Hanks said. He added, "We must have sufficient humility to approach
local communities and find out their needs and aspirations *before* we
start work. At all costs, we *must* avoid planning *upon* people, telling
them what to do without any form of consultation whatsoever."

That should be the scripture for conservationists, but there were not
many who listened to Africans, and those that did, such as Garth Owen-
Smith and Margaret Jacobsohn, who developed the community-based
ranger and tourism programs in Namibia, did not come to a meeting like
this one (they would not be in Lausanne either), because they were
working in the field. And there was not a lot of humility among those
gathered at Gaborone; nor was there much willingness to compromise.

If Hanks had been at Gaborone as the leader of the WWF delegation
(he eventually showed up, but in an unofficial capacity), he might have
been the one person who could have mediated between the warring
factions from the South and East. Though they did not have Hanks or
Cumming to help them, it was at Gaborone that the southern African
states finally entered into combat. They realized they were being slaughtered by the public relations barrage in the West, and while they could
never match the resources available to WWF, AWF and Leakey in
Kenya, they could at least make their case to their colleagues.

The essence of the southern African opposition to the ban was this:
We're managing our elephant populations well, so why should we be
penalized for mismanagement, ineffective law enforcement and corruption in East African countries? It was a reasonable question, and the
militant ban advocates didn't answer it. Instead they maligned the southern Africans by questioning their counting methods. And they said to the
southern Africans, Just wait—while you might have poaching under
control now, it will only be a matter of time before the poachers move
south in greater numbers and with more powerful weapons, and you will
not be able to stop them. There might have been some validity to this
concern—if the demand continued and the East African supply de-
creased, there would theoretically be more pressure on the southern
herds—but it was also another reflection of the low regard the Western
conservationists had for Africans: they didn't believe the "natives" were
capable of doing anything right. The more moderate and rational of the
ban advocates accepted that the southern African governments were
doing a good job, and the essence of their plea to them was: Help us save

the African elephant. More specifically, they argued that if there was a legal market for ivory, it would serve as a cover for illegal ivory. It was also a reasonable request and argument.

Zimbabwe led the opposition forces, and the one person who made it the most difficult for the proponents of a ban was Rowan Martin. A heavyset white man in his forties, with a thick black beard and thinning hair, he did not fit the image of a game warden and looked out of uniform when he wore his khaki shorts and knee socks. He was extremely bright, and he could be just as belligerent and intransigent as the ban advocates, which is probably why he was the object of their most scurrilous attacks.

Martin began his professional life as an engineer, working for Anglo American in its gold and diamond mines in South Africa. He got "hooked on wildlife" while on a safari around southern Africa, and joined the Zimbabwe wildlife department in 1972 to build a communications system. He stayed and later studied ecology at the University of Rhodesia— Hanks was one of his professors—and by 1988 he had become the department's chief ecologist and assistant director for research. Martin was irascible and abrasive. When he had been asked to contribute to the Ivory Trade Review Group study (he was the only person from southern Africa who was), he refused, saying, "My heart isn't big enough to bleed for all of Africa." When the United States sent a letter asking Zimbabwe for information about its elephants, Martin's reaction was, "the arrogant sons of bitches!"

The letter had been sent under the African Elephant Conservation Act, which had been passed by Congress in 1988, when its members were under public pressure to do something about the African elephant, and they did, even though only a handful knew anything about Africa. Congress gave the executive branch the authority to impose a moratorium on the importation of ivory from countries that were not managing their elephant populations well. To decide whether that moratorium should be imposed, letters were sent to all countries that had elephants, asking for detailed information about their elephant populations. Many African countries were offended by these requests, and it is easy to understand why. Imagine how the United States would feel if Japan demanded information about cattle on Wyoming ranches before it decided whether or not to allow American leather products or beef into Japan. The letter to the Zimbabwean authorities was passed down the line to Martin and he drafted a reply. It said that Zimbabwe was "disturbed by the entire tenor of this letter," which seemed to assume "that there are authorities within the USA who are *more competent* to determine elephant management programmes than those in Zimbabwe. We have difficulty accepting this." This was how many countries felt about the request, but they complied (not many countries ignore requests from the United States), and somewhere along the line, Martin's superiors deleted this paragraph from the more diplomatic reply the Zimbabwe government sent to Washington.

During the Gaborone summit, the United States delegation met privately with Martin and other Zimbabwean officials. The United States wanted to convince Zimbabwe to go along with an Appendix I listing. As the meeting was ending, Marshall Jones, of the U.S. Fish and Wildlife Service, told the Zimbabweans that in making their decision they should keep in mind the economic assistance that the United States provided to Zimbabwe. Stunned, Martin turned to a colleague, "Did you hear that? That sounds like a not very thinly veiled threat." Jones did not deny making the comment about aid, but, he said later, it was not intended as a threat. He was just trying to explain to the Zimbabweans about the domestic politics in the United States. "What I was telling them was that public opinion was so high in the U.S. that there might be pressure to cut off aid to countries that didn't go along with an Appendix I listing," Jones said. (The American embassy in Gaborone delivered the same "non-threat" message to the Botswana government.) Jones was right about public opinion. What he did not say was that no American official was willing to confront public emotion, to explain why a ban was not a good idea, and particularly not for southern Africans.

In spite of the threats and pressure, after five days of extended and bitter debate, the African nations could not agree that the elephant should be declared an endangered species and ivory trading banned. On the contrary, only five of the seventeen countries at Gaborone favored ending all trade—Kenya, Tanzania, Ethiopia, Somalia and Zaire. (They were, it might be noted, among the most corrupt and least democratic governments on the continent.) A dozen countries wanted the trade to continue, though they agreed there should be some controls.

If there were any mirthful moments during the Gaborone dustup, they were provided, unintentionally, by Kenya's plan to burn some twelve tons of ivory, which was to take place a few days after the meeting ended. Rowan Martin and the Zimbabwe delegation composed a limerick (which works when one remembers these people speak English with a broad British accent):

> *We cheered when they burned the first bra,*
> *Lady Chatterley was going too far.*
> *But the whole world mocks*
> *When ivory stocks*
> *Go up in smoke in Kenya.*

Kenya's ivory burn was undoubtedly the most publicized event during the ivory debate. It was also the most costly.

THE TUSKS were stacked like a tepee, twenty feet high, the design of a pyrotechnist who specialized in creating fires for movies, inside Nairobi National Park. One of the first parks in Africa, it is also about the only place in the world where wild animals are protected so close to an urban center; lions, buffalo, giraffes, zebra, gazelle and sometimes even rhino can be spotted in the savannah against the backdrop of the modern Nairobi skyline. Two large tents had been set up to protect the crowd—diplomats, government officials, Nairobi-based conservationists and the merely curious—from the Africa sun, but most preferred to wander about. A Kenyan army band entertained. Two attractive young women turned many heads: wearing shorts and halters, and barefoot, they had painted on their bodies and headbands "Burn Ivory Burn" and "Ivory Kills." Their father, Douglas-Hamilton, nattily attired in khaki slacks, a blue blazer and a dark-blue tie with white and red elephants, defended the burn as "idealistic, imaginative and moral."

Not everyone agreed. The ivory could have been sold for at least $3 million—Kenya had actually been offered that from ivory traders—and many ordinary Kenyans thought the money would be better used for the needs of the Kenyan people. "I think it was crazy," said an eighteen-year-old Kenyan. "The elephants are dead. You can't bring them back. So why not take the foreign exchange and use it for our national development." Similarly, a woman social worker in her fifties thought the ivory should have been sold: "We are a poor country. The economy is bad. There is so much we could do for our own people."

Even most of the conservationists in Nairobi thought it was "an unacceptable waste of resources in a poor nation," as the American embassy in Nairobi reported to Washington. "Stupid," was the simple assessment of one prominent conservationist when she was asked about the burn. But the conservationists again kept silent publicly.

Perez Olindo was among those who did not agree with the burning of the ivory, though he said nothing at the time, and when he did, more than a year and a half later, he spoke in his ever cautious way. "A government is the custodian of its natural resources for the people of the country," he said, explaining why he was opposed to the burn. The ivory tusks were a valuable asset, "and before they are destroyed, the people should have a say, through a referendum, or through their elected representatives." But Kenya was not a democracy.

The burn was a stunt to improve Kenya's conservation image. "Tomorrow Moi will stand up and be at the forefront of African conservation," an American diplomat remarked caustically the day before the burn. "It's pretty hard to swallow given the track record of the last ten years." To be sure that the world would be paying attention, Kenya hired Black, Manafort & Stone, an expensive and conservative public relations firm in Washington, D.C. On the day of the burn, journalists from around the world crowded on a platform built especially for them. *Life* sent a photographer from Johannesburg; Japanese television covered it; ABC's "Good Morning America" broadcast the burn live and interviewed Leakey; he was also Ted Koppel's guest on "Nightline."

The burn had been Leakey's idea, and as President Moi, against the backdrop of thorn trees and a cloudless African sky, delivered a speech before applying a torch to the tusks, few noticed that Leakey, standing attentively nearby, mouthed the speech in perfect sync with the president. There were stories that Leakey had received a large sum of money from a wealthy anonymous donor to burn the ivory. The stories were widely believed because it was hard to understand how the Kenyan government would otherwise let so much money go up in smoke. (After considerable investigation, including chasing a story that a wealthy American who had hunted elephants in Kenya many years ago had offered to raise millions of dollars for Kenya's wildlife department if Kenya would destroy its ivory rather than sell it, I have concluded that Kenya did not receive any money for burning the ivory, and that it was not offered any. There *was* an American who offered money to Kenya's wildlife department at the time of the burn—either $200 million or $450 million, depending on different people's memories—but there was no quid pro quo that Kenya dispose of the ivory; besides, he turned out to be a "fraud, a real nut case," says a lawyer who was involved.) Leakey, eloquent as ever, emphatically denied that Kenya had been "bribed." It would be hypocritical, he said, for Kenya to call for a ban on ivory trading and at

the same time sell its ivory stockpile, and he compared the burning of
the tusks to the destruction of marijuana or cocaine. This analogy to drugs
was invoked often by the advocates of the ivory ban. Asking Africans not
to make money from ivory was the same as asking South American
peasants to forgo growing coca leaves, they argued. Kathryn Fuller,
president of WWF-US, once compared the sacrifices that Africans were
asked to make from not selling ivory to those that West Virginia coal
miners make because of federal laws restricting the use of coal. These
analogies are persuasive, but only superficially. A close examination reveals a significant difference: unlike drugs, unlike the pollution from coal
burning, ivory does no harm to the person or society that consumes it.

In the end, even though Kenya lost $3 million in foreign exchange
from not selling the ivory, it accumulated tremendous favorable publicity,
some would argue more than $3 million worth. The picture of Moi setting
the pyre alight appeared in newspapers throughout the world, and it
became one of the most defining images of the ivory ban debate. And for
sure, the ivory ban advocates cheered the burn mightily. After this, how
could they lose?

BUT AS THE DATE for the CITES meeting approached, the
ban advocates faced growing support for an accommodation to the southern Africans. It would be accomplished with a "split listing": the elephant
populations in Tanzania, Kenya and other countries where poaching was
a problem would go on Appendix I, while those in Botswana, South Africa
and Zimbabwe would remain on Appendix II. This was the most just and
intellectually honest approach. It was also the legally correct one, since
the elephants in those three southern countries were certainly not endangered under international law. In fact, if there had been a legal forum in
which to bring a case, a country opposed to the ban would almost certainly
have prevailed in a lawsuit which argued that the African elephant as a
species was not endangered under the CITES definition; as evidence, it
could have presented the WWF-US memorandum written in May 1988
in which it was observed that the elephant was "not yet endangered."

In August 1989, two months before the CITES meeting in Lausanne,
the southern Africans received some unexpected backing from Olindo,
now a senior associate at AWF. In a nine-page "Discussion Paper,"
Olindo presented the case for an Appendix I listing, but he added that

because elephant populations in southern Africa had not been adversely affected by poaching, "there should be an effort made by all who may care about this problem to strike a compromise."

Olindo did not say that the southern African elephant populations should be left on Appendix II, but just the mention of a compromise was now too much for AWF. The organization that had started out cautiously, which had wanted only to educate people, which had wanted to avoid the "extreme" position of a total ban because it thought it was arrogant to tell Africans what to do, which had called for a complete ban only after considerable "soul searching," and which had done so only in May, was now a true believer willing to brook no dissent.

Olindo sent his paper to Diana McMeekin, the AWF vice-president in Washington, and he asked her to fax it to individuals who were involved in the debate. She declined to do so, because she felt it was "too sympathetic" toward the southern African position. Olindo also sent his memorandum to Marshall Jones, at the U.S. Fish and Wildlife Service. Jones, too, was alarmed, but McMeekin assured him that Olindo's paper did not reflect AWF's views. Fear of an open debate, of any moderate approach, spread through official Washington as well. The Bush administration was as inflexible on the ivory ban issue as AWF and WWF-US had become— it insisted on a straight Appendix I listing, with no compromise. It was worried, therefore, that Olindo's views might reach others, and the State Department sent cables to its embassies around the world. Olindo's memorandum "undermines the U.S. (and the Kenyan) bargaining positions," the department said, and it cabled the American embassy in Nairobi to urge Olindo "to hold his fire." Even before the embassy could arrange a meeting with Olindo, he had a copy of the cable. Olindo controls his emotions, particularly with Westerners, but this time he vented his anger on the deputy chief of mission at the American embassy, George Griffin. Olindo told Griffin that he would fight for an Appendix I listing, but that did not mean that the people who would be going to the CITES meeting should "stop thinking." He added that sovereign African nations did not like being told what to do by the United States. But Olindo backed down and did not disseminate his paper.

Olindo was not the only professional conservationist who felt strongly about protecting the elephant but saw the merit of the southern African position and above all the need for compromise. One month before Lausanne, Kenya's David Western, chairman of the African Elephant and Rhino Specialist Group, went to Harare to meet with David Cumming, who was vice-chairman. Though Western had switched his position and had come out in favor of a ban, Cumming had remained consistently against one. Now, the two men were successful in reaching an accord— they endorsed a split listing. And IUCN had concluded that a split listing was best for elephant conservation. But the hard-liners were in no mood for compromise.

THE FINAL fracas in the ivory ban war occurred at the seventh meeting of the member nations of CITES, at Lausanne, Switzerland, in October 1989, and it was marked—and marred—by hard-line positions and smear campaigns, not tolerance. The African elephant was not the only item on the agenda. Switzerland wanted to transfer the salmon-crested cockatoo from Appendix II to Appendix I, in order to save the birds in Indonesia, which are exported to the United States and West Germany. There were proposals to put the Indian rat snake on Appendix I and to transfer the sloth bear to Appendix II. The Netherlands wanted more than sixty species of orchid on Appendix I. But the African elephant dominated the conference.

A hundred-foot-long hot-air balloon in the shape of an elephant floated just above the Palais de Beaulieu, where the delegates met and where they mingled with theater crowds when the sessions lasted late into the evening. The plaza in front of the Palais was filled one sunny fall day with Swiss schoolchildren, who staged skits, wearing papier-mâché elephant heads, and read poems they had written about the African elephant. The demonstration had been organized by WWF of Switzerland and Swiss authorities had cooperated by releasing the children from school and providing buses to get them to Lausanne. There were buzzings that the advocates of the ban planned to burn elephant tusks on a raft in the middle of Lake Geneva; it was one of the few gimmicks that did not materialize.

It was thought that the fate of the African elephant would be resolved in two or three days. But the name-calling, lobbying and bureaucratic wrangling went on for nearly two weeks. There were long, often tedious, public sessions, closed-door caucuses and clusters of whispered conversations. Delegates and observers grew frustrated and irritated, and spent a great deal of money on hotel rooms and meals. The conservation organizations should match in donations to African wildlife programs what they had spent in Lausanne, Olindo quipped after the conference.

The United States delegation consisted of nineteen men and women, a "quite large" number, the State Department noted, "due to the high-level political interest in the elephant ivory issue." The head of the American team was Constance Harriman, assistant secretary of fish and wildlife and parks in the Department of the Interior. A Ronald Reagan political appointee, she knew little about Africa or elephants, but proved to be an effective politician. WWF's Bohlen was the unofficial advisor to the U.S. delegation, and his views carried more weight than those of official members.

Animal rights groups from around the world showed up in force—Friends of Animals, Animal Welfare Institute, Humane Society of the United States, United Animal Nations, EleFriends, the International Federation for Animal Welfare and more. "It's all about money," said an IUCN scientist disgustedly as he surveyed the booths and displays on the mezzanine of the Palais, just outside the main conference room, including one where WWF was selling stuffed pandas. Friends of Animals had a brass gong that sounded every five minutes, "the rhythm at which elephants have been suffering extermination at the hands of the ivory hunters for more than a decade." On the third day of the meeting, several large transparent bags stuffed with mail appeared at the Greenpeace booth; the organization said they contained 50,000 postcards and letters from Germans who wanted the elephant to be declared endangered. A continuous video ran on a television monitor at the Animal Welfare Institute booth, showing a film about poaching and the ivory trade, with pictures of dead elephants.

The animal rights people vilified the Zimbabweans. Craig Van Note, executive vice-president of Monitor, a Washington, D.C., consortium of environmental groups, called Zimbabwe's statistics on the number of elephants in the country a "big lie," and he upbraided journalists who used them in their articles. Christine Stevens, head of the Animal Welfare Institute, accused the Zimbabweans of "double counting." And they mounted personal attacks on Rowan Martin of the Zimbabwe wildlife department. "He's a fanatic," Stevens said; it was his "extreme stubbornness," she insisted, that was blocking the elephant from being declared an endangered species.

It was all-out war for the animal rights groups. "No compromise," Van Note said defiantly on the third day of the meeting. When the president of Friends of Animals, Priscilla Feral, heard rumors that WWF might be willing to support a split listing, she said, "They ought to have their asses kicked." The animal rights groups threatened to target any organization or country that did not go along with a straight Appendix I listing. "The knives will be out," Allan Thornton, the director of the London-based Environmental Investigation Agency, warned Simon Lyster, senior conservation officer of WWF-UK, and a moderate voice in the debate. The seventy-one-year-old Christine Stevens confronted Lyster, who was young enough to be her youngest son. "Do you support culling?" Mrs. Stevens demanded of Lyster. "Yes, when necessary," he answered. "Then you're for killing elephants," she snapped. She warned Lyster that she had a list of all WWF-UK members and that they would be sent letters saying that WWF-UK supported the killing of elephants.

The animal rights groups were not alone, however, in their intransigence. "The United States, Europe and several African countries came with mandates to vote Appendix I, no compromise," David Western wrote in a post-Lausanne report. There had been some discussion within the European Community before reaching this position, but not much. The economic advisor to the European Community's delegation in Zimbabwe, Michael Lake, argued that a ban would be a defeat for conservation and development. The environmentalists in Brussels insisted on a ban, failing to see any link between conservation and development, a connection the public generally doesn't understand either. And in the end, the European Community politicians bent to public sentiment.

Western and Wildlife Conservation International called for some accommodation to the southern Africans, but he and his organization didn't stand a chance. As unyielding as anyone at Lausanne was the African Wildlife Foundation, which had a full contingent on hand—president Schindler and vice-president McMeekin, who had come from Washington; Mark Stanley Price, Perez Olindo, Joyce Poole and Cynthia Moss, all of whom flew up from Kenya. Even Moss, who a year earlier had said that a ban was unfair to southern Africans, was now opposed to a split listing. No one had a more emotional attachment to elephants than Moss, but she was intellectually honest. She did not disparage the Zimbabweans, and in fact she accepted that their elephant counts were reliable and that they were managing their elephant populations well. Rather, her opposition was more pragmatically grounded. "My background is in media, so I have some sense of what people respond to," she says, explaining why she was opposed to a split listing. "You can't tell people that you can't buy some ivory, but it is O.K. to buy other. It has to be a simpler message than that." Many people may find this an unattractive justification, too calculating, but it is an honest one; she does not cloak herself in moral piety or hide behind the allegedly conclusive findings of the Ivory Trade Review Group.

In another display of the obstinacy that marked the ivory ban debate, this time by the opponents of a ban, Zimbabwe proposed a split listing in which the elephant populations in Zambia, Mozambique, Malawi, Namibia and Angola, as well as Zimbabwe, Botswana and South Africa, remained on Appendix II (while the others were put on Appendix I). Poaching was rampant in Zambia, so it was absurd to allow it to continue trading; and it was questionable whether Mozambique and Angola were managing their elephants well, given the collapse of those countries because of civil wars. The Zimbabweans argued, rather lamely, that the five additional countries had been included in the interests of southern African solidarity. The split-listing proposal was defeated 70 to 19, with one abstention. Given the forces marshaled against a split listing, it is unlikely, however, that even a proposal that included only Zimbabwe, Botswana and South Africa on Appendix II could have passed.

At the same time, in spite of the threats and lobbying, the advocates of a straight Appendix I listing did not have the two-thirds vote required by CITES for a resolution to be adopted. Indeed, the majority of African countries wanted to keep the elephant on Appendix II, which would have meant the continuation of trading. And these countries could count on the votes of a great number of Third World countries. It wasn't only Third World solidarity that had many governments from Latin America and Asia siding with the Africans who were opposed to the ban; it was more their feeling that the developed world was continually making unfair environmental demands on the undeveloped world: don't cut the trees in your rain forests, don't use CFCs, don't burn coal. The West made the demands but did not want to compensate the nations of the developing world for the costs they had to bear, which were substantial— loss of income from timber sales, more expensive refrigerators, more expensive fuel. And loss of revenue from ivory.

Horrified by the prospect of a continuation of any ivory trading, AWF's Stanley Price came up with an idea. The elephant would be declared endangered, and placed on Appendix I, but a country could get its population "downgraded" to Appendix II if a panel of experts determined that the country was managing its elephant populations well and control-ling the movement of ivory out of the country. Somalia introduced this proposal, and the vote was 76 in favor, 11 against and 4 abstentions, one of them Japan.

The elephant was an endangered species. Trading in ivory would cease. When the vote was announced, the room thundered with clapping, cheering and whistling.

Not everyone cheered, however—not the delegates and conservationists from Zimbabwe, Botswana, Mozambique, Congo, Gabon, Cameroon and South Africa. These countries had all voted against the Somali proposal. And each of these countries has more than 7,000 elephants; combined they have half the continent's pachyderms. Only five out of twelve countries with more than 7,000 elephants voted in favor of the resolution. So much for the repeated assertions by AWF and WWF that they were only doing what "the Africans" wanted.

THE BAN ADVOCATES were right about some things. After the ban went into effect, the price of ivory did drop precipitately, and there was a marked decline in poaching in Kenya. In March 1991, Robin Hurt, who leads big-game hunting safaris in Tanzania, said, "I haven't seen one poached elephant in more than a year." Before the ban, he would see "hundreds of carcasses, everywhere." He admitted that he had been skeptical but that the ban was working. Kenya claimed to have lost only fifty-five elephants to poachers in 1990, a 99 percent drop in poaching. There was an increase in poaching in some places, however, most dramatically in Cameroon's Korup Forest, where twenty-seven elephants were killed during the last three months of 1990; in the previous year only three had been shot. It was a perverse irony of the decline in ivory prices that led to the upsurge: local chiefs, who used the tusks for ceremonial purposes, could now afford to buy them, as could government officials and businessmen in neighboring Nigeria who considered ivory a symbol of affluence.

Many of the opponents of the ban acknowledged afterward that it was proving effective and that maybe it was needed, at least in the short run. Michael Wright, a vice-president of WWF-US, was one of them. But he said, "We could have ended up with the same result without the African countries feeling this was the worst kind of colonial manipulation—which I think it was." That is a fitting epithet for the elephant crusade.

After all the manipulation, after more than a year of meetings and intense attention paid to the African elephant, the most critical question still had not been answered: Who would provide the money for elephant conservation? Whenever African governments said that they needed the money from the sale of ivory, that they needed money for anti-poaching efforts, the United States and the European Community had responded, Don't worry, we'll come up with the money. At Lausanne, for instance, the United States delegation proudly reported that Congress had authorized $2 million for African elephant conservation, continent-wide. Rowan Martin pointed out that that amount would support Zimbabwe's wildlife department for only two years; it was the only time that just about everyone in the hall applauded.

Six months after Lausanne, seventeen Western governments, all of which had voted in favor of the ban, met in Paris to discuss African elephant conservation. Tanzania's director of wildlife, Costa Mlay, told the wealthy nations that East African countries required $84 million for anti-poaching alone—for training, arms, ammunition and equipment for rangers. The needs are far greater in countries like Zaire and Gabon, which lack the basic infrastructure for any meaningful conservation, and altogether, the conference was told, African countries with elephants needed an infusion of at least $500 million to protect their elephants; this was just for capital needs, not for recurring expenses.

The donors issued a lofty declaration "recognizing the importance of the African elephant both as a key species in African ecosystems and the symbol of the maintenance of the continent's biological diversity," and "recognizing also the global importance of this species as part of the world heritage." But when it came to money to match this soaring rhetoric, to preserve this world heritage, the response was pathetic. The United States offered $2.5 million, France about $1 million. Britain said it had already budgeted £3 million (about $5 million) for conservation in Africa. If the African countries wanted more for conservation, the donors said, it would have to be in lieu of money for other development projects. In other words, the burden was again on Africans—if they wanted money for conservation, fine, but that would mean less for schools or roads.

Olindo was bitter about the West's response. African countries had set aside large areas for parks and reserves—land, he noted, that would be economically more valuable as ranches and farms. African governments protected wild animals, "which raid people's farms, kill their cattle, kill their next of kin," Olindo noted. "That is a very high cost being paid by the Africans. If the developed nations don't come to the aid of these developing countries, let them not moan afterwards that they didn't know at what price the African elephant could have been saved from extinction."

"A VICTORY FOR THE ELEPHANTS," the African Wildlife Foundation exclaimed in its newsletter announcing the decision at Lausanne. Not all conservationists agreed. Many feared it would be the doom of the African elephant because hungry Africans aren't going to tolerate the damage the elephant wreaks if they don't get some economic benefit from the animal. Even if AWF was right—even if the ban on ivory trading was a victory for the elephants—what about the people of Africa? What did declaring the elephant an endangered species mean for them? Was it a resounding victory, or a devastating defeat? Few of the Western participants in the elephant campaign even considered these questions, for they ignored the African people, as if the elephant existed in some kind of human-free environment. But it doesn't, and African people, not wealthy Western-ers, are the ones who will pay the price, bear the burden, for preserving the continent's wildlife heritage. And often it is a very high cost, a very heavy burden—from loss of land to loss of life.

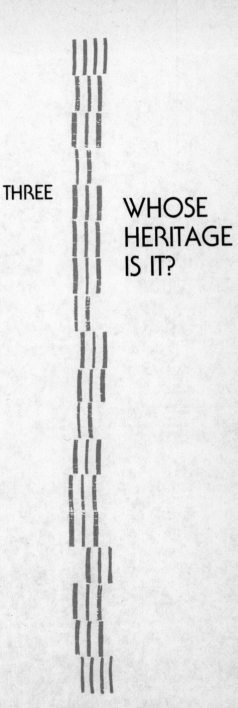

THREE

WHOSE HERITAGE IS IT?

||||| "WHEN THE LODGE goes up, we will lose this path," Parimitoro ole Kasiaro was saying. "The cattle of my village pass here and go into the crater. It is the only place we can get salt." He was standing in a quiet meadow of evergreens and thorny acacia, at a place called Kimba on the western rim of Ngorongoro Crater, in northwestern Tanzania. An international company owned by the Aga Khan had recently received permission to build a five-star hotel on the spot, and, Kasiaro went on, "We are afraid they are going to use the water for hotel purposes." The water trickles on the surface from a few small springs, and Kasiaro and other Maasai who live in this area need it for their cattle. The hotel, of course, will want it for its guests. In a competition with the tourists, Kasiaro had good reason to fear that the villagers would lose. The Maasai were evicted from the crater floor—where Kasiaro was born—in 1974, for the benefit of tourism, and many years before that, the Maasai, Kasiaro's father and grandfather among them, had been dispossessed from their land inside Serengeti National Park. Kasiaro was opposed to the Aga Khan's hotel, but not only for selfish reasons. He was also worried about the impact on the environment and the wildlife, a foreboding shared by conservationists in Tanzania and abroad, their fears compounded because another five-star hotel was also being built on the crater rim. And at the same time that the government had approved the new hotels for the crater rim, in 1990, it approved two large hotels for Serengeti, the first to be built inside the park in twenty years.

New lodges were the latest chapter in a battle over the Serengeti ecosystem. In the 1930s a British naturalist recommended that to preserve the Serengeti it should be designated a national park. It would become "a great world attraction surpassing . . . the famous National Parks of America," he was convinced. "In zoological interest it would surpass anything of its kind in the world." In time, it did become a national park, one of the first and largest in Africa. Then in the 1950s the British colonial government announced that it would break up the Serengeti, which included severing Ngorongoro. The reaction was fierce, and preservation of the Serengeti became the first test case for a nascent international conservation movement. The issue was—and still is—how much human activity, if any, should be allowed within the boundaries of a protected area. The broader question is this: Whose land is it? Does it belong to the people who live on it? Or is it a heritage that is to be protected for the benefit of all mankind? And if it is a world heritage, who is going to pay for the upkeep?

NGORONGORO IS often acclaimed—justifiably—as one of the natural wonders of the world. It arose from volcanic eruptions five to ten million years ago, and at one time, its cone may have reached nearly three miles in height. An eruption blew off the top, then a million or so years ago, the cone collapsed; today, it is the largest unbroken, unflooded caldera in the world. Its 35-mile rim is almost perfectly symmetrical. The walls, forested with dark green lichen-draped acacia trees and tangled shrubs, slope 2,000 feet down to the crater floor, a 100-square-mile bowl, or nearly five times the size of Manhattan. In the midst of the floor's natural zoo is a profusion of pink—thousands of flamingos standing on their slender legs in the shallow water of Lake Magadi, a soda lake that at one time was more than 50 feet deep. It is almost impossible to be in the crater for more than ten minutes without spotting lions stretched in the sun. There are rhinoceros and elephants, and bat-eared foxes, a nocturnal animal the size of a large house cat. Spotted hyenas camouflage themselves in shallow niches dug into the sides of mounds. Buffalo herds graze with wildebeest and zebra.

When you drive out of the crater and head west, you are soon on the grassy Serengeti Plain. They go on forever and ever—until finally, following the curvature of the planet, they meet up with the lower regions of the sky. Here, on these plains, where the sun's rays seem to arrive unfiltered, the numbers of wildlife are staggering; not thousands of wild animals, but hundreds of thousands—260,000 zebra and 400,000 Thomson's gazelle, with their brownish-red coats, dark stripes, and horns that curve back and then up. And 1,600,000 wildebeest—ungainly-looking antelope with buffalo-like horns, large heads, scraggly whiskers, and the hindquarters of a racehorse. The "clown of the plains," the wildebeest is called, on account of its looks and the way it bucks and twists.

These animals migrate every year, several hundred miles, following the rains that bring life and nutrition back to the grass. In April and May, they head north, crossing man's border into Kenya's famed Maasai Mara reserve; in September, they return to Tanzania, where calves are born. When they are on the move, their columns stretch for miles, like a wagon train crossing the American West. Lions and cheetah and hyenas and jackals stalk the animal caravans, waiting to pounce on a straggler or youngster. It is the Great Migration, and it has been going on for a million years, since the Pleistocene era, when glaciers covered much of the earth and man first appeared. "There is no comparable sight left on earth," Harold T. P. Hayes wrote in 1977 in *The Last Place on Earth*, his book about the Serengeti. It is hard to improve on that sentiment.

Kasiaro's ancestors saw all this long before the white man did. No definitive history of the Maasai has been written and much of their past is still a mystery, but the name means someone who speaks Maa, and they are believed to have arrived in what is now Kenya in the fifteenth century, after migrating south up the Nile. Along the way, they conquered other tribes and acquired a reputation as fierce warriors; the Arab slave traders were careful to go around Maasailand. At the peak of their power, at the end of the nineteenth century, the Maasai ranged over an area that stretched between Lake Victoria on the west and the Indian Ocean on the east and from north of Mount Kenya to south of Mount Kilimanjaro, some 80,000 square miles altogether. In Kenya, they occupied some of the best land, including the Great Rift Valley, the mile-high region of today's Nairobi—the word means "cold" in Maasai—and the territory over which the British, in 1895, began building a rail line to connect the Indian Ocean coast with their territory of Uganda. The British slowly forced the Maasai off these lands, and onto reserves in the southern part of Kenya. (The British referred to them as Masai, which has been the predominant spelling among Westerners, but "aa" is preferred by most of the Maasai today, especially those in Tanzania.) It is thought that the Maasai came to the Serengeti Plain and Ngorongoro Crater about the middle of the last century. At the time, the crater was occupied by another tribe, the Datoga, whom the Maasai defeated and forced out.

Today, there are about 300,000 Maasai in Tanzania and 200,000 in Kenya. And many times that number of cattle. The Maasai, like other pastoralist tribes, believe that all the world's cattle belongs to them, and some Maasai still do not take seriously the strictures of the modern state against theft; Maasai warriors stole more than 300 head of cattle and killed four people during raids around the village of Sakasaka, just south of the Serengeti, in early 1990. Maasai worship their cattle. When they meet, they ask, "How are the children? How are the cattle?" They sing to their cattle, young calves have a special place inside their small huts, and a man's status is determined by the number of cattle he has.

Westerners have long been enamored of the Maasai, who seem to fulfill the image of the "noble savage." Traditionally warriors coated their bodies with ochre, plaited their hair, stretched their earlobes, carried spears and, as part of the rite of passage, they hunted lions. "Physically they are among the handsomest of mankind, with slender bones, narrow hips and shoulders and most beautifully rounded muscles and limbs," Norman Leys, a doctor who spent twenty years in Africa at the beginning of this century, wrote about the Maasai. Isak Dinesen described the Maasai warrior as "chic," "daring," and "wildly fantastical." Many of the Maasai customs have been abandoned or prohibited by law, but it is still possible to observe Maasai who have not adapted to Western ways, particularly in Tanzania.

"Don't be romantic about the Maasai," a Tanzanian businessman and former government minister admonished when I asked about the forced removal of the Maasai from the Serengeti and their plight in Ngorongoro today. In part, his rebuke was a reflection of the tribal loyalties still prevalent in Africa. It was also good advice. There is nothing charming about much of the Maasai way of life, particularly for women. Maasai society is male-dominated, organized by age-sets: boyhood, warriors, elders. The manner in which women are treated falls somewhere between slavery and criminal abuse. Women gather the firewood, which they balance on their heads, and they fetch the water in ten- or twenty-liter containers, which they carry on their backs held by a strap around their foreheads. Women build the boma, or house, putting up the latticework of sticks, filling it with wattle and plastering it with dung, then putting on a roof of dung or thatch. What do the men do? "Supervise," says Kasiaro. And beat their wives if they do not perform their responsibilities—if the boma leaks, if there is not enough firewood. Women accept their status. "If I do wrong, my husband has the right to beat me," said a twenty-six-year-old Maasai woman as she waited in a long line with other women to fetch water that was trickling from a pipe.

But whether the Maasai are viewed romantically or harshly should not affect a judgment on how they have been treated by conservationists and governments who have coveted their land. And their story is one of how Africa's spaces have been set aside for preservation and tourism. Africa may be a vast continent, but the land that has been turned into parks wasn't idle land. Scores of tribes and millions of people have been dispossessed. And it is still happening. In 1991, 170 square miles of dense forest in southern Madagascar was set aside as Ranamafano National Park, created under pressure from American conservationists. Their desire was understandable—the forests are filled with exotic plants and animals found nowhere else on the planet, including several species of lemur, a cute, furry primate with a long tail and beady eyes. But 72,000 people lived in villages in or on the edges of the park. Many of them went into the park to cut wood, one of the few wage-paying jobs available; even more people took their cattle into the park. Now they are barred from it.

THE WORLD'S first national park was Yellowstone, created in 1872, and in the next half-century, America's national park system was firmly rooted. It became a model for African governments. But in the United States, the parks were a response to the longing for unspoiled, uncrowded places in the face of increasing urbanization and industrialization, and they were created to preserve the natural grandeur of trees and rivers, valleys and mountains. So we got Grand Canyon, Shenandoah, Mount Rainier. In Africa, the motivation for setting aside land has been to protect wildlife; indeed, the landscape of many of the parks in Africa is monotonously flat bushland that is brown most of the year, and not particularly picturesque.

The first national parks in Africa were Albert National Park, established in 1925 in the Belgian Congo, and Kruger National Park (which is as large as Israel), created a year later in South Africa. Albert, which is today Virunga National Park in Zaire, was set aside primarily to allow for the study of the mountain gorilla, and unlike national parks in the United States and elsewhere in the world, it was closed to everyone—including tourists—except scientists.

The momentum for more national parks in Africa began in 1930 when Britain's Society for the Preservation of the Fauna of the Empire sent a Major R. W. G. Hingston to look at wildlife conservation in Britain's East and Central African colonies—Northern Rhodesia (Zambia), Nyasaland (Malawi), Tanganyika, Kenya and Uganda. A surgeon who had served in the Middle East and East Africa and had been on the 1924 British expedition to Mount Everest, Hingston advanced ethical and moral grounds for protecting natural resources, as opposed to utilitarian ones. "The unique fauna of Africa must be preserved . . . its disappearance would be a crime against posterity," he told the society upon his return from Africa. He added, however, that "though the animal life should be preserved, yet it must not be allowed to injure man or to interfere with his cultivation and possessions." This dual objective—preserving nature while not inconveniencing man—could be accomplished, he said, "only by placing man and animals in two permanently separate compartments; in other words only by establishing National Parks."

The philosophy that parks and people must be separated, that a line should be drawn, with the animals on one side and the people on the other, would shape conservation thinking and programs for decades; only in recent years have some conservationists begun to challenge it, arguing that wildlife, in fact, has a better chance of being preserved only if it and people are integrated.

Hingston's findings were persuasive to the European powers with African colonies who gathered in London in 1933 to discuss conservation, as they had in 1900. The 1933 conference was necessary, the *Times* of London said, reporting on the opening day, because "The march of civilization, the increase of population, the extension of agriculture, the general progress of economic development—all these influences, fostered as they rightly were by Governments, threatened the existence of wild life." In his remarks to the delegates at the opening-day luncheon in the Park Lane Hotel, Sir Philip Cunliffe-Lister, secretary of state for the colonies, added (in the words of the *Times*, which did not quote him directly) that "the greatest danger to the animals . . . was the man who hunted for profit—the man who in 99 cases out of a hundred did not care a damn about the animals and their possible extinction, but was simply out to make all the money he could in the easiest way he could." It was the white man, not the African, who was hunting for profit, but needless to say, there were no Africans in London to discuss the solution.

At the end of a week of meetings in the Moses Room of the House of Lords, ministers and officials from nine countries put their signatures on the Convention Relative to the Preservation of Fauna and Flora in their Natural State. It superseded the 1900 treaty. To the five animals accorded complete protection by the earlier treaty, twelve more were put in Class A (the forerunner to CITES Appendix I), including all Madagascar lemurs (which the French, who colonized the island, insisted be put on the list), the gorilla, the giant sable antelope and the white rhinoceros; the *Welwitschia mirabilis*, the plant that spreads across the desert floor in the Kaokoveld, was the first, and only, fully protected flora species.

Even though Africa was still a dark and distant continent a half-century after Stanley and Livingstone, modernity was beginning to intrude, and Article 10 of the convention restricted the use of motorized vehicles. Nearly all tourists to Africa then—and for the next three decades—were hunters, and the treaty aimed to stop them from chasing their prey in cars. It also prohibited the use of aircraft, "including aircraft lighter than air," by which was meant helium balloons. Neither cars nor these balloons were to be used "in such manner as to drive, stampede, or disturb [animals] for any purpose, including that of filming or photographing." Fifty years later, Western tourists who are adamant about preserving Africa's wildlife routinely violate this early conservation wisdom. It is not only that hot-air balloons drift over the Mara and Serengeti. Just as unsettling, drivers of zebra-striped vans routinely "disturb" animals so that tourists can snap better photographs; if they did not, the tourist would consider his trip a failure and the driver would not receive a tip.

The most significant and far-reaching work of the 1933 conference, however, called for the creation of national parks. In many of the colonies, land had been set aside as reserves, but these were areas in which licensed hunting was permitted. Furthermore, reserves were created by the colonial governor, and with the power to create came the power to abolish or alter the boundaries, which often happened because of pressure from white farmers. In 1929, for example, the British, who had been given control of Tanganyika by the League of Nations after World War I (it had been a German colony), had set aside 900 square miles of the Serengeti as a reserve. The action was taken primarily to protect the Serengeti's lions; a European hunter had once boasted that his party killed fifty-two male lions. Typically, over the years, the reserve's boundaries changed as did its regulations. At one time, a license was needed to enter the reserve to take photographs as well as to hunt, and not until 1937 did the government impose a complete ban on the hunting of lions, cheetah, leopards, giraffes, rhinoceros, buffalo and roan antelope. It was still legal, it is worth noting, to shoot an elephant.

As defined by the 1933 treaty, a national park was to be a large area inside of which hunting would be prohibited, and which was to exist in perpetuity. Major Hingston had proposed the creation of several specific national parks in Britain's African colonies. The Serengeti was one. Reflecting prevailing attitudes about conservation, he noted that this could be done without upsetting Europeans because there were no significant mineral deposits in the proposed park, and the presence of tsetse fly and the scant rainfall meant that European farmers were not likely to be attracted to the land. He added, "From the two points of view, viz., that of effecting animal conservation and that of providing a world attraction to visitors, it comes very near to the complete ideal." He thought it would surpass any of America's national parks. Many would agree with him that it does.

In 1940 Hingston's recommendation was followed, and the Serengeti was upgraded from a reserve to a national park. It was the first in East Africa and it was immense. It reached from the shores of Lake Victoria on the west to beyond Ngorongoro Crater on the east; after a few changes, by 1951 it encompassed 4,480 square miles, an area nearly as large as Connecticut or Northern Ireland. All hunting was banned.

But the law creating Serengeti National Park had a special provision that allowed the Maasai who were living there at the time to remain. Even Major Hingston would have accepted this. "The existence of Masai in a National Park offers little difficulty since they neither hunt game nor cultivate the soil, and are thus better adapted than other native tribes to live amicably amongst the game," he wrote in the report of his mission. "Nor is it an important objection that the Masai kill lions, since it has been found in the Kruger National Park that a certain amount of lion destruction has to be periodically carried out." (This is because lions do not stay inside a park's boundaries but wander onto ranches, where they kill cattle.)

Tanganyika government officials frequently, and publicly, reiterated the rights of the Maasai to remain in the park. "The rights of the Masai are protected by law and cannot be abrogated," the district commissioner said during a meeting of Maasai elders and provincial officials at Ngorongoro Crater in 1952. Two years later, in a speech of the Maasai Federal Council, the governor of Tanganyika said, "I wish at once to reassure you that all Masai and other pastoralists who have been normally resident within the area of the Park will not be turned out." The promises didn't survive the decade.

THIS IS what we gave up! Kasiaro thought as he was riding through Serengeti National Park. His deep-set eyes sparkling, he exclaimed with wonderment when we passed herds of topi and hartebeest; gazelle leaped across the road in front of us, and we saw a klipspringer, a tiny antelope, perched like a ballet dancer on a few centimeters of rock. "My father used to tell me about the beauty of Serengeti, but I didn't know it myself," Kasiaro said at the end of the day, his first in the Serengeti. He grew up on the periphery of the park and had watched tourist vehicles stir up dust as they hurried from Ngorongoro to Serengeti, but until November 1990, he had never entered it. Spotting a lion with a radio collar, he asked, wonder-struck, "Who put that on him?" He was not aware that Serengeti has been one of the premier laboratories for the study of lions; today when you see a lion pride, you are just as likely to see a research vehicle with an antenna on it, and a student inside making sketches and notes. All of this was strange to Kasiaro, who as a young warrior had killed lions with a spear. After several hours' driving, as we crossed the Seronera River, where hippos were submerged up to their backs and their beady little eyes, Kasiaro had an idea. "Why didn't they give us part of this?" He laughed lightly. "Why couldn't they divide it, give us the right side of the road, and they take the left?"

From the outset, the park's trustees had hoped to entice the Maasai into leaving the park voluntarily by providing them with better grazing areas, along with wells and boreholes outside. It didn't work. Areas of the Serengeti were dear to the Maasai, rich with grass and water. One of these was the Moru Kopjes, a collection of granite boulders on the western edge of the plains; it was here that young warriors set up their camps, where they sang and danced and feasted, and set out on their lion-hunting forays. Another choice spot was Seronera, where the park headquarters is today. And the Maasai did not want to give up Ngorongoro, because that was one of their best grazing areas, one of the few places where there was permanent water. When the Maasai refused to leave voluntarily, the local authorities ordered them out, in the early 1950s. The Maasai are a tough people, and they remained intransigent. "We told them you better shoot us together with the cows; we are not going to leave the Serengeti," one of the Maasai who had been living in the Serengeti at the time, Tendemo ole Kisaka, recalled nearly forty years later.

The British government in London was reluctant to push the issue. It had enough problems across the border in its Kenya colony, where the Mau Mau rebellion, the war for independence, was in its early stages. So in 1956, in Sessional Paper Number 1, the Legislative Council of Tanganyika, whose members were appointed by the British governor, revealed a plan for the Serengeti which it hoped would satisfy the Maasai and the park's trustees. The council proposed that the Serengeti be reduced from nearly 5,000 square miles to 1,800; while this would obviously be a substantial change, nonetheless the remaining park would be as large as Grand Canyon National Park. The Maasai would leave the new park—actually it would be three small parks. Among the areas that would no longer be within the park were the central plains, which was where the animals gathered in greatest profusion and the wildebeest dropped their calves every year. The Moru Kopjes and most of Ngorongoro would also be hived off. In all these places, then, the Maasai would be allowed to put up their bomas and range their stock, goats and sheep, as well as their cattle.

The council's proposal provoked a furious reaction among whites. Many were convinced that the government officials were awed by the Maasai and had sold out to them. "We were appalled," Myles Turner, a British warden in the Serengeti at the time, wrote in his memoirs; "but luckily, so was the rest of the world."

The American Committee for International Wild Life Protection, a consortium of thirty-three scientific and conservation organizations, sent a delegation to the Serengeti to investigate. It was headed by Lee Talbot, an ecologist, who was later to become director of the International Union for the Conservation of Nature (IUCN). Talbot noted that during the season when the Serengeti's central plains were dry, zebra, wildebeest and gazelle—"with their attendant predatories and scavengers"—were attracted to Ngorongoro Crater in "spectacularly large numbers." This was because two permanent and two smaller seasonal streams flowed into the crater. Talbot believed that there was not enough water in the streams for the Maasai cattle and for the wildlife. So, Talbot concluded, if the Maasai were permitted to remain, the crater "might be denied wild life, and hence that this part of the proposed park would be denied its principal attraction for tourists." Talbot also believed that the Maasai could so overgraze the area and cut down so many trees to make their bomas that there would be serious erosion in the crater's highlands.

The chairman of the American Committee for International Wild Life Protection, Harold Coolidge, sent Talbot's report to the Committee of Enquiry that had been set up by the British government in response to the objections to the council's proposal to shrink the Serengeti. Coolidge, a prominent conservationist since the 1920s and one of the founders of IUCN, told the British committee that "as the last sanctuary for the greatest remaining concentration of arid grasslands wildlife in the entire world, the Serengeti area is a precious asset for all nations as well as for Tanganyika and the British Commonwealth." He added, "The Serengeti National Park, as it is now constituted, contains an asset which is unique in the entire world. This is the amazing assemblage of wildlife species which elsewhere has been broken into fragments if not completely destroyed." The American Committee also formally petitioned the British Colonial Office not to dissect the park.

But the most vehement objections to the government's plan for the Serengeti come from Europe, where some conservationists were so angry that they talked about having the Serengeti removed from British administration. The Fauna Preservation Society dispatched an eminent botany professor from the University of London, W. H. Pearsall, to conduct an ecological survey of the Serengeti. Pearsall prepared a 113-page report, which became the single most important document in the controversy.

It was not so important to Pearsall whether the Maasai were indeed guilty of overgrazing and responsible for soil erosion, as many charged, or whether they were in fact good pastoralists. In his view, the ecology of the Serengeti was so fragile that the effects of almost any grazing and cattle treading would be severe. Pearsall recommended that the western and central parts of the Serengeti, including the Moru kopjes, be retained as part of one national park, and that Ngorongoro become another park, with a corridor linking them. No pastoralist activity would be allowed in the parks, but humans would have limited access to the corridor.

In Africa, the paleontologist Louis Leakey was at the forefront of the opposition to the legislative council's plan to split up the park. Under the plan one area that would be excised was Olduvai Gorge. Leakey had been excavating in Olduvai—the name comes from the Maasai *ol duvai*, which means the place of the wild sisal, the plant used for making rope— for twenty-five years, having arrived in 1931 in a car, probably the first to enter the Serengeti. In 1959, Mary Leakey, his wife, would uncover the left temple of a hominid who had lived there 1,750,000 years earlier; it was one of the most dramatic findings at the time, and later discoveries at Olduvai, including the *Homo habilis* cranium, added considerably to knowledge of the origins of man.

Louis Leakey prepared a "Memorandum on the Serengeti National Park Problem," which became the basis for a submission to the Committee of Enquiry by the Kenya Wildlife Society. Leakey argued at some length that the Maasai had no legal right to remain in the Serengeti, but whatever rights they had, he said, should not be greater than the best interests of the rest of the people of Tanganyika and indeed of the world. Serengeti National Park was one of Tanganyika's greatest national assets, Leakey wrote, and he emphasized it was *"a major potential source of wealth to the Territory and for its inhabitants of all races for many centuries to come, provided that it is not destroyed now."* The wealth would come from tourism.

Underlying much of the campaign to get the Maasai out of the Serengeti was, of course, the colonial prejudice against Africans, which was particularly strong when it came to the Maasai. While many Westerners were awed by the Maasai, just as many, maybe more, found them arrogant and dirty. "They never wash," Alan Moorehead wrote in *No Room in the Ark*, which is deservedly considered a classic about African wildlife, but which reflects a colonial contempt for African people. "At certain times they streak their faces with coloured grease and dirt, and braid their hair so as to give it the appearance of a mop," he wrote. He described some of their tribal ceremonies as "barbaric," and said that the Maasai "disdains all forms of trade and ordinary labor." So pervasive was the antipathy toward the Maasai, particularly among the white wardens in the Serengeti and in Kenya, that Leakey felt compelled to stress in one of his many papers advocating the removal of the Maasai from the Serengeti, "I am not one of those who consider that the Masai should be treated with contempt and disdain or that they are unfit to survive."

Into this furor flew—literally—a man whose name would become almost synonymous with the Serengeti and a legend in the annals of African conservation—Bernhard Grzimek. A veterinarian, he had become director of the Frankfurt Zoo after World War II, during which it had been badly damaged, and built it into one of the finest in the world. Grzimek (pronounced "Jim-ek") and his son Michael landed in the Serengeti, after flying their zebra-striped, single-propeller aircraft 4,000 miles from Frankfurt. Their assignment was to count the animals in the Serengeti ecosystem and study their migratory patterns in order to demonstrate that the excisions being proposed would be disastrous. This was not their first foray into Africa. On an earlier trip, in 1953, their mission had been to capture an okapi for the Frankfurt zoo. A rare animal, the okapi is a member of the giraffe family but looks like a horse and has zebra stripes on its rear haunches; found only in the dense rain forests of the Congo Basin of Zaire, where the Pygmies live, it wasn't discovered by the white man until this century, and it was one of the species protected by the 1933 convention.

In 1956, the elder Grzimek wrote *No Room for Wild Animals*. The apocalyptic thesis was simple: human populations were expanding so rapidly, consuming resources and turning forests into deserts, that the wildlife would eventually be extinguished. "The wild animals of Africa are doomed to die," he wrote without qualification; future generations would know the magnificence of Africa's wildlife only through books, films, zoos and a few sanctuaries, he said. The book was translated into seventeen languages, and Michael made a documentary with the same title. The book and movie did so well commercially that when Grzimek offered to buy the Serengeti in order to keep the British from dismantling it, there were many people who thought he might just do it.

He didn't, of course. But his pen proved as powerful as his money. In 1959 he wrote *Serengeti Shall Not Die*, which became a best-seller internationally and has been translated into more than twenty languages. It was a clarion call to keep the Serengeti pristine, to keep man out. Again, his son made a documentary of the same name, which was awarded the Oscar for best documentary in 1959. Michael was killed before finishing the film, when the plane he was piloting collided with a vulture shortly after taking off from Ngorongoro Crater. A group of Maasai who were boring water holes for their cattle—Grzimek strongly objected to their doing so—saw the crash and alerted the authorities. Michael was buried among the evergreens on the crater rim; and when his father died, in 1987, the urn with his ashes was placed in a grave next to Michael's remains.

Grzimek was a "genius," a man who "has done more than anyone else to dramatize the plight of African wildlife," the director of the Bronx Zoo, William Conway, told the writer Harold Hayes in the mid-1970s. The director of London Zoos, C. G. C. Rawlins, said Grzimek was "one of the greatest zoo directors and conservationists of our time." The accolades may be deserved—but only if conservation is considered narrowly, devoid of any concern about people.

Grzimek insisted that he was not prejudiced against Africans. "For me a negro is an equal and a brother," he wrote in *Serengeti Shall Not Die*. Like most whites in Africa at the time, he just did not think these brothers were ready for independence. Or as he put it: "I am not sure whether the overhasty conversion of coloured colonies into independent democratic States is good for the inhabitants." The responsibility of the colonial governments, he declared, was to educate the Africans so that they would be able to live democratically. The white man's burden extended to teaching the Africans about wildlife and conservation. "*We Europeans must teach our black brothers to value their own possessions, not because we are older or cleverer, but because we do not want them to repeat our mistakes and our sins,*" Grzimek wrote, and he provided the emphasis. This was, of course, the attitude of many of the Westerners who wanted an ivory ban—that it was necessary to impose a ban on Africans or they would destroy the elephants just as Westerners had exterminated the bison and depleted populations of bears and wolves.

Grzimek was convinced that all pastoralist societies destroyed their environment, primarily because of overgrazing and tree cutting, and that the Maasai would do the same to the Serengeti. He was far from alone in this view. Even the most eminent scientists and conservationists, such as Pearsall and Talbot, believed it, and this is why they wanted the Maasai out of the park. They were wrong. "Prior to European colonisation pastoralists tended not to exploit wildlife except during periods of stock loss," says David Collett, a Cambridge-educated archaeologist who has carried out anthropological and archaeological work in Kenya and southern Africa. "Thus, there is no evidence to indicate that pastoralism is inimical to wildlife." David Western, the Nairobi-based conservationist, who has worked closely with the Maasai, goes further. "The reason wildlife has been preserved is because of the pastoralists," he says.

Whether Grzimek, Pearsall, Talbot and other conservationists of their time reached the negative conclusions they did about the Maasai because of biases they brought into their work, or whether it was because they only studied the animals and plants and did not bother to look closely at the people, is largely irrelevant. The Maasai paid the price for the

Westerners' ignorance. And the ignorance endures. European and American conservationists still trek to the Serengeti and Ngorongoro, spending weeks and months conducting expensive surveys, and then make recommendations on how to protect the land and animals.

"I wonder about these people who pretend to be educated," Kasiaro said on one occasion. "They see this good environment and just think that it happened. Oh, they don't know that those people who are living here protected it. The Maasai had a tradition that protected the environment and the wildlife." We were on the Ngorongoro Crater rim, and he cast his eyes toward a fluted tree draped with moss. "You can't just come and cut a tree without any reason. If I say, 'Oh this tree is very good for a boma,' but I don't have a use for it, I have to say, 'I'm not intending to cut you.' " He spit at the tree, a blessing in Maasai culture, and then explained that if a person cuts a tree to build his boma, but does not move in, he must perform a little ceremony. He mixes milk, honey and home-brewed alcohol in a small gourd and pours it around the boma. Then he says, "Good trees, I cut you because I thought I'd come here, but I didn't, so forgive me."

"So that's why you can always find trees where the Maasai live," Kasiaro said. "It's something spiritual—we think it's a living thing."

"We have a culture that likes animals," he said during another conversation. The one animal the Maasai does kill is the lion. Maasai warriors kill them as part of their rite of passage (a practice that the governments of Kenya and Tanzania have banned, but it continues). The warriors hunt with spears, which truly requires a display of courage, and there is no evidence that the Maasai hunters ever threatened the survival of the lion as a species, which cannot be said about white hunters. Maasai believe that if a man kills too many lions he will be cursed.

Had Kasiaro been around, he would have asked Grzimek, Leakey and the others a simple question: If the Maasai were such bad conservationists, why were these Westerners so eager to protect the Serengeti?

The British backed off substantially from the original proposals in Sessional Paper Number 1, and basically adopted Pearsall's recommendations—four thousand eight hundred square miles became the Serengeti National Park (later additions have again put it over five thousand). And they obtained concessions from the Maasai.

On April 21, 1958, twelve Maasai elders "signed" an "Agreement By the Masai To Vacate The Western Serengeti." They consented to re-

nounce their claim to the Moru Kopjes and Seronera; the agreement
further stated:

> We understand that as a result of this renunciation we shall not be
> entitled henceforth in the years to come to cross this line which will
> become the boundary of the new Serengeti National Park and which
> will be demarcated. We also understand that we shall not be entitled
> to reside in or use in the future the land lying to the west of this line,
> which we have habitually used in the past.
>
> We agree to move ourselves, our possessions, our cattle and all our
> other animals out of this land by the end of the next short rains, that
> is before the 31st December, 1958.

One of the few signers still alive is Tendemo ole Kisaka. With the aid
of two long poles, he walked to a tree, sat down on the grass and leaned
back against the yellow bark. A ring of small wire strung through a red
ball dropped from each of his long earlobes. In 1958, he was living at the
Moru Kopjes. He recalled that a few days after the agreement was signed,
six large trucks came and loaded the Maasai and their few possessions on
them and carried them outside the new park. He has never been back.
"I cry even when you ask me about them," he said, beginning to respond
when he heard the word "Seronera."

The elders signed the agreement because "We were told to sign,"
he said. "It was not explained to us." None of the elders knew how to
read or write, he said. "You white people are very tough," he said,
grinning.

The official Serengeti National Park guidebook says that in 1959 "the
few Masai remaining in the Park were resettled." That's it for the Maasai,
dismissed in less than a sentence. The guidebook was written by the
African Wildlife Foundation office in Nairobi. There is no mention in
the guidebook that the park's name, Serengeti, comes from a Maasai
word, *siringet*, which means an extended place; or that Seronera, the
park's headquarters, comes from the Maasai word *sironet*. ("They said
if you slaughtered a bull from Sironet, it's a very fat one," Kasiaro said,
recalling stories that had been handed down by the Maasai who had
lived there.) The guidebook does not even tell visitors that at the Moru
Kopjes there are Maasai rock paintings—shields, elephants, lions, in
ochre, white and black colors. For visitors to the Serengeti, the Maasai
never existed.

As Louis Leakey and others had hoped, the Serengeti became popular
with Western tourists. Kay Turner, wife of the deputy chief game warden

in the 1960s, recalls visits by "writers, actors, artists, heads of state, royalty, scientists, peers, politicians, celebrities, tycoons, and many others." Among them: James Michener and William Styron; Robert Kennedy, Robert McNamara and McGeorge Bundy; Prince Philip, Prince Bernhard and the King and Queen of Denmark; Marshal Tito and Olaf Palme; Charles Lindbergh. Most of these celebrities were also contributors to Friends of the Serengeti, the brainchild of John Owen, an Englishman who was the head of the Tanzanian parks department in the 1960s. "The jet set in America had just opened to the fact that African wildlife was worth seeing," Owen recalled many years later. Owen, who was as energetic and determined as Grzimek, raised about $5 million for Tanzania's parks—from Guggenheims, Mellons, Scaifes, Kennedys, Bechtels.

The Maasai did not fare so well.

IN EXCHANGE for giving up the Moru Kopjes, Seronera and all other parts of the new Serengeti National Park, the Maasai were allowed to remain in what became the Ngorongoro Conservation Area. It was a modest pioneering effort: instead of man and animals being separated in order to protect the animals, the needs of both man and wildlife would be attended to in the same area. Speaking to the Maasai Federal Council, the governor of Tanganyika, Sir Richard Turnbull, put it this way: "I should like to make it clear to you that it is the intention of the government to develop the Crater in the interests of the people who use it. At the same time the government intends to protect the game animals of the area, but should there be any conflict between the interests of game and human inhabitants those of the latter must take precedence." Thirty years later, it could be said that the conservation objectives have been largely successful, as anyone who gazes on the elephants, rhino, lions, knows. The human aspects have been a failure, depressingly evident to visitors who care to notice.

The first management plan for Ngorongoro, drafted in 1960, recommended that given the crater's potential as a tourist attraction, the Maasai should be moved out. When the Conservation Area's first conservator, Henry Fosbrooke, reviewed the plan, he concluded that the drafters had adopted the attitude toward the Maasai of "Daddy knows best." Little has changed. The Maasai make up more than 98 percent of the population of the Conservation Area, yet at no time have more than two Maasai been members of the Authority's board of directors (which has varied in size from eight to thirteen).

Two years after the Ngorongoro Conservation Area was created, Tanganyikans acquired their independence. (It became Tanzania in 1964 after a union with the island of Zanzibar.) But that did not mean that colonialist philosophies and practices were abandoned. On the contrary, in Tanzania, as well as in neighboring Kenya, most of them were adopted—perhaps because after generations of being told they were inferior to whites, most Africans believed that white ways were better. And over the years, the colonialist conservationists have been replaced by white expatriate conservationists and their international conservation organizations. These "experts" and their money—available to African governments that adopt the "right" policies—have had as much influence on African conservation policy as the Society for the Preservation of the Wild Fauna of the Empire ever did. The modern conservation organizations have stressed animals over people. And finally the Maasai have suffered because, it must be said, ruling African ethnic groups often mistreat and discriminate against other tribes with as much viciousness as the colonialists ever did.

In the 1970s, the Tanzanian government struck the Ngorongoro Maasai twice. First, in 1974, it evicted them from the crater floor.

"Very early in the morning, about five o'clock, three trucks full of field force soldiers stopped very close to the boma and told the people, 'Bring everything out, we are going to burn the houses,' " Tate ole Rokonga recalled. He was speaking on the southern side of the crater floor, at the edge of the Lerai Forest. "Lerai" is the Maasai name for the towering acacia, which has sprawling limbs, tiny leaves and lemon-yellow bark; the Europeans called it "yellow bark acacia," or "fever tree," because where they found it they got malaria (the tree grows near water). The Lerai Forest has become a favorite stopping place for tourists. "Can you imagine how they have damaged this?" Tate said. (The Maasai generally go by their first names; Kasiaro is an exception, because, he thinks, his first name, Parimitoro, is difficult to pronounce.) The grass was littered—toilet paper, beer bottles, cans, white boxes with the detritus of lunches packed by hotels for guests. The garbage was being picked over by grey vervet monkeys, while delighted tourists fed more of the cute primates in spite of urgings from conservationists and park wardens, throughout Africa, not to feed the animals.

The forest had been the home for Tate's extended family—twelve elders, forty warriors, altogether about two hundred and fifty people, most of them children. They had eighteen hundred head of cattle. "Here there is nice grass, water and salt," Tate said, explaining why the site had been chosen. He is not sure how long his family had been living in the crater, but he remembers that his grandfather told stories about German soldiers during World War I who had a camp in the crater, which they reached on horseback.

The Tanzanian soldiers who came to evict the Maasai—there were two villages in addition to Tate's—were armed with rifles and machine guns, Tate said. One of his brothers, Clemence, a young warrior at the time, demanded to know by what authority the soldiers were acting; he was beaten and then jailed for five days, Tate said. The soldiers went into the huts and dragged out young calves, and they opened the kraal. "They started driving the cows up, using that path," Tate said, pointing to a path winding up the crater wall. "Halfway up, most of the cattle turned back; the soldiers shot them." The people's belongings were loaded onto large military trucks. Possessions and people were dumped on the crater rim. Their village below was razed.

"No one has come clean as to who made the decision to remove the Maasai and why," Henry Fosbrooke said sixteen years later. "My personal view is that it was a political move, because the Tanzanian government didn't want tourists to see undeveloped people in hide cloths." He is probably right. Most tourists who come to Africa expect to see wild animals in the "wild"; they don't want to see cows or people living in squalid dung huts.

A Maasai can still take his cattle into the crater for water and salt, but he needs a special permit, and these days it is far easier for a tourist to pass into the crater than it is for a Maasai. One hundred and fifty thousand foreigners do so each year, ferried down and out in more than twenty thousand vehicles, using only two narrow dirt roads. It is hard to imagine that they do not cause greater environmental damage and disturb the wildlife more than a few hundred Maasai would.

The Sierra Club guide *Adventuring in East Africa* recommends the crater floor as "a delightful place to camp." Indeed it can be. One night just after dark, I detected something moving, faintly silhouetted by the nearly full moon. I twisted the head of my slim Maglite, and pointed the beam. It landed on the golden coat of a large, full-maned lion ambling not more than thirty yards away. I went to sleep to the roar of lions, and awoke in the morning to gaze upon elephants a few hundred yards from our tents.

Fosbrooke does not think that tourists should be allowed to camp in the crater. "Visitors running around is one thing, but visitors camping is another," he says. In 1934, Fosbrooke, who had arrived in Tanganyika three years earlier as a cadet in the British colonial service, walked across the crater floor with his wife, and he has dedicated much of his life to what he acclaims as the eighth wonder of the world. Fosbrooke now lives a hundred and some miles east of Ngorongoro, in a time-weathered house perched on the rim of Lake Duluti, a crater lake, formed "goodness knows when," he says; he can often be found these days sorting through his papers and books, which he has bequeathed to the University of Tanzania in Dar es Salaam, including a first edition of Joseph Thomson's classic *Through Masai Land*, which was published in 1885. Camping was "contrary to the whole spirit of the crater, that it be untouched Africa," Fosbrooke said, and he added, "It's morally indefensible that you chuck out a couple of hundred Maasai and then permit a couple of hundred *mzungu* to sleep there every night." (*Mzungu* is the Swahili word meaning white people, and is commonly used in East Africa.)

Fosbrooke gave another reason for being opposed to camping: "It spoils the atmosphere. I'll show you two pictures—of what a Maasai kraal looks like, and what a modern campsite looks like." He took out a scrapbook, with some yellowed photographs taken on the crater floor, and went on, "I'll take the Maasai over Abercrombie and Kent."

A Maasai boma is not particularly appealing to the Western eye. But one time when I camped at the crater's Fig Tree site, I understood what Fosbrooke was getting at. It was a scene like one of those lakeside campsites in Minnesota or Germany in the summer when they are jammed with campers. The Ngorongoro camp is marked by a gigantic strangler fig tree. The Maasai worship the tree, as do other African tribes, and this one is more than a hundred years old; over the century aerial roots from upper limbs have descended to the ground, new trunks have formed, and they are now all twisted and intertwined; the tree's canopy must be seventy-five feet around. A hundred yards from the tree in one direction, fifteen small brown tents had been put up. They were close to a permanent drop latrine, dug near a burial site that is at least two thousand years old. This tourist company had dug a temporary garbage pit under a young thorn tree, and this time when I heard a noise at night and shone my light, I caught the sparkle of the eyes of a jackal scavenging in the garbage.

In another direction, it was a village of green canvas—tents for sleeping, a tent for cooking, a tent for eating. These belonged to Abercrombie & Kent. Five of the A&K tents were guest quarters, each with two beds, with a hanging shower in the back. Only two of the tents were being used, so the others could have been taken down. When a guest arrived at the A&K camp, he found cold beer, and ice for his scotch—thanks to the company's generators, which whine in the morning and in the evening, breaking the crater's silence. "With the generators blaring all night, the animals never get a rest," said John Bennett, the owner of his own small safari company. "At least the Maasai gave the wildlife twelve hours of peace," he added wryly. A short, bearded Tanzanian fond of his black woolen stocking cap, Bennett, son of a Chaga woman and an English coffee grower, can talk about the Maasai, Tanzanian politics and wildlife with equal and impressive knowledge. Even though he took his clients to the floor for camping—he pitched his tents when he arrived and took them down upon departing—he felt just as strongly as Fosbrooke that all camping in the crater should be banned, and in February 1992, the Tanzanian government decided to close the crater floor to camping for an indefinite period. A&K argued against the action, but, in fact, it had been largely responsible for it. "Major tour operators organize large camping parties which impose environmental impact on the campsites, and the lights of those camps constitute a form of pollution of the serenity of the crater at night," the Ngorongoro authority said when it announced the closure. Although camping was discontinued, no one entertained the idea of allowing the Maasai back onto the floor of Ngorongoro, and life outside the crater was difficult because of laws for the benefit of wildlife.

One year after the Maasai were expelled from the crater, the Tanzanian government ordered an end to all cultivation in the Ngorongoro Conservation Area. It was another victory for conservationists. While pastoralist societies might be able to live in harmony with wildlife, agricultural ones by and large cannot. Wild herbivores, particularly elephants and buffalo, can quickly destroy a person's maize crop, and to protect his field from the marauders, the farmer either wants to put up a fence, which interferes with the animals' migratory patterns, or even worse, he wants the animals shot.

When the Tanzanian government announced the prohibition on cultivation, the Maasai complained bitterly, particularly the women. Contrary to the popular image, the Maasai do not subsist entirely on milk, blood and meat from goats and sheep; though those are the staples of their diet, they have long eaten grains, generally maize, and particularly so during droughts when their livestock herds are depleted. And as the Maasai have become less traditional and pastoralist—by the pressure of "development" and government policies, as much as by choice—they have gradually become more agriculturalist. The government responded to the complaints with more promises—to provide veterinary services for the Maasai cattle, to build roads that were needed to bring in grains and other food from the outside, and to build grain-storage facilities. The promises remain largely unfilled—there are still no grain-storage facilities, and what few roads exist are in a deplorable state, often impassable in the rainy season. The prohibitions, on the other hand, have been enforced. During one special police operation, in 1987, six hundred villagers were arrested for illegally cultivating; their tiny plots were destroyed and they were fined between 1,000 and 2,000 Tanzanian shillings each, a stiff amount (200 shillings was roughly one dollar). Tendemo ole Kisaka, the old man who had signed the agreement under which the Maasai left the Serengeti, said that during another crackdown, several people from his village had been jailed for six to nine months because they were caught cultivating.

The ban on cultivation has been exacerbated for the Maasai by a devastating decline in their cattle herds. The number of cattle per person today in Ngorongoro is less than half what it was in the 1960s. One reason for the decline has been a substantial increase in the number of wildebeest. When the wildebeest gives birth, the ground is fouled by the afterbirth, a malignant catarrhal secretion that is fatal to cattle. A greater cause of cattle deaths, however, has been bovine cerebral theileriosis, the most serious tick-borne disease. Traditionally, the Maasai dealt with this disease by moving their cattle from the affected area for several years, burning the grass—which harbors the tick—and grazing the area with sheep and goats. Now, of course, the Maasai have fewer areas to move to, since so much of their former land is park.

Kasiaro comes from a wealthy family. His father had owned more than 500 cattle, which was enough to support his five wives and all their children. When his father died in 1982, Kasiaro inherited some of the cattle and within three years he and a brother together had a herd of more than 300. Then the diseases hit. By 1990, they possessed fewer than 75 cattle. It was probably a fourth of what he needed to support his extended family. Kasiaro has three wives—"They were booked for me," he says; his father had secured the engagements with gifts of cattle. Each wife has borne Kasiaro one child; his brother, who also has three wives, has seven children. They all live in Kasiaro's boma, fourteen dung huts surrounding a large kraal, a few hundred yards from the crater rim. Kasiaro has taken in one full sister and one half-sister "simply because they had no cattle left." Kasiaro gave the full sister three cattle a few years ago, and she now has ten, but these must support her four children, her husband and her husband's other wife, all of whom live in the boma. The half-sister has three cattle and six children. Twenty-two children were living in his boma, Kasiaro said, after silently counting to himself. Then, he added, "There might be more than that." It looked as if there was not a healthy child among them. Two of them were severely malnourished, with stick-thin arms and legs. All were caked with dirt, covered with flies. Flies in the mucus running from noses. Flies on their lips. Flies in infected eyes. And Kasiaro is one of the better-off members of his community. The same sickening sights exist in virtually every boma. A child's diet is maize meal porridge, twice a day. When Kasiaro was a child, milk was added. These days, there is little milk, and the porridge is thinned with water.

One afternoon, along the crater rim road where it begins to twist down into the Olduvai plains, there was a group of about thirty Maasai. They lived in the huts in a cut in the hills behind them; on rainy days, children slide down the hill, laughing, on pieces of calfskin. Most of the Maasai here were women, colorfully attired, and children. They were beckoning to the white people in the passing minivans and Land Rovers, hoping that the tourists would be enticed into taking a picture of a Maasai—and paying for it.

It is the ubiquitous scene, the one that disturbs most tourists, in the Caribbean islands, in bustling Bangkok, at the pyramids in Egypt, at Machu Picchu: impoverished people begging, selling their culture and their dignity. They tug at you. "Buy this bracelet. I give you good price." You feel sorry for them, but you also get angry because they won't leave you alone. As my wife and I hiked up the mountain to see the gorillas in Rwanda, we were followed by children with dirty faces and torn clothes beseeching us to give them some food or money. When we returned many hours later, a larger number were waiting, their hands out. The images of these sad children has lingered with her as long as the thrill of visiting the gorillas.

"I used to cry when I saw them standing on the road like this," Kasiaro said. "It pains me. Now, I say, OK, there's no other alternative. But actually I don't like it at all. It is not good to get money you don't work for. It is changing the young people just to depend on that, without working; it is destroying them. We have tried to stop them, by talking to them, telling them, 'This is not good.' But stopping somebody who is hungry and has nothing to eat, it is hard. It is the only way they can survive."

One of the women along the road was Naloya. She was born in the crater and was living there in 1974 at the time of the evictions. She did not know how old she was, but an acquaintance remembered that she was born in 1960. Her tall, statuesque body was draped in a purple cape. Long, beaded strings dangled from her ears. She wore a fez-like cap of colorful beads and a broad, flat band of bright-colored beads around her neck. She has five children. The oldest looked to be about twelve. She too stood erect, and was adorned with necklaces, earrings and circles of copper wire on her ankles. One of Naloya's daughters, maybe four or five years old, was wearing a wool sweater that reached below her knees. It was torn and soiled, and had probably been left by some well-meaning Western woman; Naloya tried to conceal it under the girl's cloak, for she understands that tourists want to photograph "natives" in their traditional garb, that children in Western rags do not appeal to them.

When asked if she liked having her picture taken, Naloya hesitated, then said, "No, I feel that they are taking my picture because I am like a wild animal. It's not good, but I need the money."

She said that on most days she got only 100 or 200 Tanzanian shillings; on a very good day, 600; at most, 1,000. With the money, she buys food for her children, she said. One kilogram of corn flour costs 100 shillings; it will feed her family for a day. One kilogram of sugar costs 200 shillings; that will last three days.

Four teenage boys were standing off to one side. They were wearing black togas and their faces were painted white, masklike; flat, fan-shaped frames stuffed with the feathers from ostriches and smaller birds extended above the backs of their heads. The attire said that they had recently been circumcised and would soon be warriors. In answer to a question, one of the boys said tourists were good because they gave them money when they took pictures of the Maasai. Another added, "We can buy our clothes and spears with this money we get." This meant that their father did not have to sell any cattle, they said.

Kasiaro said that when he was a warrior, he would never have allowed a tourist to take his picture. But now, even warriors are beggars. They stand with their spears, their red togas flowing, at the choice spots, such as the entrance to the crater and even on the crater floor.

One day, along the rim, a group of warriors and elders from Oloirobi, Kasiaro's village, had gathered in the tall grass, in the shade of a large, leafy tree. Sixteen spears were stuck in the ground; Maasai spears are about five feet long, pointed on one end and swordlike on the other. The matter of going into the crater came up. With special permission, a Maasai can go into the crater with his cattle, for salt and water, but the government does not want him to pose for the tourists. "If you don't stop going into the crater to be photographed, we will lose the permits for our cattle," the village chief said, gesturing with his staff. Warriors were coming from thirty miles away to make money from the tourists; they spent the night in a boma near the crater, then went down in the morning. One of the Oloirobi warriors spoke: "It is not good to welcome these warriors from other places. We better tell them not to go into the crater, and if they don't listen, we must report them to the Conservation Authority."

Not far away stood a boma where the warriors perform for tourists. "WELL-COME TO SEE OUR MAASAI TRADITIONAL DANCES" said the sign on the road. The idea was Kasiaro's and Tate's, a way for the Maasai warriors to earn money so that they did not have to beg. Tourists are charged 1,000 shillings per camera, 2,000 for a video camera, and a portion of the proceeds is distributed to the poorest families; Naloya was one of the beneficiaries the first year. But Kasiaro is uncomfortable with the project. "The warriors are the young people who should look after their family and the cattle," he said, walking toward the boma. "Having them dance just to get some money, I think it will change them."

There was another sign on the road, letters neatly etched into reddish wood: OLOIROBI WOMEN HANDCRAFT PROJECT. In front of a small thatched hut, a group of women sat on the ground, chatting and stringing beads while their children played in the dirt nearby. This was another of Kasiaro's and Tate's ideas. In addition to providing women with some money, the project has had some indirect benefits. When the women earn money, they buy things for their family and this is good for the economy; when Maasai men get money they are more likely to buy booze. But Kasiaro was worried that the craft project would not succeed. The price of one necklace—twenty-four strings of orange, blue, white and red beads—was about 8,000 shillings. "It's too expensive," he said, looking at the beaded jewelry draped over a wood rail. It was the equivalent of roughly $40 and that probably is more than most tourists would be willing to pay (unless perhaps, as Margaret Jacobsohn has done in Kaokoveld, the tourists can be made to realize that when they buy crafts they are contributing to conservation). But the beads cost 6,000 shillings, and a woman sits for four days stringing them to make this necklace. Kasiaro pointed out a belt. It takes a woman seven days to make it, "working early morning until late at night," he said. The price was 9,000 shillings; the beads cost about 6,000. The beads were expensive because they were made in Czechoslovakia and exported to Kenya, and the Kenyan company then sold them to the Maasai. Kasiaro thought something should be done so that the beads didn't cost so much. "It is up to the world community to help these people who are living here survive because they are the ones who are benefitting from this land," he said. He did not sound like a defeated man begging, nor a radical demanding.

It is a delight to spend time with Kasiaro, with his twinkling eyes and genuine joy when he encounters new experiences. And the more time one spends with him, the more hopeful one becomes for Africa. He is humble but not obsequious, and a person who cares deeply about his people, about wildlife, about the environment. He is a leader in his community, but his leadership skills are self-taught and one has to wonder how far they will take him when he faces powerful international conservationists and wealthy private businessmen who want to determine the future of Ngorongoro. If only he could go to the United States or Canada or Britain for a couple of years of study, I often thought when I was with him.

At a Catholic primary school Kasiaro received a good educational foundation, including English, which he speaks fluently. He started secondary school, but did not finish because his brothers, who were warriors, thought school was a waste of time—the traditional Maasai attitude. Kasiaro became a warrior when he was fifteen. "I was a very young warrior," he said; circumcision does not usually take place, he explained, until a boy is eighteen or twenty. In spite of his youth, the elders selected him from the more than a thousand warriors in the group to be one of the leaders. In the modern world of government, he was elected to the

Ngorongoro District Council in 1985, and reelected three years later. Kasiaro had been asked to serve on the council by a more established Maasai leader, Morige Parkipuny, who was a member of the national parliament from Ngorongoro. Parkipuny is one of only twenty or so Tanzanian Maasai who have university degrees, and he has traveled widely—in 1989 he was a visiting scholar at Dartmouth and Hampshire colleges, where he acquired a fondness for baseball, or at least a Boston Red Sox cap, now faded by the African sun. "We were looking for people committed to community interests," Parkipuny said, explaining why he had approached Kasiaro. "I think it was very, very difficult for him at first. He was very timid." Kasiaro is still timid, though he slowly seems to be acquiring confidence.

What he lacks is some worldly experience. Not until he was thirty years old did his world extend even four hundred miles away to Dar es Salaam, his country's political, financial, academic and cultural center; on his fourth visit, in December 1989, he was still confused by many aspects of the city, including how to get an airplane ticket. Reading a magazine that I had given him, he once asked, puzzled, "What is this 'Cold War'?" The article also talked about the demands for multiparty democracy that were sweeping Africa (after decades of strong one-party rule), and Kasiaro asked where the idea of multiparties had come from. He was fascinated, but completely baffled, and understandably so, when I suggested that if Tanzania were the United States, a good lawyer would go to court and probably win compensation for the Maasai for the land that was taken from them.

During Kasiaro's first visit to the Serengeti we stopped at Seronera Lodge. On the stone pillars in the lobby were informative posters about cheetah, spotted hyenas, lions and wild dogs. The one about wild dogs most interested Kasiaro. "Wild Dogs Need Your Help," urged the Frankfurt Zoological Society, which is where Grzimek began his work and which today funds research in the Serengeti. "Wild Dogs are among the most endangered canids in the world and are the RAREST AND MOST ENDANGERED of the large carnivores in Serengeti," the poster said. Park visitors were asked to help by recording where and when they spotted any wild dogs, and they were also requested to make donations to the "Serengeti Wild Dog Project." Kasiaro read all this slowly; then he said quietly, "They care only about the animals; they say nothing about the people. They could have said there are also people, the Maasai, who were living here for many years. They are living outside now and they are suffering. They don't have water. Even they need help. Not just the wild animals."

There are only four primary schools in the Ngorongoro Conservation Area, so many children do not attend because even the nearest one is too far. "They have to run and run, for several hours," Kasiaro said, pointing across the hills to where the school is for the children of his village. "And these are very, very young boys." The schools are perpetually short of the most basic supplies, including tables, chairs, and even chalk. There are no secondary schools. The health care system is even more deplorable. There are four dispensaries for the 25,000 Maasai in the 3,000-square-mile Conservation Area. They are in poor physical condition, understaffed, have insufficient drugs and often lack essentials such as scissors, mattresses, blankets and sheets. There is only one hospital, operated by Roman Catholic missionaries. A person who needs treatment either has to walk a long distance or pay an extortionate amount to someone who has a vehicle. "When you have sick children, you have to sell your cattle to hire a car to take them to the hospital," said Clemence ole Rokango, a junior elder who lives on the crater rim not far from Kasiaro. The owner of the car will usually charge 10,000 shillings, he said, recalling that the family of one warrior who had been gored by a buffalo had to pay 15,000 shillings to the Conservation Authority, owner of the only available vehicle.

The Maasai remain poor while living amidst a very valuable resource, the wildlife—which is the case for most rural Africans. Tourism has steadily increased in the Ngorongoro Conservation Area, and in 1989 the number of visitors reached a record level, as did the Conservation Authority's revenues—nearly $1 million. (This is in addition to what the hotels and safari companies earned and the income generated by Serengeti National Park, which is separately administered.) Obviously almost none of it has been spent to help the people. Nor have there been many, if any, indirect benefits for the Maasai.

"I want a job as a ranger or a guide to take those tourists down the crater, but they don't want me," Clemence said. "I know the crater very well." He was born there in the 1950s and lived there until the evictions in 1974. He speaks fluent English, punctuated with American slang he picked up during his friendship with an American woman who was doing graduate research in Ngorongoro in the 1970s. He is charming and gregarious and can entertain and educate with stories about his life as a warrior. But Clemence can't find employment. Ngorongoro Crater Lodge and Ngorongoro Wildlife Lodge, the only major lodges on the crater rim (until 1992), have never hired a Maasai, according to Kasiaro. Out of a work force that has exceeded three hundred for many years, the Ngorongoro Conservation Authority has never had more than a dozen Maasai on the staff at any one time.

Though the Maasai receive no benefits, they pay the price of living with the wildlife, as a story Clemence told reveals.

"I was sitting here near the boma," Clemence began; to ward off the chill, he was wearing a red-checkered shuka, a robe-like garment, over a red toga. "My brother's child and my sister's child were walking to meet other children in that boma," he said, pointing across a shallow draw, where two of his sisters and their husbands and children live. "The leopard came—he was just laying in the long grass there—and caught one child near that boma. The other child cried. We heard this, and we saw the leopard running in the bushes there with the child. We took our spears and we ran and chased it. We tried to find it, but it became very dark. We turned back home. It was raining and misty."

The next morning they took up the pursuit again, following bloodstains on the grass. They found the girl's skull. They continued looking for the leopard. "We saw him and he jumped, and he made a sound"—here Clemence made a low, rumbling sound from deep in his throat, which sounds different from the one he makes when imitating lions he has cornered. "We tried to follow it in the bushes, but we didn't see it again." During the next month, the leopard continued raiding people's bomas, killing calves and goats, and eluding Conservation Authority rangers who had rifles. Then one day the leopard returned and killed three goats near Clemence's boma. "We saw him, and we ran after him. He ran away. We said, 'We must kill it today.'" Clemence and his friends cut some branches and made a small hut, and tied a goat to it. A man hid inside. That evening, the leopard came and tried to seize the goat. The man threw his spear, hitting the leopard in its side, killing it.

When the Conservation Authority officials came to take the dead leopard—it would sell the skin—Clemence and other elders talked to them. "We said, 'The leopard killed many goats, and we said nothing. But now it takes a ten-year-old girl. Now the government must pay.' But they said no."

. . .

A FEW YEARS AGO, Western conservationists decided it was necessary to take a close look at the Ngorongoro Conservation Area after it had been in existence for nearly three decades and to develop programs that would contribute to both conservation and the needs of the people. The project was initiated, in 1987, by IUCN, and cost $250,000. IUCN hired consultants—nutritionists, economists, ecologists, engineers, foresters. They produced eighteen "technical reports"— "Wildlife Ecology," "Livestock/Wildlife Interactions," "Water Development Impact Assessment," "Assessment of Forest Produce Needs of Local Communities," "Analysis of Vegetation Change" and "Nutritional Status and Food Security."

The project bewildered Kasiaro. "I don't see why IUCN needed all that time and to spend all that money to find out the conflict between the people and wildlife and the environment. There is no conflict," he said. "I don't see why they needed two years to do these scientific things while the basic needs of the people are not fulfilled. It is just a matter of the government or world community coming here to look, and to help the people."

It is, of course, not that simple, and some scientific studies are necessary for intelligent conservation. Still, Kasiaro has several ideas for helping his people, ones that don't involve spending money on consultants or infrastructure, and in January 1991 he wrote a letter to the Ngorongoro Conservation Area Authority board of directors. He proposed that the tourist hotels at Ngorongoro be required to employ a fixed percentage of local people. "This will make them more productive than lazing about nearly the whole day waiting to perform traditional dances for tourists," he wrote. He also proposed that a percentage of the proceeds from each hotel be given to the villagers "as compensation for the loss of their grazing land." He justified this proposal by noting that the Maasai had been "cheated and deprived" of grazing land in the Serengeti and the most fertile areas of Ngorongoro Crater, as well as other places. "We have very little remaining now and most of us are already starving and desperate."

He received no reply, which was not surprising—the idea that hotels should share some of their profits, even a minute amount, with local people is a revolutionary one which has been proposed and rejected in other places, including Kenya.

But the revenue-sharing and employment proposals were not the most contentious subjects Kasiaro raised in his letter. After noting that the Maasai had already given up their land for the benefit of tourism, he added, "And as if that is not enough, we are now being asked again to give way to yet more tourist hotels and it is all done without prior notice or consultations." He was referring to the two new hotels to be built on the crater rim.

In spite of their popularity, Ngorongoro and the Serengeti had remained relatively pristine—relative, that is, to what has happened to most natural attractions developed in order to generate tourist revenues. For a long time, there were only two hotels on the 35-mile crater rim; even more extraordinary, only two in the 5,600-square-mile Serengeti. Then the restraints broke. In 1990, the government authorized the building of two hotels on the rim and two in the Serengeti. The Maasai had been evicted from the Serengeti and Ngorongoro Crater in the name of protecting the environment. Now everything that conservationists had fought for was being sacrificed on the altar of tourist profits.

THE CONFLICT between development and conservation has plagued governments and conservationists since the concept of setting aside land for parks was born. In the United States, the first director of the National Park Service, Stephen Mather, once remarked that the agency's job was "to keep the national parks . . . close to what God made them." At the same time, Mather advocated developing the parks for tourists, which meant building lodges and roads, and in his time, the 1920s, the latter was one of the most controversial issues, since roads would bring more people into the parks. While lodges and roads and other development of American parks has been limited, nevertheless the prevailing principle is that the parks are to be used for recreational purposes—fishing, whitewater rafting, kayaking, backpacking. In contrast, most African parks are sanctuaries of solitude.

In Tanzania, it was not until the end of the 1980s that the issue of conservation versus tourism was seriously joined. Under Julius Nyerere, Tanzania's president from independence in 1961 until 1985, the country pursued a socialist economic policy—foreign investment was discouraged, and without it, it was difficult to develop a world-competitive tourist industry because local companies lacked the financial resources and expertise. It did not bother Nyerere that tourists were not flocking to his country. He was fiercely nationalistic and he feared that Western culture would destroy the cultures of the Tanzanian peoples. Changing attitudes about development were accelerated following the collapse of communism, and as Tanzanian officials recognized the benefits of capitalism, the country began courting foreign investment and tourists. It has decided it wants to bring 1 million tourists annually—it had fewer than 200,000 in 1991—and it has begun allowing private companies to build lodges around the country to attract them.

The appeal of tourism is understandable: it could finance the country's development and could do so more quickly and with fewer capital costs than probably any other industry. But tourism is necessary not only to finance Tanzania's general development. As the director of Tanzania's National Parks, David Babu, put it in 1992, "What is the future of wildlife in Tanzania without tourism?" In other words, tourism can generate the revenues for park maintenance.

Many Third World countries see tourism as their economic savior; most are dreaming. Not Tanzania. The country has more elephants, more rhinoceros, more lions, and more of just about every other species, than Kenya. Four Tanzanian areas are World Heritage sites, a designation under a 1972 United Nations convention calling for the recognition and protection of natural and cultural areas of "outstanding universal value." Throughout the world, only seventy-seven natural sites have been granted this status, and none are in Kenya. Ngorongoro Crater was the first place in Tanzania to go on the World Heritage list (in 1979), and it was included for its cultural significance as well—there are Stone Age ruins buried deep under the crater's floor. The Serengeti was proclaimed a World Heritage site two years later. The next year the Selous Game Reserve, in the southern part of Tanzania, made the list. It is one of the largest protected areas in Africa—22,000 square miles—and one of the wildest. In 1986, Mount Kilimanjaro achieved the honor. Rising more than three and a half miles, it is the highest mountain in Africa, and a mile higher than any peak in the continental United States. It is a freestanding inactive volcano, not far from the equator, yet perpetually crowned with snow. It is an awesome and majestic sight.

Underlying the World Heritage Convention is the premise that some places are the heritage not just of the political entity in which they happen to be located, but of all mankind. It is a noble ideal. But if places are part of the "world heritage," then the world has an obligation to come up with the millions and millions of dollars needed to preserve them.

The white settlers in Africa and the men who set up the conservation organizations like AWF and WWF were certain that once the Africans became independent and were free to run their own governments, they would destroy their natural heritage. How wrong they were: 8 percent of Zambia, 7 percent of Zimbabwe and 6 percent of Kenya are set aside as National Parks and Reserves. In contrast, in the United States, 7 percent of the land is National Parks and Reserves; in the United Kingdom, 6 percent; in Australia, 5 percent, and in Canada, 4.5 percent. New Zealand has the best record in the developed world, and still it has set aside only 9 percent. Twelve percent of Tanzania is National Parks and Reserves, according to IUCN, which maintains a worldwide list for the United Nations. (Tanzania says that 25 percent of its land is protected to some degree, but like nearly all countries Tanzania uses its own definition of what is a protected area. Under the IUCN definition, a National Park is a relatively large area that has not been materially altered by human exploitation and that contains plants or animals of special scientific, educational or recreational interest or contains a landscape of great beauty. A Reserve is usually a smaller area, in which a specific species or habitat is protected.)

Like most Third World countries, Tanzania cannot afford to protect all of its parks and reserves, not given the demands and needs of its population—for schools and textbooks, health clinics, roads—and the country's paltry resources. Tanzania is one of the poorest countries in the world, fourth from the bottom in terms of per capita gross national product, below even Bangladesh and Haiti, according to the World Bank. If the cost of maintaining a park and protecting against poaching, particularly of elephants and rhino, is between $200 and $400 per square kilometer, as is generally accepted, Tanzania needs $24 million to $48 million annually; the amount available for the parks and wildlife departments in fiscal year 1991 was less than $5 million. If the Serengeti alone spent $200 per square kilometer, $3 million a year would be needed; entrance fees, the main source of revenue, were less than $400,000 in recent years.

In the past Tanzania has not attracted more tourists because it has lacked the infrastructure. Arusha is the jumping-off point for trips to Ngorongoro and the Serengeti, but the paved road ends 50 miles out of town; the next 70 miles are dirt, and it takes four hours to reach Ngorongoro. In the dry season, by the time you arrive you are caked with dust. It is another uncomfortable drive over 90 miles of rutted road from

Ngorongoro to the Serengeti. On the crater rim, Crater Lodge and Wildlife Lodge offer guests truly spectacular views, but the condition of the rooms and the quality of the food do not begin to match the vistas. The same is true for Seronera and Lobo lodges in the Serengeti.

So, it might be hard to argue against more tourist facilities in the Serengeti and Ngorongoro. But the story behind the building of two large hotels in each place is another chapter in a long history of greedy developers, who may destroy the very thing that brings them their riches. It is also the story of contemporary Africa: corruption, strong-man rule, weak institutions and lack of accountability. "They were forced down our throats by the president's office—by the president himself," says a Tanzanian government official about the new lodges at Ngorongoro and Serengeti, which he opposed.

Two companies are putting up the new five-star lodges. One is Serena Hotels, owned by the Aga Khan. One of the world's richest men and leader of the Ismaili Muslims, a small and moderate sect, the Aga Khan has long been an investor in Africa, displaying a confidence in the continent that few Westerners have, building schools and hospitals as well as hotels, including several in Kenya. The other builder is Consolidated Tourist and Hotels Investment Limited, a holding company wholly owned by a British citizen who lives in Kenya, which for tax reasons is registered offshore on the English Channel island of Jersey.

At Ngorongoro, the Aga Khan's hotel will be on the western rim, at Kimba, the place were Kasiaro stood and worried aloud about what the hotel would mean for the Maasai. Consolidated's hotel is across the way at Lemala.

The members of the Ngorongoro Conservation Area Authority board were unanimously against both hotel projects on the crater rim, but when the board's chairman informed the minister of lands, natural resources and tourism of this opposition, "the Minister said that there was very little he could do to stop it because it was a Presidential Order." The board members then tried to get the president to reverse his orders. They were rebuffed. In a final effort to protect Ngorongoro, the board, noting that "some businessmen were hurriedly out to build hotels and lodges in the Ngorongoro Conservation Area and the Tanzania National Parks notwithstanding their ecological impact in these areas," decided that a tourism master plan was needed. But even before the consultants hired to prepare the plan had begun asking questions, Consolidated was cutting trees, laying cement and putting up beams.

Consolidated's lodge, which is called Ngorongoro Sopa—*sopa* is the Maasai word for welcome—includes two circular buildings, one of which serves as the dining room, the other as the bar and lounge. Just below these buildings, on the slope down to the crater, is a small swimming pool. While paddling in the pool, drinking at the bar or just resting in their rooms, guests have stirring views of the crater.

"The idea is to introduce a new idea of sophistication into safaris in Tanzania," said Consolidated's general manager in Tanzania, George Crossland, standing among the construction debris. "It's for people who want a hot shower, wall-to-wall carpeting, imported tiles and a fluffy towel. Safaris are hard." The standard room—a "suite," he insisted—has an outer room with a couch, desk and mini-bar, but no window. Nor is there a window in the bathroom, but, Crossland noted, it does have a bidet and imported tiles. Off the bedroom—with five-foot-wide beds, Crossland boasted—is an alcove with paned windows for views into the crater; only two of the windows open, and then only slightly. The ceilings are low.

"Fantastic overpretentiousness" is how Henry Fosbrooke, the first Ngorongoro conservator, describes the lodge. It may, of course, be what many people who come to Africa on safari want. Indeed, John Bennett, the safari operator, who was very much opposed to any lodge being built on the rim, had to admit after he stayed there that the service and food were "excellent."

That doesn't faze John Stephenson, an Englishman who was a warden in Tanzania between 1962 and 1974, when he played a role in establishing four of the country's national parks.

"It ought to be torn down, brick by brick, stone by stone," Stephenson says of Consolidated's lodge. In 1991, he was asked by the Conservation Authority to study the impact of the new lodges on the crater rim. He concluded there should be no lodges there. "That is one of the most beautiful places in the world, and it should not be defiled by man," he says. "It's a World Heritage site; it should be kept as pristine as possible. The beauty of that country, its magnificence, belongs to you and me, as well as to the Tanzanians."

From an ecological point of view, the most acute anxiety is about water. "The current water supply system [in the Ngorongoro Conservation Area] is inadequate to meet the demands of over a quarter of a million head of livestock, and some 25,000 resident pastoralists," a 1990 Tanzanian government report on the future of Ngorongoro warns. It was, of course, concern about the scarcity of water that had led Lee Talbot and other scientists to conclude in the 1950s that the Maasai should be moved out of Ngorongoro. One of the very streams that Talbot believed did not have enough water to supply the Maasai cattle and the wildlife was the Munge River, which flows into the crater near the Ngorongoro Sopa. This river will be the principal source of water for Consolidated's hotel. When pampered Western tourists, paying $200 a night, start making demands on Ngorongoro's limited water supplies for hot showers and cold drinking water, what will most probably happen is what Kasiaro fears: the Maasai will be forced to go without. Even before the hotels were completed, there was evidence of too little water in dry years. Nineteen ninety-one was such a year. The powdered dirt on the roads was several inches deep; water had to be trucked into the village where lodge employees lived, because the regular supply was drying up; Lake Magadi, in the center of the crater, was shrinking almost visibly every day. On a visit to the crater in December 1989, friends and I could see only the backs of elephants as they swished through tall green reeds in the swamp near Lerai Forest. In October 1991 the reeds barely reached an elephant's sagging underside.

The sides and floor of the crater will inevitably take a beating from the substantial increase in tourists that the new lodges will generate. Only one road takes tourists into the crater; another brings them out. They are twisting, narrow dirt roads, and a doubling or tripling of the number of vehicles passing over them—or the use of heavier vehicles, carrying more passengers—will accelerate their deterioration. Once on the crater floor, those vehicles will do untold ecological damage. And what will so many more tourists mean to the wild animals in such a confined space? Undoubtedly they will become more tame, less wild. Already it is possible to get closer to the wildebeest and elephants in a vehicle on the crater floor than in the nearby Serengeti, where the wild animals are less accustomed to humans.

COSTA MLAY, who has been director of Tanzania's wildlife department and a member of the Ngorongoro and Tanzania National Parks boards, understands his country needs tourism. "But at what cost?" he asks. "Is Tanzania's heritage for sale to the highest bidder?" The son of a schoolteacher, Mlay, a soft-spoken man, is a graduate of the East Africa College of Wildlife and served as a personal assistant to President

Nyerere for ten years before becoming head of the wildlife division in the Ministry of Tourism in 1989. "Lodges are a way of taking advantage of wildlife, but you can site them in such a manner that they are not in conflict with conservation," Mlay said. And the new lodges on the crater rim and inside the Serengeti "are not in the best interests of conservation."

Mlay, who became director of the Serengeti Wildlife Research Centre in 1992, was particularly upset about the new lodges in the Serengeti. In the early 1970s, he explained, after two lodges were built, the board of trustees adopted a policy that any new facilities would be built outside the park; visitors would be taken in for the day, and if they stayed longer they would camp.

Stephenson, who was the senior warden in the Serengeti in the early 1970s, is opposed to any lodges in the Serengeti—indeed, to any buildings at all. Seronera Lodge is a model of building that fits in with the surrounding landscape. It is low and follows the contour of the land. Yet, even allowing it to be built was "one of the biggest mistakes we ever made," Stephenson says. Nor does he think that the Serengeti Research Institute should have its headquarters inside the park, also at Seronera. "It is a place of absolutely unparalleled beauty," Stephenson says about Seronera. It truly is. There are streams and the yellow acacia, date palms, and animals all around, especially lions.

However deeply Stephenson might feel about preserving nature in as pristine a state as possible, the reality is that there is going to be more tourist development in the Serengeti. The task, therefore, is to control and manage it so that the damage to the country's heritage is minimized. To that end, a team of eighteen scientists and conservationists prepared a "Serengeti National Park Management Plan," to guide development in the park from 1990 to 1995. In contrast to Kenya, where white expatriates dominate the conservation planning, all but a few of the members of the group were Tanzanians; the group was chaired by the chief ecologist for Tanzania's parks, and included the chief ecologist for the Serengeti and three Serengeti wardens.

The management plan allows for small tented camps inside the park, but says that "major tourist facilities" should be built *outside* the Park." The hotels being built by the Aga Khan and Consolidated are definitely major facilities.

Moreover, as part of its effort to control development, the Management Plan divides the Serengeti into five zones, defined by the degree of human intrusion that will be allowed. The Wilderness Zone will be "the least developed and most natural areas of the park," and "no physical development will be allowed" in this zone. Consolidated's Serengeti Sopa is in the Wilderness Zone. It rises on the side of the elongated Nyaraboro Hills, in the southern part of the park, not far from the Moru Kopjes.

"The concept of lodges blending in with the environment has been abandoned," John Bennett said, angry and disappointed, emerging from a thicket of trees, slapping at tsetse flies and staring at Consolidated's lodge, then in the early stages of construction. "It sticks out like a sore thumb." The two lodges in the Serengeti that were built in the early 1970s, Seronera and Lobo, are so well designed to blend in with the surrounding environment that it is almost impossible to see them until you are inside.

At Consolidated's site, in November 1990, Sammy Singh, the construction supervisor, noted proudly that guests at the Serengeti Sopa, who pay $200 a night, would have the use of a video room and a sauna. In case they have come for nature, they will also have sweeping views north across the Serengeti Plain, where the wildebeest and impala, the elephants and the giraffes will surely be playing. The animals, though, will be disturbed—Singh said the company would build an airstrip on the plains, so that it would be easier to bring tourists, on the company's planes, from the international airport at the foot of Mount Kilimanjaro.

IT IS UNDERSTANDABLE that Tanzania wants to build more facilities to attract more tourists. It looks across the border to Kenya and sees gold. In 1990, for instance, more than 800,000 foreigners traveled to Kenya, leaving behind $500 million. Only 150,000 foreigners took a holiday in Tanzania that year, generating $65 million. David Babu, in 1992 the director of Tanzania's National Parks and formerly a chief warden in the Serengeti, defended the concept of more lodges there (though he objected to Consolidated's hotel) by pointing to the Maasai Mara. The Serengeti and the Mara are part of the same ecosystem and it is impossible to know where one ends and the other begins, the two being divided only by a line on a map first drawn when the British and Germans created Kenya and Tanganyika. There are six lodges and luxury tented camps in the Mara, which can accommodate 600 people a night, and 150,000 tourists entered the reserve in 1989. Serengeti National Park is forty-five times larger than the Mara. There were 55,000 visitors to the Serengeti in 1989, and even with the completion of the new lodges, there will be fewer rooms for tourists in the Serengeti than in the Mara. So Babu's point seems valid. Yet, does Tanzania really want the Serengeti to become like the Mara, where a common sighting is twenty minivans, packed with tourists sticking out of sun roofs, their cameras clicking at a lion pride?

Maybe Tanzania is going about the development of its tourism industry in the wrong way. Instead of asking how many tourists it can attract, maybe it should ask how much money can be made from tourism. It is the question economists and good businessmen would ask. The answer might be to raise park fees.

The number of people who can visit the mountain gorillas in Rwanda is severely limited by concerns about the impact on the gorillas, and the government charges the equivalent of nearly $200 to enter the park. That is a numbing amount to pay for the privilege of hiking through dense jungle, stumbling, tired, wet and cold, in order to spend forty-five minutes with a gorilla family. It is worth it.

The entrance fee for Tanzania's parks is $15. Could it charge more? "If you have only one day in your life to visit an African game park, that day should be spent at Ngorongoro," the Sierra Club guidebook, *Adventuring in East Africa*, exclaims. With that kind of an endorsement, the answer would certainly seem to be yes, a lot more. Could not the government charge $30 or even $50, given the uniqueness of the experience—if it remained unique? During one trip to Ngorongoro Crater, my wife and I watched two adult rhino and their offspring. Though we'd been in Africa more than a year, and had seen lions, elephants, giraffes, hyenas, gerenuk and just about every other species, this was the first time we'd seen rhino, and it was the closest we would ever get to them— maybe thirty yards away. After twenty minutes, we were ready to leave, when John Bennett, ever knowledgeable about wildlife, suggested that we might want to wait a bit longer. He refrained from telling us why, but we took his advice, and soon we were observing the rhino mating. There was not another tourist in sight.

Many people are rightly uncomfortable with high fees because the effect is to make an African game park the preserve of the elite. I gulped when I was asked for $15 at the Ngorongoro gate. And I was appalled at how much it costs to visit the gorillas in Rwanda, noting that for a family of four it would come to almost $1,000, and it would surely be beyond the means of a backpacker trying to see as much of the world as possible with as limited a bank account as imaginable, as I once had. But the lower fees do not raise enough money to pay rangers and maintain the parks, which means in effect that Africans are subsidizing the parks for the benefit of Western tourists.

IT IS EASY to rail at Consolidated and the Aga Khan for building their lodges, and to censure the Tanzanian government for allowing them to do so. But because these projects so obviously abuse the environment, they divert attention from the more fundamental and difficult question: Should any lodges be allowed inside the Serengeti and on the rim of Ngorongoro Crater? Stephenson doesn't think so, and if Grzimek were alive, there can be no doubt that he would scream "No!" and he would rally the international community against the lodges.

More than thirty years ago, in *Serengeti Shall Not Die*, Grzimek cried, "Must *everything* be turned into deserts, farmland, big cities, native settlements and dry brush? One small part of the continent at least should retain its original splendour so that the black and white men who follow us will be able to see it in its awe-filled past glory." Then followed his prayerful declaration: "Serengeti, at least, shall not die."

On the book's final pages, he wrote:

> Men are easily inspired by human ideas, but they forget them again just as quickly. Only Nature is eternal, unless we senselessly destroy it. In fifty years' time nobody will be interested in the results of the conferences which fill today's headlines.
>
> But when, fifty years from now, a lion walks into the red dawn and roars resoundingly, it will mean something to people and quicken their hearts whether they are bolsheviks or democrats, or whether they speak English, German, Russian or Swahili. They will stand in quiet awe as, for the first time in their lives, they watch twenty thousand zebras wander across the endless plains.

His cry has more resonance today, on a planet more crowded and more polluted, with fewer and fewer spaces to escape to. We need silence, places where we can stand in awe of that which God or Nature created. But who is going to pay for these places? Is it fair to put the burden on the Maasai, on the people of Africa, which has been the effect of the policies in the past? These glorious spaces *are* part of our heritage, and so we—New Yorkers and Berliners, Japanese and French, Canadians and Australians—must pay. Yes, Africans, too, must pay, but they are paying already. If we in the West don't meet our responsibility, if we don't match our rhetoric about the urgency of preserving Africa's wild animals and wilderness with money, then the future for the grandeur of the continent is grim. "The advance of civilization . . . is fatally disturbing to the primitive forms of animal life," the *Times* of London noted in calling upon the European nations to take action to preserve Africa's wildlife. That was at the beginning of this century, in 1900; now we are at its end. The dire prediction may become a sad reality, as modern civilization, which has marched slowly in Africa throughout most of this century, begins to gallop.

FOUR

SPACE
FOR
LARGE
SPECIES

||||| *SAFARI* IS A SWAHILI WORD meaning "to travel," and an African will ask someone who returns from a trip to Europe or the United States, "How was your safari?" In the West, however, safari means a vacation to look at wild animals in Africa. And the country that has been synonymous with a wildlife safari is Kenya— now on the brink of a million visitors a year. Going back to the beginning of this century, Kenya has seemingly had it all. Writing in the Fauna Preservation Society's journal in 1905, an eminent British zoologist, P. L. Sclater, declared that the elephant, rhino, giraffe, eland and zebra required special efforts in order to reserve them; and, he noted, there was one place in Africa where all these animals were to be found—Kenya (or the East Africa Protectorate, as it was known then). But as much as Kenya represents the grandeur of the past, it is also the reality of the future, a future with less room for wildlife and with whatever wildlife remains confined to a few parks; in other words, a bleak future—unless radical conservation programs are undertaken.

Though safaris were popular in Kenya at the turn of the century—in high season, it was hard to find a guide—the safari era is often said to have been launched by Theodore Roosevelt. Two weeks after leaving the White House, in March 1909, he sailed from New York and twenty-nine days later steamed into "the beautiful and picturesque harbor of Mombasa." Then Roosevelt and his party, which included his son Kermit (whose own son would later become one of the founders of the African Wildlife Foundation) took the train, climbing slowly from sea level to mile-high Nairobi. Built by the British, beginning in 1895, and connecting Mombasa with Lake Victoria, 581 miles west, the Uganda Railway "pushed through a region in which nature, both as regards wild man and wild beast, did not and does not differ materially from what it was in Europe in the late Pleistocene," Roosevelt wrote in *African Game Trails*. "It was literally like passing through a vast zoological garden." Roosevelt

described the scene as his train moved across Kenya's Southern Game
Reserve:

> At one time we passed a herd of a dozen or so of great giraffes, cows
> and calves, cantering along through the open woods . . . still closer,
> four waterbuck cows, their big ears thrown backward, stared at us
> without moving until we had passed. Hartebeests were every-
> where. . . . Huge black ostriches appeared from time to time. Once
> a troop of impala, close by the track, took fright; and as the beautiful
> creatures fled we saw now one and now another bound clear over the
> high bushes. A herd of zebra clattered across a cutting of the line not
> a hundred yards ahead of the train.

The year before Roosevelt's trip a young British politician named
Winston Churchill vacationed in Kenya. He, too, rode the train from
Mombasa. "The plains are crowded with wild animals," Churchill wrote
in the first installment of his account of the safari, which appeared in *The
Strand Magazine*, a leading journal of the time, a classy illustrated with
reportage, fiction, humor and art. Churchill's articles were collected in
My African Journey, and 12,500 copies were published in Britain in
1908, an extraordinary number back then; there was also an American
edition. Churchill wrote, "From the windows of the carriage the whole
zoological gardens can be seen disporting itself. Herds of antelope and
gazelle, troops of zebras—sometimes four or five hundred together—
watch the train pass with placid assurance, or scamper a hundred yards
further away, and turn again." He described the "long files of black
wildebeeste and herds of red kongoni . . . and wild ostriches walking
sedately in twos and threes, and every kind of small deer and gazelle."
He did not spot any rhinoceros from the train, and so one day he and a
friend went in search on foot. After hours of trudging through high grass
and over rocky plains, they were about to turn home, disappointed, when
they saw "three beautiful oryx, great, dark-coloured antelope with very
long, corrugated horns." Churchill, like Roosevelt, was on a hunting
safari, and he and his friend began stalking the oryx, hoping to shoot one.
They followed them for a mile, and then abruptly they found themselves
practically on top of a rhino. "The impression was extraordinary. A wide
plain of white, withered grass stretched away to low hills broken with
rocks. The rhinoceros stood in the middle of this plain, about five hundred
yards away, in jet-black silhouette; not a twentieth century animal, but
an odd, grim straggler from the Stone Age."

With the vivid writings of Roosevelt and Churchill, no wonder a Kenyan safari became popular.

After World War I, British royalty added their endorsements to the adventure. Though his brother and his wife had been on an earlier safari to Kenya, it was the safaris of the Prince of Wales that captivated the British. On his first visit, in 1928, Edward shot a lion and an elephant and was nearly killed by another elephant when he debated with his companion over who should shoot it; a game ranger finally fired when the charging elephant was only twenty feet away. (The Prince's visit goes down in Nairobi's social history for his partying at the Muthaiga Club, where the white settlers drank and carried on. During a dinner, Lady Delamere, wife of one of the most prominent settlers, threw pieces of bread at the Prince, one of them missing and giving Isak Dinesen a black eye.) The Prince's safari was cut short when he received a telegram that his father, King George V, was seriously ill. But as for so many after him, one journey into the African vastness was not enough for the Prince, and when his father had recovered, Edward returned. The man who would become King Edward VIII, and then abdicate to marry an American divorcée, had as his guides Bror Blixen and Denys Finch-Hatton, two of the most famous white hunters at the time (one the husband of Isak Dinesen, the other her lover). They pursued one elephant for three days, walking seventy miles over rugged terrain. When they finally spotted it, they knew it was a really big tusker, its head so bowed down with the weight of its tusks that Blixen thought they weighed four hundred pounds. Just as the men were getting in position to shoot, the Prince stepped on a dry twig, and the elephant spread its ears wide and charged off in the other direction. The disappointed Prince then decided to "shoot" wild animals with a camera, and he got an elephant with relative ease. A rhino proved more difficult. When one was spotted, it was sleeping, so a game warden made noises to wake it. Finally aroused, "he glowered at the Prince's camera," Blixen wrote, describing the scene. "The living tank rolled forward to the assault on the Prince, who went on quietly clicking his roll of film. The rhinoceros grew swiftly on the picture, which was just what was wanted." The game warden fired a warning shot. That didn't deter the massive beast, which Finch-Hatton felled, several tons of animal falling six feet from the Prince, who remained remarkably calm.

World War II kept British royalty and just about everyone else at home, and certainly off the high seas, which was how most people traveled. Then, in 1952, Kenya received what would become the most famous royal visit—by Princess Elizabeth, elder daughter of King George VI. It took nineteen hours and one stop for refueling in Libya aboard the *Royal Argonaut* for the Princess and her husband, Prince Philip, to reach Kenya. The city of Nairobi presented the royal couple with a dinner gong of nickel-plated brass hung between elephant tusks, with the striker resting on two miniature elephants. They visited Nairobi Royal National Park, where the highlight of a three-hour game drive was a large male lion, his mane dark on top and tawny ginger below. The couple's driver maneuvered the wood-paneled, four-door station wagon to within ten yards of the animal, which was feasting on a large wildebeest. The royal activity and the delights of an African safari were broadcast over Cable & Wireless Limited; the service also transmitted photographs, and the world saw more pictures of Kenya during the royal visit than it probably ever had before. On the sixth day of their safari, while staying at a lodge north of Nairobi where they had tracked a herd of thirty elephants, the royal couple received a tragic message—King George VI had died in his sleep. The twenty-six-year-old woman who came as a princess left as the Queen of England.

About this time, Americans were being introduced to Kenya and the romance of safaris through films. MGM's *Mogambo* starred Clark Gable as a white hunter pursued by a purring playgirl, played by Ava Gardner, whom he runs off with, leaving behind his wife, played by Grace Kelly. The film was released in 1953, one year after Twentieth Century–Fox's *The Snows of Kilimanjaro*. Ava Gardner was in this one, too, along with Susan Hayward and Gregory Peck. The film was based on Ernest Hemingway's novel of the same name, which he wrote after his safari to Kenya in 1933. That same safari also resulted in his nonfiction work *The Green Hills of Africa*. In 1953, Hemingway returned for another safari in Kenya, and wrote about it for *Look*, one of the most widely read magazines of the era.

In addition to all this attention from royalty and "commoners," Kenya had other advantages that made it the premier wildlife attraction for both luxury-oriented and more ordinary travelers. As Britain's favored colony in Africa, it had more and smoother roads, more reliable and faster communications, more efficient administration. And it had the ocean port at Mombasa, a distinct advantage before the days of the jet. In the 1970s, Tanzania might have surpassed Kenya, had President Julius Nyerere's policies not discouraged tourist development. Uganda, too, would have lured more Westerners looking for remote, exotic Africa: wildlife abounded; it was the source of the Nile, and one could go by boat along the river, among hippos and monstrous crocodiles, to the bottom of Murchison Falls, a rival to Victoria Falls in grandeur; the Ruwenzori mountain range has several peaks above fourteen thousand feet. But in the 1970s Idi Amin destroyed just about everything—the people, the wildlife and the country. By the time he was overthrown, in 1979, Kenya had a new international airport, the largest and most efficient in East Africa. (It is still the largest, but few tourists leave praising the manner in which it is run.) Three hundred thousand tourists left their money in Kenya in 1983. That was a bonanza for the country, but then in 1985 came Robert Redford (as Denys Finch-Hatton) and Meryl Streep (as Isak Dinesen) in *Out of Africa*. By 1990 the tourist numbers had climbed to nearly eight hundred thousand, which is probably more foreigners than visited all other countries in sub-Saharan Africa combined.

For today's tourists, however, the Kenyan experience is not the same. Like Roosevelt and Churchill, they can still take the train from Mombasa to Nairobi (it is a bit scruffy—but then, the Orient Express isn't what it used to be, either). But along the way, passengers won't see the vast herds of game that Roosevelt and Churchill saw. Those days are gone, but then everyone is forever remembering what Kenya used to be. Thirty years ago, J. F. Lipscomb, a colonial legislator and a member of the small Wild Life Preservation Trust Organizing Committee, which considered buying the national parks, convinced that the Africans once they gained independence would destroy them, looked back on the 1920s. Those were the days, when "there were still vast stretches of country completely given over to game, where man never or rarely penetrated, and where the number of animals was only limited by the balance of nature and the toll of occasional droughts," he wrote. "These conditions have gone and will never return. They remain as happy and exciting memories in the minds of a few people of the older generations who have watched, during the ensuing forty years, a steady diminution in nearly all varieties of wild life in East Africa, particularly in most species of plains game, including the carnivores."

Thirty years later, in 1992, David Allen looked back nostalgically on the 1950s and 1960s, when he had been a professional hunter, guiding Europeans and Americans in search of their trophies. "You could still go somewhere new and say 'God, this is fantastic.' You could still do that in

Kenya. You would go into new virgin territory. It was absolutely fantastic. You could go to places and find game that you never imagined was there—herds of oryx, herds of zebra, elephants, rhino, everything." Today, he conducts photographic safaris for select individuals. "The game is gone now. You only see a quarter of what you used to."

POACHERS HAVE TAKEN their toll on the game, especially the elephants and rhino. But even if there had been no poaching, the herds would have thinned, and even if poaching is brought under control, the wildlife will continue to vanish. It has and will because Africa is changing. When Roosevelt came to Africa, when the game was plentiful and the spaces wide open and it seemed almost inconceivable that either would ever disappear, the population of the African continent was 100 million; today, it is 450 million. Kenya's population has tripled just since independence in 1963.

But it is shortsighted to think, as most Westerners have—and still do—that the reason for the vanishing of the game is simply that there are too many people. That is one factor, but only one, and maybe not the most significant one. In spite of having one of the highest growth rates in the world, Kenya's population density is still only half that of France's and a fifth of Italy's. Many Westerners, when presented with this information, say yes, but so much of Kenya is arid land, not suitable for supporting human populations; so, they argue, there are too many people for the good land. This, too, is partially true, but who would have imagined that Israel, so much of which is desert, could support the population that it does? And three generations ago, it was absurd to think that southern California, where there are no major rivers, could be home for millions. You might keep the number of people down, but you are not going to halt the Africans' desire for modernization. Nairobi is already a city of skyscrapers and traffic jams, and the modernization will continue, with other countries catching up. You cannot have lions and elephants in shopping malls.

Keeping people down on the farm isn't the solution either. "Smallholder farming totally excludes wildlife as does large scale cereal farming," Holly Dublin, a Nairobi-based conservationist, wrote in a report for the United States Agency for International Development a few years ago. "If wild herbivores enter these areas they are killed. The smallholder stands to lose the entire harvest in one night, and it is naive to suggest conservation to him."

Dublin's observation is sobering, but very real. It is a reality few Western champions of Africa's wildlife have contemplated. And for the advocates of the ivory ban, the real conundrum is going to come if indeed the ban does work, if poaching is brought under control, if elephant populations recover and grow. Cynthia Moss, the noted elephant researcher, puts it straight: "Elephants and man cannot coexist where agriculture is practiced because elephants will eat and trample crops." If it is possible to deliver a more alarming judgment, David Western does. "Hungry African farmers . . . would gladly see all elephants eradicated," he once wrote, contrasting this with the view of many Westerners that no elephants should be killed for any reason.

These statements are even more unsettling when considered against the background of another African reality. There is often loose talk about some African country's becoming another Taiwan, or Singapore, or Thailand—that is, a country where cheap labor produces exports. But this is fantasy, mostly by Westerners who are looking for some hopeful signs in Africa. Kenya has tried to develop "export processing zones" to attract foreign companies that want to manufacture there for export abroad, and it hasn't been successful; there are only a handful of African countries, at the most, that will ever develop export-led economies. Without exports, there is no money for imports. Therefore, what most African countries must strive for is self-sufficiency. Simply stated, then, the choice that African countries face is this: Do we feed our people, or do we keep thousands of elephants because they are a "world heritage" and Westerners want to come see them?

ONE OF the largest populations of elephants in Kenya is not found in a park or a reserve but in Laikipia, an agricultural region north of Nairobi. Between 2,000 and 3,000 elephants roam in the area, which may not seem like very many, but it is too many for the Laikipia farmers. At one time, the district consisted primarily of cattle ranches, 5,000 acres and up, owned by white Europeans, most of whom were descendants of early British settlers. The elephants knocked through their fences, tore up their water pipes and smashed their dams. Some ranchers erected fences, but most simply absorbed the elephant damage.

None were very happy, and when Richard Leakey became director of the Kenya Wildlife Service in 1989, he inherited disgruntled farmers demanding that something be done.

Leakey retained Christopher Thouless, a young zoologist who had a doctorate in animal behavior from Cambridge, to look into the problem and suggest solutions. When Thouless went to Laikipia, he quickly discovered that the government was faced with a far more serious situation than had been perceived. Over the years, many white ranchers had sold their properties, and many of the purchasers, most of whom were Africans, realized—as have capitalist entrepreneurs and land owners everywhere—that there was more money to be made in subdividing and selling off small plots than in farming; often three to four times more. As a result, Laikipia is now crowded with thousands of small shambas, or plots, each no larger than three to five acres. Many of them are on marginal farming land, and in some of the poorest areas the average shamba produces only enough maize to feed one person for six months; with an average family size of eight, this means that the shamba feeds one-sixteenth of the family for a year. "These people are really getting stuffed," Thouless says. "They've settled on poor land, and then the elephants come." The animals not only trample the fields, but often destroy the simple structures where people store what little maize they have harvested.

Simon Mwangi and his wife own five acres in Sipili, in western Laikipia. "We settled there in 1981, but to date, we have never harvested any maize or potatoes," Mrs. Mwangi wrote Leakey in 1990. "Our casuarinas have never thrived, our bananas have been uprooted by the same jumbos you are protecting. . . . Come June/July/and August, the jumbos are there to share what we have toiled for and to uproot what we have planted. . . . Please consider that thousands of wananchi [people] are suffering because of these same jumbos you are protecting."

The farmers' antagonism toward the elephants could be contained if they were compensated for their losses. Until a few years ago the law did provide monetary compensation for damage by wild animals. The law was repealed in 1989, because the claims were excessive and there was massive fraud—the year before the repeal, claims had reached the equivalent of $10 million, which was far in excess of what the department could afford to pay. In some cases, owners claimed compensation for damage to crops on land that "had never been tilled since God made the world," said Perez Olindo, director of the wildlife department at the time. "It became a highly refined, crooked system." In order to deny compensation to the crooks, the Kenyan government now denies compensation to those with legitimate claims as well. Even before the law had been repealed, the department was unable to pay claims in a timely fashion—if they paid them at all—and there had been an outbreak of a kind of vigilantism. On the edge of Amboseli National Park, for instance, a farmer once poisoned a pride of six lions. The lions had killed one of his prize steers, and the farmer retaliated by putting a deadly chemical that is used for killing ticks into the carcass. When the pride returned to feast, all died. In other parts of the country, farmers also poisoned lions that were raiding their stock, but most of the incidents were never made public.

Since Leakey could not pay compensation to the farmers in Laikipia and since he did not feel he could go around shooting all the elephants that were causing damage, he had to find other solutions. One was to put up fences. Throughout time, farmers have tried various barriers against elephants and none have proved completely effective. Elephants have been known to use their tusks to simply break an electric fence if it is only one or two strands of wire and the voltage is not high enough. Moreover, zoologists object to fences because they interfere with migratory patterns, not just of elephants, but of other animals as well. When Leakey took over the wildlife department, he said publicly that all of Kenya's parks might have to be fenced. That brought a tremendous outcry from conservationists, and he backed down (it was also unlikely that he could have raised the millions of dollars necessary). Nevertheless, Leakey decided to erect electric fences in Laikipia. The first one, 30 kilometers long, runs along the eastern boundary of Ol Ari Nyiro, a 90,000-acre spread owned by Kuki Gallmann, a chic Italian who has acquired international acclaim because she protects rhino and elephants on her ranch with her own security force (at a cost per animal that far exceeds anything the government could afford to spend). The fence cost about $100,000, the money provided by the European Community.

Along with most conservationists, Thouless had serious reservations about the fencing scheme from the outset. "It is not appropriate technology for rural Africa," he said during the planning stage. "It's a solution dependent on a sophisticated infrastructure." It requires money to build and a commitment, as well as money, to maintain. Those may exist now, but whether they will in, say, ten years, is problematic, he said.

But worries about the future quickly became academic once the fence was finished, in October 1992. "It is completely unsuccessful," Thouless said a month later. "The elephants have been breaking through every night." He went on to say that it was uncertain now what kind of fence or barrier might work, but that whatever it was would require spending "enormous amounts of money."

Another solution to the problems in Laikipia—sustainable utilization projects—would have cost the government almost nothing, and, in fact, would have generated revenue. Because of the ivory ban, the government could not have introduced a scheme to sell ivory, which would have been the most profitable. But it could have allowed for some culling of, say, impala and zebra and then distributed the proceeds from the sale of the skins to the people of Laikipia.

There was, however, a major obstacle to any utilization schemes. In 1978 Kenya had banned all trading in wildlife products (it was the effort to stop the poaching, after the ban on sport hunting imposed the previous year had failed to do so). The sale of wildlife products to tourists was a big business in Nairobi, with the most popular item being zebra skins, but merchants also sold everything from ostrich eggs, which are enormous, to impala horns. Once again, corruption was pervasive. In order to obtain more items to sell, merchants bought from poachers, who were thus encouraged to kill even more animals. When government inspectors asked store owners for proof that they had legally acquired the wildlife skins—or horns or eggs—the owners simply bribed the inspectors.

Leakey believes in sustainable utilization—there isn't a serious conservationist in Africa today who doesn't—and that therefore Kenya's laws and policies must be changed, that there must be "consumptive utilization" of wildlife. Consumptive utilization (which is something of a euphemism for killing wild animals for commercial purposes) is a "mechanism for getting benefits to people who conserve wildlife," he said in the report by his department in 1990 that examined the past and projected the future of wildlife conservation in Kenya. Leakey noted, "As pressure for land and resources grows, the support of rural people for wildlife conservation will depend increasingly on the tangible benefits they gain from it." Given his beliefs, Leakey launched some "experimental" utilization projects, but he did so quietly and timidly, because he was worried about international reaction.

One major utilization scheme has been realized on a Laikipia ranch owned by Guy Grant; it is a 1,200-acre savannah bushland filled with birds and wildlife—more than 4,000 gazelle, impala, waterbuck, zebra and giraffes. The wildlife add to the beauty of the land, Grant says, but they also make his life as a rancher more difficult. A rugged individualist, Ian Guy Patrick Grant bought the land in 1963, at the time of Kenya's independence, a time when more whites were leaving the country than buying in. He borrowed money, paid it back, then borrowed again to add to the size of the ranch and buy livestock. The property was called El Karama when he bought it, which means precious possession, an answer to a prayer. "We realized we couldn't improve on it, so El Karama we've remained," he said in his soft, slow voice; he has a silver beard, thick, wavy silver hair and penetrating pale blue eyes. "It's a place of inspiration or refreshment for anyone who finds their way here, and what keeps us going is that I think we're keeping it that way," he said, sitting on his veranda; mounted on the wall were antlers from oryx and eland, dusty and draped with spiderwebs. He looked out into his yard filled with flame trees, cactus plants, acacia, and an orchard of banana, lemon, orange, custard apple, and at least nine other types of fruit tree.

From time to time, elephants pass through El Karama, but zebra and giraffes are Grant's principal nemeses. When he bought the place, there were only 25 zebra. Today, he has more than 1,000, and he figures the ranch should have between 300 and 500 at the most. The zebra population must be controlled because they like the same grass as the cattle and a zebra eats more grass in day than a cow does. As for the giraffes, they spend up to twenty hours a day eating, and eventually they can eat a tree to death. "We'd be better off if we had more trees," Grant said. This is because the tree's canopy slows evaporation, and in dry periods, the last green grass is under the trees. Without the wildlife, Grant figures he could double the number of cattle he has. One of Grant's neighbors has put up an electric fence to keep the game out. In the neighbor's mind, a ranch should be a ranch, a park a park.

Grant likes having the game, but he would also like to derive some monetary benefit from it, especially since it costs him so much. He used to sell rights for sport hunting on his land, of the buffalo, elephants, zebra, waterbuck, and even warthogs. Safari hunting provided about a third of his income. "I lost it overnight," he says about the government's decision to ban hunting. He also sold hides, mostly from the zebra, and biltong (strips of air-dried meat). He lost that income the next year. "It had always been a struggle to make ends meet. My tractor is thirty-two years old, the Land Cruiser twenty-two years old." Electricity is supplied by a generator; he has no telephone.

In 1991, with permission from Leakey, Grant began shooting zebra again, for economic gain. He had the right to shoot twelve a month; he sold the skins. Grant is careful about which zebra he shoots; he selects each one as he would select a steer he was going to send to the butcher. He does not shoot a female if she is with a youngster; an immature zebra; or a prime breeding male, which he can recognize because it is the dominant male in the herd. And he does not shoot from a vehicle or even from near a vehicle, because he wants the tourists who visit El Karama—he has a few simple cottages—to be able to go on game drives and not have the animals flee in terror. Grant is an expert marksman, and he nearly always brings the zebra down with one shot. The zebra thus drops on the spot, and the other animals move off slowly, without realizing what has happened.

It would be hard to imagine a more responsible approach to the utilization of wildlife than Guy Grant's, whose oldest daughter has decided to study wildlife utilization at Oxford. Yet Leakey, who is voluble on just about all other subjects, has not talked about it much, for fear of international protests. His fears are not irrational—it is easy to imagine animal rights groups demonstrating in front of tour companies that book safaris to Kenya, holding signs that proclaim: "Kenya murders zebra." Still, if Leakey is to be a leader in conservation, then he has an obligation to lead in the direction of what he knows is best for conservation instead of following the emotion-driven public herd; and given Leakey's credibility in the West, he could contribute immensely to the public's understanding of the need for sustainable utilization as a conservation policy. To keep the project on Grant's ranch as invisible as possible, the skins of the zebra shot by Grant have not been sold in Kenya. Instead, they have been shipped more than a thousand miles, across several countries, all the way to Botswana, where they are treated, tanned and then sold to customers in Europe and Japan. This is the equivalent of Kansas farmers sending their wheat to Canada to be ground into flour and then having the Canadians sell it to bread buyers in Europe.

THE IDEA THAT Africans should be permitted to make money from the sale of wildlife products in order to convince them to preserve the wildlife confounds Westerners. To them, it is obvious why Africans should save the game: tourism. During the ivory ban debate, the Ivory Trade Review Group, which had been set up by WWF and other conservation organizations, even hired an economist to determine what value Kenyan tourists put on seeing an elephant. Using questionnaires, the economist, Gardner Brown, chairman of the economics department at the University of Washington, concluded that tourists were willing to pay an additional $100 in order to protect elephants, and that overall the "viewing value" of elephants was $25 million (this last amount determined by asking how much people would pay for a safari if there were no elephants, or only half the number of elephants). While there is good reason to be skeptical about how a tourist would respond if he were in fact asked for an additional $100, there can be no doubt that elephants are valuable for tourism. It does not follow, however, that this value would be lost by allowing an ivory trade: you could shoot a very few selected elephants for their ivory and still have thousands for tourists to view.

Westerners have been preaching tourism as the salvation for Africans for decades. In the 1950s, Alan Moorehead, the British writer whose many books about Africa remain classics, lobbied the colonialists in Kenya with arguments about the money to be made from saving the wildlife. "I was armed with a booklet of official statistics which stated that the tourist trade was worth about £6 million to East Africa every year—quite an important item in this limited economy," he wrote in *No Room in the Ark*. To convince the game department officials that they should spend more money and enact tougher laws to protect animals, he advised them, "People don't come to Africa to see the cities and the factories and the farms. They want to see the buffaloes and the elephants." In one of his *Observer* articles in 1960, Julian Huxley wrote, "I would prophesy that the revenue to be derived from tourism in East Africa (which already runs to well over £10 million) could be certainly increased five-fold, and probably ten-fold, in the next ten years." He added that it could be done "without overcrowding the national parks, which would spell their ruination."

Huxley was right that there was big money to be made in tourism. But there are questions about what that has meant for the parks, for conservation and for Africans. Many of Kenya's parks have become overcrowded with people, vehicles and lodges, leading to their "ruination" in the eyes of many visitors. Fifteen years ago, the Mara had a wonderful feeling of wildness about it. Now, it is overburdened with buildings, cars and tourists. "Severe congestion has created an ugly network of tracks . . . and other notable problems include unplanned settlement around lodges and tented camps, associated pollution and the harassment of predators by tourist cars," says a 1988 report about the Mara; the number of tourists has increased since.

And while the African safari has become a lucrative industry, who exactly has benefitted from the bonanza is far from clear. Most safaris are expensive—$250 a day and up is typical—and most tourists assume this money is good for Kenya. As surprising as it may seem, given the obvious importance of the information, Leakey says that he is aware of no studies that have been done on how much of the tourist's dollar actually remains in Kenya. He believes that of the, say, $5,000 that a tourist spends on a safari, no more than half actually remains in Kenya; the other half—or more—goes to the airline and other foreign-owned companies. And when the cost of the Kenyan holiday is £600, which British tour operators have offered, Leakey says almost none of that sum actually benefits Kenya.

Nevertheless, it is true that tourism has become Kenya's most important industry, bringing in more foreign exchange than either tea or coffee. But very little trickles down to the local people. Leakey says flatly, "With few exceptions, people living in areas with wildlife receive few or none of the economic benefits of tourism." As inconceivable—and unconscionable—as it may seem, the amount of tourist industry revenues that has directly benefitted rural Kenyans is less than 1 percent, according to Leakey.

More than 100,000 tourists a year visit Kenya's Maasai Mara, generating millions of dollars in revenues. But the revenues "do not find their way back to the Mara Area in any substantial form as better services or infrastructure," the 1988 study concluded. Less than 10 percent of the gross tourism revenues remained in the district, the study found. Most of the money went to the owners of the lodges and camps (43 percent), travel agents and tour companies (13 percent), operators of balloon safaris (12 percent), and air charter operators (11 percent), with the remaining 10 percent divided among a variety of recipients, including the government (as taxes). Nor were there the indirect benefits that Westerners assume flow from tourism. The Maasai Mara is actually owned by the Maasai, and it is they who live in the areas around it, yet fewer than half of the employees in the lodges and camps were Maasai.

The question becomes obvious: Why should Africans want to continue putting aside land for parks and reserves? "What value are the wild animals to us?" asks Hussein Isack, a Boran who grew up as a pastoralist in northern Kenya but was sent to school by his parents and managed to get to England, where he earned a doctorate in zoology. He notes that the Boran can no longer utilize the wildlife as they did traditionally—for meat, ornaments or necessities. And the parks are seen as a luxury intended for foreigners. "They know that the wildlife is being protected for the *mzungu*—they don't see any of their own people watching the lions," Isack says about the Boran. Though Isack has moved to Nairobi— he works at the National Museums of Kenya—most of his family still live in the north around Marsabit National Reserve. It is a spectacular place, with a 5,000-foot-high forested volcano rising out of the desert, and elephants with large tusks. Not many Boran have ever been in the park, however. "There's a beautiful forest and a beautiful lodge," says Isack. "But who of us can afford to pay to go there?"

Seeing an African on a game drive in one of Kenya's parks is more rare than spotting a rhino or a leopard. Fewer than 5 percent of the visitors to Kenya's parks are Kenyans, and that is a higher percentage of use by a country's citizens than in any other African country (with the exception of South Africa, which hasn't had many foreign visitors). The parks are either too far from where the people live and they do not have cars, or they cannot afford the entrance fees, to say nothing of the lodging.

Africans do not use the parks and they do not receive any significant benefits from them. Yet they are paying the costs. There are indirect economic costs—government revenues that go to parks instead of schools. And there are direct personal costs.

A man who lives near Kenya's Meru National Park wrote to a Nairobi newspaper:

> On December 1, 1990, a marauding elephant killed three people in Naathu, Sub-location of Meru's Ntonyiri Division.
>
> Since that fateful night, the whole sub-location has been gripped by fear—a fear exacerbated by the fact that the elephant got away with no signs yet that it will be tracked down and shot.
>
> Naathu at present resembles an area under dawn-to-dusk curfew, for no one dares to go outdoors between 6 pm and 6 am. One of the dead was my cousin and he left behind a widow and one young child.
>
> His father believes it will be difficult for the loss of his son and the added burden of caring for his widow and child.
>
> In fact, many here think the Government attaches more importance to tourism than to human life.

This notion has been reinforced by the fact that it is Government policy to protect the elephant which is an endangered species worldwide.

And here is a sampling, from just a brief period in 1991, of what conserving wildlife means for local people.

"Leopards Maul Children, Woman" was one headline in a Kenyan newspaper. Two weeks letter, in the same newspaper:

> A woman, who was eight months pregnant, was gored to death by elephants in Wundanyi District on Friday morning. . . .
> Ms Henrita Mkankjala Mwamburi (40) was trying to scare the elephants which had invaded her maize plantation. . . .
> One of the elephants charged at Ms Mwamburi and hurled her about 10 metres away.
> Her stomach burst open and the unborn child was thrown out.
> Both died on the spot.

Two weeks after that, another newspaper reported, "Straying jumbos in Taita Taveta District have killed four people in the last ten days." The district is on the edge of Tsavo National Park, the country's largest; it was this park that the African Wildlife Foundation had raised an alarm about in its "Urgent Memorandum" that launched the ivory ban campaign. AWF said that where 30,000 elephants had once "roamed peacefully," there were now only 5,000 and those might be dead in a couple of years. They did not roam so peacefully in the neighbors' minds, and it might have been fine with them if all of the elephants were dead, and the sooner the better.

"Our people realize that the elephant and rhino and lions and buffalo are fewer than before, but the fewer there are the better, so they aren't concerned that the numbers are declining," Isack says. "I'm not saying that they aren't sympathetic. They believe that these animals are created by God, so they are unhappy when one dies, but it doesn't affect their daily life. It's like if somebody dies, they are sad, but life goes on. The animals aren't critical to them, because they can no longer hunt them."

Leakey has realized that "a fundamental obstacle to conservation is the very small fraction of tourism revenue which goes to local people." Consequently, in 1990 he announced that 25 percent of park entrance fees would be shared with people living around the country's parks. That was a marked departure from the past, when the contiguous residents received nothing, but Leakey knew that it was only the beginning, that much more would have to be done, particularly if two of Kenya's most popular parks, the Mara and Amboseli, were to be saved. These parks, Leakey noted, are "ecologically viable only because [the people living on the borders] tolerate the wildlife on their land."

That last statement needs to be ingrained into the consciousness of everyone who wants to save Africa's wildlife. Underlying it is the zoological fact that many species need space to roam: an elephant clan's home range can easily cover 600 square miles; neither lions nor impala are going to stay within a park's man-made boundaries. One way to keep them in the park is to erect fences. But fences reduce the animal's forage range and shrink the reproductive pool, and tourists don't like them because they give the park the feeling of Disneyland. Therefore, if wildlife preserves are to remain "wild" the people living around them must tolerate the wild animals coming onto their land. Moreover, and this is even more critical—and contrary to the general perception in the West—80 percent of the wildlife in Kenya lives *outside* parks. So the future for Kenya's wildlife is in the hands of Kenyans, and their willingness to tolerate it.

That willingness fades when people discover they can make more money as farmers, which is easy to do when they receive such an infinitesimal amount of tourist revenues. In 1981, a million acres were planted in wheat in Narok, the district where the Maasai Mara reserve is situated; it is now more than three million. These lush wheat fields attract herbivores. One year one farmer shot 3,000 animals that had invaded his fields; during the annual migration of the wildebeest from the Serengeti, a hundred animals a night are often shot.

Amboseli's future might not be much brighter. A freeway could bring people living in Amboseli ranch-style houses—a view of Mount Kilimanjaro from their patio—within a two-hour commute of Nairobi. A preposterous fantasy now. But remember the orange and lemon orchards close to downtown Los Angeles in the fifties?

"AMBOSELI is unique. It can have no rival in the rest of Africa. Nowhere is it possible to see so much big game in such a small area under conditions which are ideal and so suitable to the photographer." Thus wrote the director of the Royal National Parks of Kenya in his report for 1955. The local pride was permissible; Amboseli was a special place. There were more rhino than in any other place in Kenya—the warden once counted twenty-two adults and nine calves during a two-hour drive—including Gertie, who had the strange, four-foot-long horn and would be featured in WWF's initial fund-raising appeal, and her friend Gladys, who had a similar horn. But what made the park so magical, so enticing, was Mount Kilimanjaro. The majestic mountain rises in Amboseli's backyard, and the perfect safari photograph was one of the elephants or giraffes captured in the frame beneath the mountain's snow-capped peaks. The mountain is still there, of course, and one morning I watched a herd of some fifty elephants, including several youngsters, amble from the base of Mount Kilimanjaro, barely visible, across the fields until they were only a few hundred meters away. What a pageant! But that is about all that is still appealing at Amboseli.

"This is the last of the woodlands," said David Western, pointing to a small patch of trees as he piloted his single-engine plane over the park. Moments later, "All this swamp was surrounded by thicket." It is now only swamp, surrounded by dead trees. "That was dense thicket, it used to be called kudu corner," he said, as he banked the plane again. It is barren now and there are no kudu in the park today.

On the ground, as he drove in the park near Ol Tukai Orok, Western said, "It was so thick, I couldn't drive a vehicle in here. You couldn't get to that tree," he said, pointing to one a hundred meters ahead of us.

Once an area of lovely yellow-bark acacia, it is devastated now. The earth is littered with tree trunks. Only a few trees remain standing, and most of them are dead or dying, their skeletal limbs bleached white. A family of elephants wandered about, searching for food, like orphans in the ruins of a bombed-out city; a couple of them, with big tusks, ate at the trunks of two standing trees. Much of Amboseli looks like this, like someone has gone through the park with a tank-mounted flamethrower or dropped napalm on it.

And what is responsible for the vandalism of the woodlands, the destruction of the park? The elephants. Elephants pluck seedlings; push over or snap trees smaller than two feet in diameter; strip the bark off larger trees, which eventually die because water does not reach their upper branches. At least 90 percent of Amboseli's woodlands have been destroyed in the past twenty years. Whether this is good or bad depends on the beholder. Many tourists visiting the park these days are appalled at what they call a "tree holocaust."

But by destroying the trees, the elephants have opened up the park, and it is full of grazing animals. Cynthia Moss, whose Amboseli elephants are her family, thinks this is wonderful. "In all the twenty years I've been in Amboseli, I've never seen animals like this year," Moss said in 1991. "It's become incredibly rich—there are so many zebra and wildebeest—even though it's no longer a woodland."

Western acknowledges that there are more zebra and wildebeest, but the price for that has been too high for him. "We've lost diversity," he says. The woodlands were home for many species. Today, Western points out, there are no kudu, no bushbuck, no mongooses or genets, hardly any giraffes or reedbuck, and very few primates, such as vervet monkeys or baboons.

Western, who has the build of a rugby player and poster-Marine posture, remembers well the early days, for it was in Amboseli that he began his conservation research and career, in the 1960s, several years before Moss arrived. His father was an Englishman who came to East Africa during World War II to train British troops for the Somali campaign, then remained, working as a building surveyor in Dar es Salaam. The elder Western loved the outdoors and worked as an honorary warden; he was killed in 1958 by an elephant he was trying to shoot because it was destroying people's crops. Two years later his widow took the family back to England, but David—who as a member of a childhood bush gang had adopted the nickname "Jonah" (from a British comic strip), the name by which he is still widely known—was intent on returning to Africa, which he did in 1967, with a degree in biology from the University of Leicester. He studied for a doctorate in zoology and ecology at the University of Nairobi, doing his field research in Amboseli, where, with the permission of the Maasai who were living in the reserve at the time, he built a house.

When Western first came to Amboseli, there were seventy rhino in the park. "There were forty rhino just over there," Western recalled, pointing to a thicket of low shrub a mile or so from his ramshackle house. Poaching reduced the number in the park to seven or eight by 1977, but then the poaching stopped and the rhino population started to recover, eventually reaching fifteen. But there was not enough browsing to support even that many, and they left the park in search of food; once outside the park, they were vulnerable to poachers.

Western and Moss agree on one thing: there are too many elephants in Amboseli. Too many, that is, for a park of only 150 square miles—one of the smallest in Africa. Amboseli's elephant population is 800, which is probably twice the park's carrying capacity. What Western and Moss and other conservationists cannot agree on is what to do about the problem. Western has a couple of ideas. One is to limit the elephants' access to swamps and waterholes by erecting fences around them, in effect creating an artificial drought and thus forcing some of the elephants to leave the park. Or, he suggests, allow the Maasai who live around the park to move in with some of their cattle. This, too, would force some of the elephants to migrate, because elephants and cattle eat the same grass and elephants do not like grazing with cattle. Moss is against these approaches; among other things she fears that if the elephants do leave the park, they will become easy targets for poachers. This is probably true, in part because the Maasai living around the park have no incentive to protect the elephants.

Another option is culling. Though Moss very reluctantly accepts culling in theory, she is adamantly opposed to any culling of Amboseli's elephants; she has even said that she would rather see all of Amboseli's elephants killed than see them culled—an extreme statement, but one that reflects her attachment to the elephants, almost every one of which she has named.

Leakey has also rejected culling the Amboseli herds, at least for the moment: "Having led the vanguard on saving the elephant we can't be slaughtering adult elephants and female elephants and baby elephants." But Leakey knows that something will have to be done to reduce the size of the Amboseli elephant population. "We cannot lose the habitat that supports biodiversity," he says. He will not let happen in Amboseli what happened in Tsavo in the seventies.

What Leakey is hoping for is the development of some form of birth control for elephants. Startling as that idea might seem at first, it is a subject of serious scientific research in Britain and the United States, and in 1992 there was a conference in Nairobi on "Elephant Demography and Fertility Control." But success seems unlikely. "None of the existing forms of human contraception is suitable," according to the British medical journal *The Lancet*. "Male methods are not even worth considering; vasectomy is precluded by the intra-abdominal location of the elephant's testes; and the very thought of condoms stretches the imagination too far. Female methods—daily, weekly, or even monthly administration of a pill or an injection—are equally impractical." Therefore, the best hope for controlling population, the journal says, is to develop an abortion-inducing drug. In addition to the public furor that would likely erupt over the introduction of an abortion pill for elephants, any form of birth control would raise again the issue of whether man should interfere with nature.

An even greater storm is brewing, however, if a birth control method is not found: Leakey is prepared to cull. "If we cannot control the numbers by any other method, we will have to cull," he says. He thinks Kenya has about five years before having to decide whether it must cull in order to avoid a catastrophe like the one in Tsavo, before too many elephants bring about their own self-destruction. "At the end of five years we will either be able to control most of our elephant populations by a new technique or we will know that it cannot be done, having invested several million dollars in research. And if it cannot be done, having tried, I think we can defend ourselves against the militant animal rights movement." Leakey may be underestimating the power of that movement, just as the Zimbabweans did during the ivory ban debate.

There is another potential solution to the Amboseli elephant problem, and it is not controversial, though it may be the most difficult to carry out: get the Maasai who live around Amboseli to tolerate the elephants on their land, in order to take pressure off the park. "We can't have that many elephants in Amboseli if we can't use the Maasai land," says Kadzo Kangwana, a Kenyan in her mid-twenties who has a degree in zoology from Oxford and has been doing field research in Amboseli for a doctorate. "The most important issue for the future is whether there will be room for elephants and people," she continues. "Both are large species demanding space. The ivory trade and poaching—they can be stopped. But do we have space for elephants?"

Kangwana's research in Amboseli focused on the interaction between the elephants and the people. She went from boma to boma talking with the Maasai, to learn how they felt—something, she notes, AWF and most other conservationists had not done before. "We've been trying to work with the Maasai without knowing what they think," she says. The Amboseli Maasai are not antagonistic toward the wildlife. "They are positive about the wild animals; they have always lived with them," Kangwana said. "One woman told me, 'The wild animals were created by God and therefore we should live with them.'" But, Kangwana said, "they are very negative about the national parks and the conservationists." The bad feelings aren't surprising: conservationists have taken the land from them for parks and elephants, and even now most of them do not pay much attention to the Maasai and their needs.

The story of the Maasai and Amboseli is similar to the story of the

Maasai and the Serengeti—eviction for the benefit of wildlife and tourism, and unfulfilled promises. Amboseli was declared a reserve in 1947, but the Maasai, who had been living on the land for several hundred years, were permitted to continue grazing their cattle within the boundaries. Over the years, however, as the reserve became more popular with tourists and as the size of the Maasai herds increased, there was pressure to have the reserve declared a national park and the Maasai evicted. Western was about the only conservationist opposed to this, and in 1974, Kenyan president Jomo Kenyatta, siding with the other conservationists, abruptly declared that Amboseli was a park and the Maasai would have to leave. The Maasai warriors responded with a campaign against the wildlife. They speared leopards, even hyenas, but the main victim was the rhino; a sluggish animal with not very good eyesight, a rhino is far easier game than an elephant. The Maasai also went after the rhino because they were the most popular with tourists.

After some negotiations, the Maasai agreed to leave the park, which meant they would lose one of their best watering spots, at Ol Tukai. The government promised to construct a pipeline to carry water from the spring at Ol Tukai to Maasai land outside of the park, and with money from the New York Zoological Society and the World Bank, the pipeline was built; but it was soon neglected and fell into such a state of disrepair that it became virtually useless. The Maasai were also promised annual payments to compensate them for having lost their valuable grazing land inside the park and for tolerating the wildlife on their property. When the first payments were made, the poaching stopped. After a few years, however, the payments stopped, when the government, reeling from the second oil crisis, was badly short of funds.

Given these experiences, the Maasai have been reluctant to enter into new agreements with the government that would allow wildlife to roam over their lands. And the task of getting the Maasai to accept the wildlife is compounded because there has been a dramatic change in the way of life for the Maasai around Amboseli: they have become agriculturalists. This transition from pastoralism to agriculture is welcomed, indeed it is encouraged by the Kenyan government and many international development agencies. They want a modern, capitalist society in Kenya, and that cannot be built while large numbers of people are herding cattle and goats. And while pastoralists and wildlife are able to coexist, agriculturalists and wild animals are enemies.

One of the most successful of the new breed of agriculturalists is thirty-nine-year-old David Maitumo. He lives in a solid, neat four-room house with a corrugated tin roof and has ten acres of land just outside the Amboseli park boundary. Much of the land looks like a checkerboard, divided into two-foot by four-foot plots, which are separated by low ridges, with irrigation ditches running between them. Maitumo grows tomatoes and maize, but his favorite crop is onions. "The onions from here are the best in Nairobi and Mombasa," he said proudly. He plants onions twice a year, and got ten bags each growing season in 1991, which brought him 1,500 shillings (about $600), a considerable sum for people who have almost no other income.

Maitumo and his neighbors look at Amboseli and are anxious, worried that the wildlife will wander over and trample or eat everything. Some years, Maitumo said, the community has lost three-quarters of their crops because of the animals, with elephants and buffalo causing the most damage. In an effort to protect their fields, in 1989 Maitumo's community of two hundred families erected six miles of fence. Each family contributed 300 shillings toward the cost, and it was a rather simple project—four strands of wire electrified by solar power; the panels were placed on Maitumo's roof. After two years it had proved successful against elephants—in marked contrast to the much more expensive fence Leakey and the international community erected in Laikipia.

Maitumo does not own the land where his house sits and his crops grow; nor do the other families in his community own their land. But they might before long, and that really frightens conservationists. Since the early 1970s, the land around Amboseli has been divided into "group ranches." Roughly the equivalent of cooperatives, they are a cross between communal land, which was the traditional land tenure system for the Maasai and other tribes, and individual ownership. The largest group ranch around Amboseli is Olalarashi, where 3,000 families, including Maitumo's, live; it nearly surrounds the entire park. As part of its modernization drive, the Kenyan government wants the group ranches broken up into smaller plots, to which individuals will have title. For many of the families, the idea of subdividing and acquiring title is appealing because it would mean that a person would have collateral if he wanted to borrow money, or he could sell his land to raise money.

"If they subdivide, that's it—the game is over," Western says. "If the ranch is subdivided, cheerio Amboseli," says another conservationist.

Every landowner could then put up a fence, and that would play havoc with wildlife migrations. But what Western and other conservationists most fear is that many of the new owners would sell their plots. Many of the buyers would probably be Kikuyu, Kenya's entrepreneurs. They do not have a cultural affinity for wildlife, and they would almost certainly put fences around their plots. Moreover, one person might buy many plots and combine them into one vast cattle ranch or farm and put up a fence, keeping the wildlife out of a very large area.

"If we get money from wildlife, we won't subdivide," Maitumo said. "If we don't, then we will."

In 1991, Olalarashi negotiated an arrangement with Abercrombie & Kent and Ker & Downey, two of the largest safari companies in Africa. For the right to use eight sites on the ranch for camping, the companies agreed to pay the equivalent of about $20,000 a year. That may seem like a lot, but as Western noted it was a pittance when compared with the $250 to $500 a day that a tourist paid the company. Western also believes the lodges located inside Amboseli should contribute a "bed tax" of 30 to 50 shillings (less than $2) per guest per night to the group ranches. "Considering that forty percent of the viewing is of animals that migrate from the ranches, that doesn't seem like too much, does it?" he asks. Nor did it seem unreasonable given that the average rate for a room was about 2,300 Kenyan shillings. The lodges, one of which is owned by the Aga Khan's company, declined to contribute the bed tax.

The group ranches have begun to realize some benefits from tourism, however. As part of the revenue-sharing scheme that Leakey instituted— to give 25 percent of gate receipts to people living near the parks—they received 3.5 million shillings (slightly more than $100,000) in 1991. They planned to use the money to build schools and cattle dips. But the first thing they did with the money was hire fourteen of their own game rangers to protect the wildlife—the very wildlife that is such a menace to them, which suddenly becomes an acceptable menace when there is money to be made from it. It was proof, if any were needed, that if Africans see there are financial benefits from wildlife, they will do more than just tolerate it; they will protect it.

Leakey describes revenue sharing, and pilot consumptive-utilization schemes, like the one on Guy Grant's ranch, as "radical new policies" and "bold steps." When looked at in the context of how rural people have been treated historically, they might be bold and radical. But if one looks to the future, then the schemes are conservative and cautious. If the visitor to Kenya in 2020 is not to look back to 1990 with the same nostalgia for the profusion of game with which we now remember 1900 and 1960, there will have to be a fundamental change in thinking about conservation. It will have to begin with an examination of the stereotypes and prejudices about who are good conservationists and what are good conservation practices.

FIVE

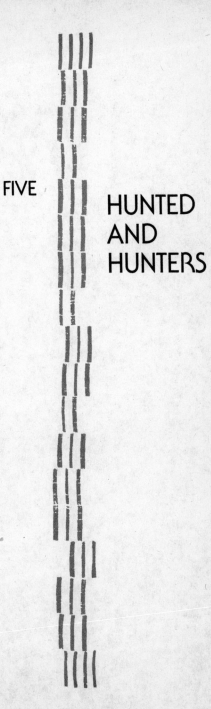

HUNTED
AND
HUNTERS

||||| MASWA GAME RESERVE is an 800-square-mile acacia woodland on the southern edge of Serengeti National Park. Twenty years ago, when Robin Hurt, a Nairobi-based safari operator, took his clients there, it was a great place to find wildlife. Elephants and rhino were everywhere. There were great numbers of roan, a majestic antelope with scimitar-curved horns; greater kudu, another member of the antelope family; and eland, the largest of the antelope, six feet at the shoulders, with corkscrew horns. On any day, Hurt and his clients would see a hundred lions. Leopards were bountiful.

After an absence of twelve years, Hurt returned in 1985, and was sickened and appalled. The elephants were gone; so were the rhino; and just about all the game seemed to be on the brink of extinction. There were only small herds of roan and kudu. Hurt walked and drove around the woodlands for two weeks before he spotted his first lion. And that one had only three legs. Its other leg had been cut off by a poacher's snare. It was the use of snares that was devastating the game. Hurt found twenty lion skulls in one snare line. He found lines that extended for two miles.

Something had to be done and Hurt came up with a plan to pay villagers living on the edge of the Maswa reserve rewards for turning in snares and poachers; he would also pay them to work as rangers, and he would give the village council money from his safari clients which it could use for community projects. It doesn't seem like a very radical program, but it had never been tried before, and the establishment conservation organizations declined to support it.

The first village Hurt approached with his proposal was Makao, a scattering of small, rectangular mud huts, most with thatch roofs, on the eastern side of Maswa. In the shade of a large sausage tree—so named because the fruit hangs like large sausages—was the community center, which was crumbling; the mud walls on one side were held up by poles.

There was one primary school, three churches, and a small general store. The village population was about 800, a melting pot of Wasukuma, Maasai, Mbulu, Barbai and even a few Watindiga, a click-speaking tribe of hunter-gatherers. Most of them migrated here, beginning in the early 1950s, because the land was good for growing maize. Because of tsetse fly, cattle herds were small, and for meat, the villagers killed wild animals, as they had long before they moved to Makao. The traditional means of hunting was bows and arrows, and they are still used (even though it is illegal in Tanzania to shoot an animal without a license). The best material for the bowstring is the tendon of a zebra or wildebeest, villagers explained. The sinew is dried, then covered with fat, making a very strong string. The arrowhead is coated with a poison that is extracted from the bark and roots of the acocanthera tree by boiling them. The Wakamba, from Kenya, and the Wakuria, who live on the northwestern edge of the Serengeti, are the principal makers of the poison, and they sell a small cupful in exchange for two goats. Before buying it, a man will test the strength by pricking his forearm and letting the blood run down toward his wrist. Then he puts a drop of the poison on the blood; the speed with which it runs up the blood trickle, turning it black, indicates the freshness and strength. It is highly toxic; there is no known antidote. An animal, including an elephant, usually dies within five to ten minutes after being hit with a poisoned arrow.

The favorite prey was eland and buffalo. A bull eland weighs 900 to 1,000 pounds, and will produce 60 to 70 pounds of meat, even after being dried, enough to feed a family of ten for a week. The hunters also killed zebra—a mature adult will yield about 30 pounds of dried meat—and wildebeest, because these animals existed in greatest numbers.

The villagers were no threat to the survival of any species, in part because they used the bow and arrow, and also because the poison was expensive, and so a man was forced to exercise discretion and discipline. Then they started using snares; no one seems quite sure when. One villager said it was when the animals "got too wild"—that is, when it was becoming more and more difficult to get close enough to shoot them with an arrow. It might also have been when steel cable became more readily available, from mining operations in the area. The snares are fashioned from cable either three-sixteenths or three-eighths of an inch thick. The thinner wire is used to catch leopards, because thicker cable slips too slowly and the leopard can escape before the noose is tightened. To make a snare, the cable is twisted into a loop, four or five feet in diameter to catch the larger animals, and it has a slip knot. The poachers set the snares along the trails the animals use—over time, thousands of hooves wear a very clear path, often leading to a water hole. They also lay them in bushes, then cut tree branches to channel the animals along the path where the snare has been placed. Poachers often work in three teams— one sets the snares; the second skins the animals and prepares the meat, drying it and cutting it into strips of biltong; and the third carries the meat to the villages, where they sell it.

For the people of Makao (which is also spelled "Makau"), as for most Africans living near wildlife, it has been "poaching for the pot"—to provide food for their families or to sell to other villagers. Only occasion- ally did they poach a rhino or an elephant. Until the early 1970s, that is, when the world price for rhino horn and elephant ivory began to rise dramatically. Then, rhino and elephant poaching got out of hand. "We went completely berserk," one villager recalled. "It was total slaughter." He said that sometimes there were relays of people bringing the horns and tusks out of the Serengeti. Buyers from everywhere descended on the remote area. Somali traders from Kenya brought cattle across the border and put them in holding pens; for a rhino horn, they paid a man two head of cattle. Middlemen from Dar es Salaam, the Tanzanian capital, paid 100,000 shillings for a rhino horn, or 150,000 shillings for a really big horn; it was a lifetime fortune for an illiterate rural Tanzanian. A good pair of elephant tusks was worth four head of cattle. How much money a man might get depended on whether he was a good bargainer. "If they realized I was reluctant to sell, they would offer ten thousand, but if I showed no reluctance, they would pay me only two thousand," one villager recalled.

Twenty years ago, there were so many elephants in the area that "we were not able to move around freely," another villager remembered. "The elephant was just like the grass," he said. By 1985, it was too late to do anything about the elephants and rhino—except to hope that someday others might come—and Hurt concentrated on trying to save the antelope, the cats and the rest of the game by gathering up the snares. Even if one accepts the right of local people to hunt wild animals for subsistence, as Hurt does, using snares is an inefficient method of ob- taining meat. Before the poacher gets back to the snare, a lion or leopard or hyena has often finished off the kudu or roan. And snares catch animals that are not the intended quarry, such as lions. People do not eat lion meat, though the Makao villagers said that they did boil the paws and use them in medicines, and lion fat is considered a good ointment for flesh wounds. Using snares is also cruel. The snare is intended to seize the animal around the neck and strangle it. Often the animal is caught by the leg, which is what happened to the lion Hurt found. It was not only the survival of the remaining wildlife that propelled Hurt into action, however. His livelihood was at stake. Robin Hurt is a professional hunter.

"Wildlife is my business," he said one quiet morning, sitting in the mess tent at his camp among sprawling yellow bark acacia at the base of a kopje. He had just returned from a dawn hunt with his clients and was wearing matching leaf-green shorts, shirt and jacket. Hurt, who owns his own hunting company, has been very successful financially as a professional hunter. "I feel very fortunate to have had so many years of doing what I like to do," he said. "But I didn't go into the hunting business because of the money. I love the wildlife." A big, bespectacled man now with a boyish face, Hurt grew up with the wildlife. His father had come to Africa as a young army officer in 1929, served with the King's African Rifles, and then stayed on, eventually becoming a game warden in Kenya. When Robin was barely a toddler, his father shot a lion on the Nairobi golf course, and as a teenager, Robin went with his dad tracking hundred-pounders along the Tana River. For three generations, the eldest son in the Hurt family had attended Sandhurst; Robin, however, wanted to be a game warden or hunter, and at eighteen he had his professional hunter's license. Hurt has been called the "hunter's hunter." He is also an ardent conservationist.

For most people, the notion that a hunter can be a conservationist falls somewhere between oxymoronic and unfathomable. But Hurt's conservation ethic springs from more than a desire to make money. When he says, "I love the wildlife," I believe that he is sincere, and that he cares about the wildlife as much as any hotel owner or tour operator in Africa, and probably more so.

Hurt is careful about which animals he shoots. Though he has been an avid elephant hunter and elephant hunting is permitted in Tanzania, Hurt does not hunt them these days because he says there are not enough big bulls; the poachers have killed too many. For the first two years after he returned to Maswa, he did not allow his clients to shoot any leopards, because there were too few. He will still not shoot a female leopard. One morning, after his client had missed bagging a leopard that she so desperately wanted, he explained why. "Let's say she has two cubs a year—that's a minimum—and she'll be able to produce for ten to twelve years—that's twenty to twenty-four cubs. And half her cubs will be males—that's our off-take."

Not all hunters are this responsible, of course. During his safari in 1908, Churchill sat on a seat in front of the engine as the train moved from Mombasa to Nairobi. "As soon as we saw anything to shoot at—a wave of the hand brought the train to a standstill & sometimes we tried at antelope without even getting down," he wrote to his mother. "On the first day I killed 1 zebra, 1 wildebeeste, two hartebeeste, 1 gazelle, 1 bustard (a giant bird)." Hunting was banned in Kenya because of abuses, and for every Robin Hurt in Tanzania there are too many irresponsible hunters. "They shoot everything that moves—cheetah, lion and leopard cubs, and every form, shape and sex of antelope," a Tanzanian who makes money from hunting safaris wrote in 1991, about a group of hunters from the Middle East who regularly came to Tanzania. "A bunch of them ran down a wildebeest in a vehicle and then practiced pistol shooting on the exhausted beast," he said. And he added, "Anybody who is in the least concerned about conservation has been appalled by this completely un-controlled wholesale slaughter of game." (It was uncontrolled because the men who were engaged in it apparently had the same protection from government officials as did the men who were building the hotels at Ngorongoro and the Serengeti over the objections of responsible govern-ment officials who wanted to protect Tanzania's heritage.)

ON THE MATTER of hunting elephants, Beryl Markham once wrote, "It is absurd for a man to kill an elephant. It is not brutal, it is not heroic, and certainly it is not easy; it is just one of those preposterous things that men do like putting a dam across a great river, one tenth of whose volume could engulf the whole of mankind without disturbing the domestic life of a single catfish." Churchill also seems to have had second thoughts about hunting, after shooting a rhino. His first shot, from a hundred yards, hit the animal but didn't kill it, and in *My African Journey* he described how the rhino "bore straight down upon us in a peculiar trot, nearly as fast as a horse's gallop." Everyone in the party then fired. "Still the ponderous brute came on, as if he were invulnerable; as if he were an engine, or some great steam barge impervious to bullets, insensi-ble to pain or fear." Finally the rhino was brought down, only a few feet away. After all this, Churchill felt differently: "There is time to reflect with some detachment that, after all, we it is who have forced the conflict by an unprovoked assault with murderous intent upon a peaceful herbivore; that if there is such a thing as right and wrong between man and beast—and who shall say there is not?—right is plainly on his side." And the young man who had already seen combat in the Sudan and in South Africa went on, "In war there is a cause, there is duty, there is hope of glory, for who can tell what may not be won before night? But here at the end is only a hide, a horn, and a carcass, over which the vultures have already begun to wheel."

The eloquence of Markham and Churchill sum up how I feel about hunting. I do not understand what it is that drives a man, or woman, to pick up a rifle and shoot an elephant, or a lion, or a leopard, or a kudu, for sport. And whatever "sport" or physical challenge might have been involved in the days when Churchill, Roosevelt and Hemingway went on their hunting safaris, when it was necessary to hike for miles and days, is certainly gone now when most hunters reach their farthest points in Land Rovers and walk only a few miles as they stalk their prey, and then return by vehicle to camp, where the beer is cold. But whatever one thinks about hunters and hunting should not cloud a judgment about whether they can be good for conservation.

There can be no disputing that hunters have long been leaders in conservation. It was hunters who founded the Fauna Preservation Society and convened the 1900 London Convention. And in America, in 1887, five years before John Muir established the Sierra Club, twenty-eight-year-old Theodore Roosevelt gave a dinner party for some of his hunting companions and out of it came the Boone and Crockett Club; one of the club's objectives was "the preservation of the large game of the country." Membership was denied to anyone "who shall not have killed with the rifle in fair chase . . . at least one individual of one of the various kinds of American large game." When he became president, Roosevelt did more for conservation than any American head of state, before or since.

Sport hunting presents conservationists with an uncomfortable dilemma. They do not like killing animals, and they know that hunting is deplored by most people who give money to conservation organizations; at the same time, they realize that hunting has a place in conservation. "I support hunting as a conservation tool," says David Western, who hunted until he was sixteen, when he voluntarily put away his rifles and has not hunted since. "To me it's the survival of the wildlife that matters."

Because of his beliefs, Western spoke at the 1988 New York preview of *In the Blood*, a film by George Butler (who had achieved fame with

Pumping Iron). Though Butler is a political liberal, it was a pro-hunting documentary, built around photographs of Theodore Roosevelt with his son during their 1909 hunting safari in Kenya. In the film, Butler takes his young son on his first hunting safari, and it ends with the boy killing a buffalo; Robin Hurt smears the animal's blood on the boy's face, a ritual followed by the Maasai and other tribes to mark a first kill. When the film came out, Western was director of Wildlife Conservation International, the field research arm of the New York Zoological Society. The society was worried about the reaction of the animal rights groups to the film and upbraided Western for lending his reputation to it. "I took more than a little heat," Western says. Nevertheless, he thinks he acted responsibly. "My commitment is to African conservation, and periodically you have to speak your mind."

When it comes to sport hunting, however, not many conservationists or conservation organizations are willing to. Russell Train, the chairman of WWF-US, believes elephant hunting provides "the most efficient and cost-effective form of producing economic benefits for local people that you can find." And WWF gives money to a conservation project in Zambia in which safari hunting is the major source of revenue. Yet a WWF member reads the organization's public reports about the project in vain to find any reference to hunting. Esmond Bradley Martin, the ivory and rhino horn trade expert and leader in the worldwide campaign to save the rhino, has said privately that if a license to shoot a rhino could be sold for $50,000 (which many hunters would surely be willing to pay; in South Africa, the fee to shoot a rhinoceros is $30,000), he would not be opposed. That amount of money could hire several rangers just to protect rhino, or to monitor the illegal rhino horn trade. A conservationist with AWF has concluded that the sale of 200 or 300 elephant hunting licenses in Zambia a few years ago would have brought in more money than the country received from the World Bank and all other international donors for conservation.

Along with Western, one conservationist willing to accept sport hunting is the chairman of IUCN's cat specialist group, Peter Jackson—though with a heavy heart. "I can't bear hunters," he says. "The hunting mind is something abhorrent to me." But Jackson has concluded that trophy hunting is probably the only way some cat species will survive. As an example, he points to the Siberian tiger. Only some 400 Siberian tigers still remain, most of them prowling outside protected reserves, in areas inhabited by people, where they kill humans and domestic stock.

The people want the tigers shot. The only way to ensure the tiger's survival in the unprotected areas, Jackson says, is by giving it an economic value, and the best way to do that is through sport hunting. Jackson cites the recommendation of a Russian biologist who has studied the Siberian tiger: "If the leaseholder of hunting land has a material incentive for having tigers, he will not only protect them, but, as one game manager has said, he will hand-feed them."

It is a similar story with the cheetah in Zimbabwe. The speedy, powerful cat is protected in reserves in the eastern and western parts of Zimbabwe, but there are also cheetah populations living on farmlands between these reserves. These populations are the biological link between the populations on the reserves, so if the cheetah on the farms are killed off, there will be two isolated populations; that would result in a shrinking of the gene pools and ultimately the deterioration of the species. The cheetah on the farms have become a very serious threat to cattle, however, and most farmers would like to shoot them all. Vivian Wilson, a Zimbabwe biologist who has studied the cheetah, has concluded therefore that safari hunting should be permitted. "I personally hate the idea of having to 'shoot' the animal, but cannot think of any other way in which we will ever be able to persuade farmers to see its value," says Wilson, who runs an animal orphanage in the southern Zimbabwe city of Bulawayo, taking in lion cubs, small wild dogs and the offspring of other cats that have been killed. Like Tanzania, Zimbabwe allows sport hunting, including of elephants.

Kenya banned hunting in 1977, and many conservationists think it is time to permit it again. The ban was not imposed for moral or ethical reasons, but in response to pervasive corruption. Some professional hunters would obtain a permit for their client to shoot, say, one leopard or lion, but they would shoot several, bribe rangers in the field not to report them and then file false reports with the game department. They also shot animals from their vehicles, which was illegal. "It got so bad in some areas that wildlife took off at the sound of a vehicle," recalls Perez Olindo, who was director of Kenya's national parks department at the time the ban was imposed. Olindo supported the decision to ban hunting, but he notes it was never intended to be permanent; it was to last only until the poaching could be brought under control. In 1988, soon after returning to the department, Olindo thought the time had come to reintroduce some hunting—of the plains game, such as zebra and impala, and predators like lions, though not of rhino or elephants. Olindo did not succeed in getting hunting reinstated before he was replaced by Richard Leakey, but it seemed that Leakey would do so. In interviews after becoming director, he made it clear that he intended to permit hunting. "I'll probably reopen sport hunting soon," he told *Audubon* magazine in early 1990.

"Sport hunting appears to have the potential to generate more income for land owners from a given number of wild animals than do wildlife cropping or ranching, and possibly more than viewing tourism," Leakey concluded in the report released in June 1990 that detailed the five-year program for the Kenya Wildlife Service. To illustrate, the ranchers around the Mara could earn $2 per hectare from selling hunting concessions, whereas from tourist operators they earn about seventy cents per hectare.

Leakey not only believes in hunting in general; he has even said that it is OK to hunt elephants. Indeed, in a meeting with U.S. officials in May 1989, Leakey urged that the elephant not be classified as an endangered species under U.S. law because that would preclude trophy hunting. That, of course, wasn't something the man who campaigned so hard for the elephant to be declared endangered under CITES ever said publicly.

In a study for Leakey in 1989, Robin Hurt concluded that hunters would generate almost $20 million annually for Kenya. They would pay $4 million to the Kenyan wildlife department in license fees alone; that is four times more than the department had ever earned in a single year from park entrance fees. Given the wildlife department's pressing need for revenues and Leakey's repeated assertions that people who live with the wildlife must benefit if Kenya's wildlife is to be preserved, one would have expected him to move quickly and forcefully to allow hunting. It is not only because Leakey is unwilling to subject himself to international opprobrium that he has cut his convictions to fit popular opinion. At home, Kenya's powerful tour operators are opposed to hunting. They fear that hunting will damage the country's image.

From a conservation perspective, it might be wiser to promote hunting over tourism, however preposterous the proposition might seem on first examination. Ecologically, tourists are more destructive than hunters. They speed across the plains in their minivans, in pursuit of a lion pride or rhino, tearing up the grass and in rainy periods cutting ugly ruts. In

Amboseli, the tourists have contributed as much to the park's deterioration as the elephants have. There have simply been too many tourists for the small park, and they turn the place into a dust bowl in dry years, in addition to a Disneyland in high season.

Very little research has been done on the impact of large numbers of tourists on the wild animals, but what research has been done should disturb anyone who believes tourism is the panacea for conservation. For one thing, tourists are taking some of the "wild" out of animals and Africa. A visitor can practically pet the elephants in Amboseli. As recently as the 1970s, the lions in Ngorongoro would "hide from tourist vehicles," one researcher noted; today, the lions have become so accustomed to man and his car that they yawn and pose. But the consequences of too many tourists may be far worse than the taming of the wild. "Harassment of the lions by camera in Serengeti has led to so many kills being missed that lion cubs sometimes starve," Norman Myers, a British conservationist, observed, and that was twenty years ago, when the number of tourists was a fraction of today's. Cheetah have also been seriously harmed by camera-clicking tourists. The cheetah hunts in the daytime, and tourists love to follow one as it stalks a gazelle or an impala. The vehicles often scare off the prey, and the cheetah itself will react to the vehicle by either lying down and waiting until it leaves or running away from it; either outcome deprives the cheetah of its meal. The cheetah "no longer lives like a wild animal," Leakey said in 1991.

The final argument for hunting over tourism is an economic one. A lucrative hunting industry can be established with a limited capital investment, without large hotels and minivans, or even a road network to get hunters to their destination. And hunters spend prodigious amounts of money. Robin Hurt's clients easily spend $50,000 for a safari, and most of it stays in Tanzania; even a top-of-the-line photographic safari is not likely to cost more than $20,000.

Costa Mlay, the director of Tanzania's wildlife department, figures that one hunter is worth a hundred nonhunting tourists. This is his rough calculation, but it is easy to see how he arrived at it. Hurt's hunters paid an average of $12,327 each directly to the Tanzanian government during the 1991 season. Every hunter must pay $200 a day to the Tanzanian government; this is in addition to what he pays Hurt. The hunter also has to buy a license, one for every animal he wants to shoot, and they are expensive; on top of that he has to pay an amount equal to one-third of the license fee into the Wildlife Protection Fund, which is used by the game department for rangers and anti-poaching. In 1990, these fees came to $4,000 for an elephant; $2,000 for a leopard or a lion; $1,300 for a lesser kudu or sable antelope; $840 for a hippopotamus; and $600 for a buffalo. The Tanzanian government took in a total of $2.3 million from license fees alone in 1990, which is more than the gate fees tourists paid to enter the country's parks.

In the final analysis, however, it is not an either/or proposition—either tourism or hunting. Some land can be set aside for tourism, other land for hunting. The prime Kenyan tourist circuit is Amboseli, the Maasai Mara and a few places north of Nairobi, while vast areas of the country northeast of Nairobi to the Ethiopian and Somali borders are largely untouched by tourists. This region, which is sparsely populated by humans, would be ideal for hunting. Moreover, some areas are not suitable for tourism because there is not enough game. A tourist who drives all day and sees only five animals is disappointed, if not angry with the driver of the van. A hunter needs to see only one animal of the sort he is pursuing.

TANZANIA BANNED hunting in 1973, for the same reasons Kenya did a few years later—abuse of the system and corruption—but reinstated it in 1984. It was because of the ban that Hurt had been out of Maswa for more than a decade. In his absence, poaching had escalated. In part this was because there were no hunters. The game department did not have enough rangers to patrol all the parks and reserves, and with no one else around, "the people had a free hand in poaching," as one Makao villager put it.

When Hurt started up again, he and his clients conducted their own random anti-poaching effort. They destroyed poachers' camps, even captured a few poachers, and they picked up snares they found while they were out hunting, between five hundred and a thousand each season. "But we just weren't winning, we weren't getting anywhere," Hurt recalled. "Our presence was helping to reduce poaching, but it wasn't enough. So I thought the only solution was to involve the local people, to give them something so that they're on the side of the wildlife for a change."

The core of Hurt's program was a reward scheme—$2.50 for a snare; $75 for a poacher's rifle; and $100 for information leading to the arrest and prosecution of an elephant or rhino poacher. In addition, Hurt proposed setting up village anti-poaching teams; each member would be paid a salary and provided with a uniform and equipment. When he sketched out this program, Hurt concluded that the total annual cost would be $65,000.

He realized that the villagers had to receive something positive from the wildlife, something in addition to the rewards. The effect of Tanzania's game laws was that impoverished local villagers like those in Makao could not kill a wild animal for food, but a wealthy foreigner, like Hurt's clients, could kill one for sport. "Why should they tolerate us hunting if they get nothing out of it?" Hurt asks, raising the obvious question. To address the injustice, Hurt decided that his clients should contribute an amount equal to 20 percent of the license fee, and that this would be given to villages on the edge of the reserve. "This will give the local people a real interest and benefit from their wildlife and I believe will prove to be a successful long-term conservation benefit," Hurt said in a letter to Costa Mlay, outlining his proposal.

Hurt had ideas, but he needed money. On a cold evening in New York, in January 1989, when his thinking was still in its embryonic stages, he was at a dinner party given by Bartle Bull, whose *Safari: A Chronicle of Adventure*, an expensively produced book with magnificent photographs, had just been published. Bull was a lawyer and liberal activist; he had been the New York campaign manager for Robert Kennedy in 1968 and George McGovern in 1972, and publisher of *The Village Voice* in the 1970s. As a young man, he had been an avid hunter, but he had given it up in his twenties. At Bull's Manhattan apartment, Hurt met Joseph Cullman III, the retired chairman of Philip Morris. Another big-game hunter/conservationist, Cullman was on the board of WWF-International in the 1970s, was a member of WWF's 1001 Club, and has given more than $50,000 to the United States chapter of WWF. During the dinner conversation, Hurt sketched his idea to Cullman. Cullman was intrigued, and invited Hurt to his Park Avenue office to discuss it further; Hurt went the next day and left with a commitment from Cullman to support Hurt's scheme with his own money and to raise more.

Cullman sent Hurt's proposal to the African Wildlife Foundation, which Cullman had also supported with substantial donations over the years. AWF was not being asked for money, but merely to act as a conduit for contributions. This would save Hurt the trouble and expense of establishing a nonprofit organization in the United States. It was all perfectly legal, but once again the internecine jealousy in the conservation commu-

nity surfaced. AWF's president, Paul Schindler, was piqued that Hurt
had not consulted with Mark Stanley Price, the head of AWF's office in
Nairobi. "After all, they only live about a stone's throw apart in Nairobi,"
Schindler wrote Cullman. Then, Schindler offered a number of reasons
why AWF would not get involved.

Hurt had been careful to discuss the project with the director of the
Tanzanian wildlife department, Costa Mlay. Mlay was enthusiastic, but
he wanted the donations to come to his department (whether or not
they were first passed through AWF was unimportant to Mlay), and the
department would then disburse them to the village. It was a way for the
department, which had to enforce anti-hunting laws against villagers, to
be seen in a more positive light, and for the project to have less of a
"white-man-helps-the-Africans" air about it. Hurt considered Mlay's desire reasonable. AWF did not. Though Schindler assured Cullman that
"Costa is most honorable," Schindler said that AWF could not release
any funds to Mlay because there was no assurance that they would be
sufficiently accounted for. But Schindler's "greatest problem" was with
the reward scheme. "There is all too great a likelihood that poachers in
a village . . . would finger some sad sack as the 'poacher' and turn him
in. Not only could they keep some of the ivory/rhino horn, but they'd
get a reward while dispensing with a village enemy," Schindler wrote.
"Not only would some innocent character get a virtual death sentence
(which is what jail can mean all too often), but his enemies would get a
reward in the process."

Hurt addressed Schindler's objections in his own letter to Cullman, a
response which reveals much about the difference in attitudes between
conservationists who try to make policy while sitting in the comfort of
their offices in the city, whether Washington or London or Nairobi, and
those who get out in the field with the Africans affected by the policies.
After dismissing Schindler's complaint about AWF's not having been
consulted as "sour grapes," Hurt gave the reason he was confident that
the reward scheme would work and would not be abused. "I am the man
in the bush rather than in Washington or Nairobi and I am able to get a
feeling on these things," he wrote. And he certainly had more respect
for Africans than Schindler did. "I know the people of Makau village and
I think it is most unlikely that they would finger some sad sack as the
poacher." Hurt closed with the observation that if Schindler's way of
looking at things "was the attitude on everything to do with wildlife
conservation, we would never get anywhere—we have to try new ideas."

WWF-International was also cautious. It was not that the organization did not agree with the concept. Indeed, the International's senior program officer for Africa, Rick Weyerhaeuser, said, in a letter to Hurt, that involving local people in conservation "is probably the only way that conservation in Africa has any realistic hope of long-term success." Nor did—or does—the organization object to sport hunting. Indeed, Weyerhaeuser noted that WWF was supporting local conservation programs in Zimbabwe and Zambia in which "safari hunting is the principal means of generating revenue and benefits for local people." Why then would WWF not support Hurt's program? Because it was not "institutionalized," Weyerhaeuser wrote; rather, it "relies on the good will of a few individuals" and therefore "is not sustainable in the long-term."

It was certainly true that Hurt's program was not institutionalized, but if one looked at the millions of dollars that WWF has sunk into "institutionalized" programs that have failed, it is not at all clear why that should be a criterion for support. And it would also seem appropriate to examine how effective programs are once they do become "institutionalized," with all the bureaucracy, record-keeping and reporting to superiors that inevitably follows.

Though the "leaders" in conservation stayed away, Cullman gave Hurt $10,000, and Hurt was able to obtain $10,000 contributions from Herbert Allen, the New York investment banker and one of Hurt's hunting clients, and from Lynn Foster. Foster, who had made her money as a financial analyst and institutional broker in Boston in the 1980s, had been introduced to Hurt at a fund-raiser for George Butler's *In the Blood.* Foster and her husband, John, later went on a hunting safari with Hurt, their first in Africa. Lynn Foster was so impressed with Hurt and his project that she gave another $10,000 of her own money and she and her husband hosted a dinner party at their Park Avenue apartment; they invited thirty-two people, who ultimately donated $80,000 to Hurt's program. Cullman, Allen and Foster received no tax deduction for their initial donations, which went directly to Costa Mlay's department (where they weren't stolen, to the best of my knowledge), but later donors channeled their money through American Friends of the Game Conservancy, a small organization in Shreveport, Louisiana, which offered to play the role that AWF had declined to.

When Hurt had the initial commitment of $30,000, he set up a meeting with the Makao villagers, in May 1990. All the elders and leaders, including the village's only teacher and only health worker, crowded into the mud-walled community center to listen to Hurt. Outside, it seemed that just about the entire village gathered to learn what they could. "Robin explained to us the value of the game and what benefits we could get by protecting the game instead of poaching, and he offered to help us," one villager recalled. At one point, Hurt said, "You people see the Maasai, they are very rich. Why?" Because they have many cattle, the villagers said. Hurt then went on, "Well, you don't have cattle, but the wildlife are your cattle, and if you look after that wildlife it can be very valuable to you." Hurt told the villagers that he had money from America for them and he outlined the reward scheme for turning in snares and poachers; further, he said, the hunters were going to give money to the village, which the village could use as it wished.

The village leaders were skeptical, and for three hours they questioned Hurt. Then they decided to sign on, and before they adjourned, the elders selected the men to make up the anti-poaching team. Almost all the new rangers were once poachers. They are provided with uniforms, rations, medical care and bicycles, which they need to move around the area on patrol, pedaling on the paths made and hardened over the years by the wild animals. The rangers are paid 500 Tanzanian shillings a day, which is far better than a government ranger's salary of 2,500 shillings a *month*.

It might not have been institutionalized, but Hurt's program was immediately successful. In the first six months, sixty-eight poachers were caught and convicted, seven poachers' camps were discovered and destroyed—five of them inside Serengeti National Park. Two thousand snares were turned in, including eighteen leopard snares. Based on his experience, Hurt believes that each snare traps five to ten animals; thus the 2,000 snares represented the saving of at least 10,000 zebra, wildebeest, buffalo, impala, lions and other wild animals. The cost, after paying the rewards and salaries, worked out to $2 per animal.

The program has had a deterrent effect as well. "There used to be a lot of poachers in the reserve because there was no control," one member of the anti-poaching team said. "But now, because there are hunters there and the anti-poaching teams, there has been a great reduction in poaching. They're afraid of being caught."

And the benefits Hurt promised have been realized. In the center of Makao stands a shiny new corrugated tin shed. Each day, the women line up with a hodgepodge of containers—a woven wicker basket, a shallow green plastic pail, a tall, rusting tin can—filled with maize, waiting to have it shelled by the automatic machine inside the shed. Most women in rural Africa are still grinding corn by hand, as their ancestors did—they shove a rock back and forth over the corn on a stone slab to remove the hard kernel; then with a mortar they pulverize the kernels into flour.

When the women get inside, they see a sign, in English and Swahili:

> The Cullman Wildlife Rewards & Benefits. This Mill was paid for by
> the wildlife of Makau and Maswa. Such are the rewards of the correct
> utilization of wildlife.

The villagers bought the grinding mill with the money Hurt's clients donated in 1990, just as Hurt had promised. The next year, they had enough money to buy a tractor.

"IT REMAINS my fervent dream that this arrangement which started so quietly will grow to engulf the whole country," Costa Mlay wrote to Joseph Cullman in September 1991. His dream was quickly coming true. Word of the program spread rapidly throughout the area, and villages besieged Hurt to be allowed to participate. When Hurt responded to the invitation from the people of Saka Saka, a village on the northern edge of Maswa, four hundred people turned out to hear him. In 1992, the village bought a Toyota Hi-Lux with money it received from Hurt's hunters.

Mlay hopes that eventually the program will not be dependent on the voluntary contributions of hunters. He wants the government to direct that 25 percent of the hunting license fees be allocated to villages adjacent to reserves and parks. "I am convinced that it is the right way to go about winning the hearts of local communities to actively participate in conservation work," Mlay says about the rewards and benefits program. "With their support, survival of the wildlife is certain; without it, it is doomed as surely as the dodo."

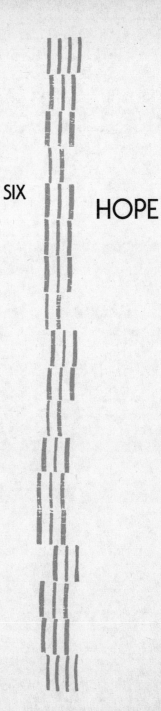

SIX

HOPE

||||| IN JANUARY 1989, as the international campaign to ban ivory trading was gaining momentum in the United States and Europe, the people in Nyaminyami, in northwestern Zimbabwe, were granted authority by the state to exercise dominion over the wildlife in their district. There were no front-page headlines, not even any news stories, but it was a critical step in a radical conservation program—one that will do more to save the elephant than the ban on ivory trading, and one that goes farther toward giving people the benefits of wildlife than anything being tried in Kenya or anywhere else on the continent. The people of Nyaminyami can cull impala herds, or sell concessions to hunt lions or elephants, or set up tourist joint ventures—and they get nearly all the financial returns, not just a small share. What enables them to do this is CAMPFIRE—the acronym used (mercifully) for the Communal Areas Management Programme for Indigenous Resources. The communal lands, which are akin to the Maasai group ranches in Kenya, make up about 40 percent of Zimbabwe's land area. During the colonial period, the communal lands were the tribal trust lands, where the colonialists told the blacks they had to live; not surprisingly, they are the poorest lands in the country. In many of the communal lands, as in much of rural Africa, wildlife is the only valuable resource.

Nyaminyami—it is pronounced "nee-ah-mee nee-ah-mee"—is rich in natural beauty. Its rolling hills are forested with thorn trees and stands of mopane, with its small, butterfly-shaped leaves; according to Shona legend, after God made all the animals, the butterflies complained to Him that they were being eaten by the birds, so He made the mopane tree, where the butterflies can hide. Nyaminyami also has a wealth of wildlife. During an hour's drive through the woods near Lake Kariba, a tourist encounters elephants at every turn. A hippo once ran across the path of my vehicle, then plunged into the lake, creating a huge wake, to the amusement of onlookers. On the cliff above the lake sits the Bumi Hills

Safari Lodge; from the bar or rooms with sliding glass doors, guests can gaze down on elephants drinking from the lake as the sun sets. On another visit, I departed the lodge just before sunrise for a game drive and walk. Within minutes, the lanky guide directed his spotlight into the bushes and caught the soulful eyes of a dozen slumbering buffalo— massive beasts with thick flat horns. Farther on, in an open field, hundreds of buffalo were grazing, along with impala, kudu and zebra; warthogs scampered about, their long tails erect and whipping in the air. The guide shone his light at the base of a cliff a few hundred yards away and the glistening eyes of a leopard answered back; it quickly dashed off. Across the field in a copse were two lionesses, a mother and daughter. "Powerful lady," the guide commented with admiration as the mother got up and sauntered off; he had seen her mating several months before, and now two four-month-old cubs tottered toward our vehicle, stopping ten yards away. During the walk, we came upon a family of elephants. When they detected our presence, they froze, and spread their ears wide. Deciding we were not a threat, they returned to cracking off tree limbs with their trunks as they ambled past the rocks where we were perched.

The "big five" on most safari-goers' checklist are elephants, lions, buffalo, leopards and rhino; most people leave disappointed, with the last two species the most elusive. I had just seen four of the five in a few hours, and though we did not come upon any rhino, our guide said that if we had gone into nearby Matusadona National Park, we surely would have. There are forty rhino in Matusadona, and another twelve to sixteen rhino live in Nyaminyami outside the park; together that is more rhino than in any unfenced area of Kenya. The guide said that 90 percent of the guests at the lodge were people who had been to Kenya and now wanted a safari experience where there were not so many vans and people. He added that the owners of the Bumi Hills lodge had been talking about expanding from twenty-two rooms but that the staff had threatened to resign. "We don't want to become another Kenya," he said. To avoid that, he said, no more than two vehicles were out on a game drive at the same time, a welcome contrast to Kenya and even Tanzania's Ngorongoro, where minivans leave the lodges in convoys in the morning, again after lunch, and once more just before dusk. Tourists are enthralled by the wildlife in Nyaminyami, and sport fishermen angle for tiger fish in Lake Kariba—the record is nearly thirty pounds and fourteen-pounders are not unusual.

But nature's endowment has not meant much for the people of Nyami-nyami, who are Shaangwa, a Shona-speaking tribe, and Tonga. Agriculturalists, the Tonga were living along the Zambezi River when David Livingstone explored it in the middle of the last century. The Zambezi's headwaters are in Angola, and 1,600 miles later they empty into the Indian Ocean off the coast of Mozambique. At one point, the waters plunge 600 feet, roaring and sending up a constant spray, forming Victoria Falls. In the 1950s, the British, in order to provide hydroelectric power for their colonies of Northern and Southern Rhodesia (today Zambia and Zimbabwe) and Nyasaland (Malawi), dammed the Zambezi at Kariba, 300 miles below Victoria Falls. As the waters rose, Lake Kariba was formed—the largest man-made lake in the world at the time; its length is comparable to the distance from New York to Washington—and the Tonga were forced off their lands. The name Nyaminyami comes from a mythological water snake that the Tonga believe lived in the Zambezi and during droughts came to help, curling itself on the bank of the river and allowing the people to cut nutritious meat from its body.

Nyaminyami could be just about any place in rural Africa. The people live in mud-and-wattle huts; they survive as subsistence farmers, coaxing maize, sorghum and a few vegetables out of soil that is shallow and sandy; there is little rainfall, less than thirty inches in the best years. The wildlife and the tsetse fly make their lives even more difficult.

ONE MORNING, Nyaminyami's executive officer, Simbarashe Hove, talked about CAMPFIRE and the people's attitude toward the wildlife. He was sitting in his office in Siakobvu, the district's administrative center, which consisted of a few cinder-block buildings, a police post, a health clinic and a general store. Hove's corner office had a cement floor and was sparsely furnished with a wooden desk and a high-back, vinyl-covered chair. It was a few weeks after the international ban on ivory trading had been imposed at Lausanne, and Hove said, "The decision was, let me put it bluntly, irresponsible. All these organizations, if they really wanted to come up with something, they should have talked with us. You know what this ban means to the local people? There will be too many elephants. The elephant population is growing. You don't need surveys, you can just see it. It means the people are exposed to more danger than they are now." Hove reached for a book in which he filed reports from villagers about damage by wild animals. Reading from one, he said that in the last growing season, elephants returning night after night to one man's plot had destroyed 264 bags of maize, 24 bags of groundnuts and 4 bales of cotton.

About this time, a district councillor, Wilson Nebiri, who is also a village chief, came in to talk to Hove about something, and when he realized the conversation was about the problems with wild animals, he mentioned that the previous night lions had killed twelve goats in hamlets in his constituency. A half hour or so later, a clerk brought in a note handwritten on a half-sheet of lined paper which had just arrived in Siakobvu. "Dear Chairman. Manyandu was nearly killed by an elephant and the women could not fetch water because of these elephants. There are two of them."

Also present in Hove's office was Elliot Nobula, the senior game officer for Nyaminyami, and after listening to Nebiri and reading the letter, he set off to investigate. He had already been at work since dawn, following up on last night's reports of wild animal attacks, much as a police officer coming on duty pursues the previous shift's crime reports. In Nobula's office, down the outside corridor from Hove's, the top of a low bookshelf was lined with animal skulls, and one wall was covered with a topographical map of the district. The map was overlaid with transparent plastic, and on the plastic were little dots, each one indicating where a wild animal had invaded someone's field—green for buffalo, blue for leopards and lions, red for elephants. In some places—near the lake and several small streams, most of which exist only in the rainy season—there were so many dots that they merged into a big mass. Most of the dots were red. In Mola, the largest of the four traditional chieftaincies in Nyaminyami, elephants and buffalo destroyed between six and seven tons of maize during the 1989 growing season.

After he left his office, Nobula's first stop was two miles down the dirt road, at a small hamlet where a man, his wives, their sons and their wives, and lots of children lived. Their huts were made of mud packed between a ribbing of rough posts, which was then covered with a thin layer of mud; the roofs were thatch, which extended over the sides of the hut to provide some shade. In this hamlet, as in most, there was a granary, a small circular structure raised off the ground, and a slated platform about four feet high where the women put their pots and pans to dry—a simple, and ancient, kitchen counter. Near a smoldering fire several women were sitting on the ground, sorting vegetables, some with tiny children held in slings on their backs. A brown dog limped about, an open wound on its rear left leg, the evidence that it had barely survived the swipe of a lion's paw the previous night.

Picking up faint paw marks, Nobula now tracked the lion's path through the hamlet and around the circular goat pen. Only one goat had been taken, but Nobula believed that it was probably the same lion—an adult male, he said—that had killed fourteen goats in a nearby hamlet two days earlier. "It is probably an old lion," Nobula remarked as he followed the tracks through the scrub before coming to a spot, two hundred yards from the huts, where the lion had stopped to feed on its catch. "He can't go around chasing impala, so he looks for a goat; goats are easy," Nobula explained. Before leaving the hamlet, Nobula assured the women that they would be compensated for the goats the lion had killed.

As part of its CAMPFIRE program, Nyaminyami set up its own wildlife department, which is called the Nyaminyami Wildlife Management Trust. One of the wildlife trust's first acts was to search for a warden. Twenty-five men applied, and after interviewing six of them, the trust, in 1989, chose Nobula, who was approaching thirty.

When he was fourteen, Nobula left school and went to work as a stock checker for a chemical company where his father was a security guard. He did not like the work. "I grew up in the communal lands and coming to town and sitting in a plant was boring," he says. "I didn't want to be confined. I wanted to be in the bush." He was also determined to get an education, and through correspondence courses, he earned his high school diploma; then he took a test and was admitted to Zimbabwe's national-parks college. After graduating, he worked as a game ranger in a wildlife reserve near Victoria Falls, and was then assigned to Chizarira National Park, which is just south of Nyaminyami. Within two years there, he advanced from ranger to acting warden. He had done well, but he left that promising future to work with CAMPFIRE in Nyaminyami. "This was a chance to work with the people in the communal lands," he explained. A quiet, but assured, lean six-footer, Nobula speaks Tonga, Shona, Xhosa and English, an invaluable skill in Zimbabwe's multilingual nation. As he goes from village to village, Nobula seems like a cross between a family doctor and a politician, soothingly talking to villagers about the importance of wildlife in order to enlist them in his cause to save it.

Leaving the hamlet where the lion had taken the goat, Nobula drove on the dirt road past fields of charred stumps and smoldering tree trunks. (To clear the land for cultivation, the men hack a notch in the base of a tree with a machete, and then prop the ends of burning logs against the notch; eventually, the fire burns through the base and the tree crashes.) In most of the fields there was a small log platform, perhaps ten feet off the ground, supported by not very sturdy poles. From this perch women and older children stand guard, throwing rocks or banging on pots to drive off animals, such as baboons, which forage for seeds, and even buffalo, which often stampede through a field. The men who had sent the letter about the elephant attack were lounging under a tree; nearby, women were doing daily chores—a typical picture of rural Africa, where the women do the heavy work, hauling firewood on their backs and water on their heads, and planting, weeding and harvesting.

The men, most of whom were barefoot, with mud caked on their cracked feet, described what had happened the previous evening. They had been drinking beer—a home brew made from sorghum—and communicating with their ancestors, they explained. About seven o'clock, the party broke up and Manyandu, the man referred to in the note to Hove, headed home. As he rounded a bend in the road, he saw the elephant, an adult bull, twenty yards away and ambling in his direction. Manyandu stopped, but the elephant continued moving toward him, and when it was only a few feet away, Manyandu, who is not sure of his age but looked to be in his fifties or sixties and has silver stubble on his chin, took off, running as fast as he could through a furrowed field. The elephant chased him. Reenacting the harrowing experience the next day, Manyandu pointed to two places where the elephant had scooped its tusks into the dirt to seize its prey; one time the dirt sprayed over Manyandu. He managed to reach a guard tower; the elephant gave up.

The elephant remained in the area, and the next morning it had frightened other villagers, about two hours before we arrived. This time, it had charged twenty-six-year-old Tobias Changwedera while he was clearing logs from his field. "They're just there, they're just there," Changwedera and the other men now said excitedly to Nobula, motioning toward the trees. They wanted Nobula to set out in pursuit of the elephants and kill them. Nobula takes every opportunity to explain to villagers about conservation, and he did so now. The wildlife belongs to them, he told the men. It is valuable, and if they look after it, it will benefit them and their children, he said.

The next day, Nobula drove to Mola, the commercial center of Nyaminyami; it consisted of four cement-wall general stores, painted in pastel colors and sparsely stocked with soap, pots, blankets, peanut butter, and of Nyaminyami. Maybe they don't fully understand yet why it is important to conserve the elephant, but when they begin to see the economic value of the resource, we are very, very sure that eventually they'll understand. But the ban means they won't receive the economic benefits of the elephants; they won't have the meat and they will not be able to sell the skins and the ivory."

As another pot of coffee bubbled on the open fire, two men in yellow jumpsuits came through the trees, with tanks on their backs. They were spraying for tsetse fly. Nobula reacted with a few expletives, then said, "It is bad for the wildlife."

It might seem hard to imagine how anyone could be against eliminating the tsetse fly, but the tsetse fly is the wildlife conservationist's best friend. The reason is somewhat complex. To begin with, the tsetse fly transmits a disease that is fatal to cattle (the strain that causes sleeping sickness is virtually nonexistent in Africa today), so farmers stay away from areas with tsetse flies. Without humans and cattle, wildlife flourishes. Conversely, when the tsetse fly is eliminated, farmers move in. Then the battle with the wildlife begins because the farmers do not want zebra and giraffes competing with their grazing animals, elephants and buffalo destroying their crops, and lions killing their cattle.

The tsetse organism *Trypanosoma* is borne in the blood of wild animals, which share the woodlands and dense bush that the fly inhabits. Traditionally, Africans cleared small areas around their villages in order to get control of the tsetse fly. When the colonialists came to southern Africa, they had another approach to opening up tsetse-infested lands. They destroyed the game on a large scale. In the early 1930s, for instance, Southern Rhodesia adopted a tsetse fly eradication policy that resulted in the killing of 25,000 wild animals a year.

The Zimbabwe government still wants to eliminate the tsetse fly, because there is a shortage of good farming land, and also because the government wants ranchers to raise more cattle, primarily for export to the European Community. Once the tsetse is controlled, the people of Nyaminyami will have a choice: wildlife or cattle. It will probably be a fairly easy decision, as it would be for most Africans. In modern society, cows are private property; wildlife is not—you can't brand a kudu. You can go to the bank if you have cattle and borrow money; you can sell it. If the people of Nyaminyami have any doubt that their lives would be richer if they had cattle, they have only to look at their neighbors. The tsetse has been eliminated just outside Nyaminyami for several years,

a hodgepodge of sundries, most of which languish on the shel
weeks because they are too expensive for the people of the distri
one hamlet, a mile or so from Mola, a small woman named Tenes M
told Nobula about a tragedy that had happened just a few weeks ea

One evening, after dinner, four small girls had gone into a fi
hundred yards from their huts in order to go to the bathroom,
Mutare began. Moments later, the villagers heard screams and the
came running back. But there were only three; Mrs. Mutare's se
year-old daughter was not with them. She had been seized by a l
When Mrs. Mutare went to look, she found only her daughter's in
tines, and farther away, pieces of her legs.

"If my husband had followed that lion and killed it, he'd be in
now," Mrs. Mutare said, becoming increasingly agitated. Several oth
women expressed their anger to Nobula. Buffalo and elephants had d
stroyed their maize and sorghum, but the government did nothing, the
said. When the people tried to protect themselves by killing the animal
they were put in jail. Or if a man shot an impala or a zebra in order t
get meat for his family, he was arrested by the rangers and beaten. A
far as these women were concerned the government's conservation laws
and policies meant that wild animals were protected while people were
persecuted and prosecuted. "That is the feeling we want to break
through," Nobula remarked as he left the hamlet.

Nobula combines a concern for people with his commitment to conservation, an attitude far too rare among rangers, and on another occasion,
he discussed his views of conservation and what he and CAMPFIRE
hoped to accomplish. It was first light, and sitting in front of his "home"—
a large tent, to which he had added a thatched porch—we could see in
the distance the bright-orange meanderings of disconnected brush fires
started by farmers to clear areas for cultivation. Nobula's rimless glasses
were pushed down on the bridge of his nose, and he was wearing leaf-
green shorts. "The concept of conservation is to conserve for the people
of this country, but in actual effect it has been the visitors who have
benefitted more," he said. "The people of the communal lands have been
hunting for hundreds of years, so we have to educate them that the
animals have a right to live and that they will be a benefit for the people.
We have to educate them, not just arrest and beat them." In the past,
national park rangers routinely beat poachers or suspected poachers, he
explained. It has been the same throughout Africa.

Asked about the ivory ban, Nobula said, "It is not good for the people and in that area, where cattle are grazing, the homes are substantial—rectangular, with white-washed bricks and glass in the windows, rather than squat mud-and-wattle structures.

Conservationists, of course, hope that the Nyaminyami villagers can be persuaded to choose wildlife over cattle, and they might if they can make money from wildlife as they do from cows. And that is the purpose of CAMPFIRE. "They have never had the opportunity to know the potential value, the full value, of wildlife," says Simon Metcalfe, who has worked with CAMPFIRE in Nyaminyami since its inception.

ALONG WITH NOBULA, Metcalfe stands out as the person to be recognized for the success of CAMPFIRE in Nyaminyami. He was the catalyst for getting it started and remained as the advisor. And successful it has surely been, so much so that nearly every district in Zimbabwe where there is wildlife has instituted CAMPFIRE programs—Metcalfe became the national coordinator—and conservationists throughout Africa realize that CAMPFIRE is a model conservation program.

What is striking about Metcalfe is that he is not a professional conservationist or an ecologist. His work with wildlife is motivated by a desire to save humans. "I only came into this project because I wanted to try to do something for the needs of the people," he says, without an air of righteousness. An angular and intense man whose hair was beginning to grey and thin when he turned forty in 1991, Metcalfe is not a patrician by heritage, education or attitude. His father was an agricultural extension officer in the British colonial service who served in the Sudan before moving to Rhodesia in the 1950s. He didn't send his son away to England for schooling as so many whites did, and Simon graduated from the University of Rhodesia, with a degree in political science. That was in 1972, when the white Rhodesian government was drafting young men for its war against the black independence movement; Simon left the country rather than fight against a cause he sided with. He worked for the social services department in the London Borough of Lambeth.

As soon as Zimbabwe had achieved its independence, in 1980, Metcalfe returned and went to work in Nyaminyami for Save the Children, the nonprofit humanitarian and development organization. At that time, malnutrition was so severe that most Nyaminyami children were physically and mentally retarded. Metcalfe remained with Save the Children until 1988, leaving only after he was approached by a local nonprofit development organization, Zimbabwe Trust, to help get CAMPFIRE started. After studying the CAMPFIRE policy, Metcalfe decided that it would be a way to increase the wealth and improve the nutrition of the people in Nyaminyami, and he signed on.

"Simon's brief for the first year was just to run around and talk to people," said Robert Monro, who as director of Zimbabwe Trust in Harare recruited Metcalfe. Metcalfe did precisely that, reluctantly leaving his wife, who managed a rock band, and two children behind in Harare, to spend long weeks in Nyaminyami sleeping on the ground and eating canned food heated over an open fire.

Zimbabwe Trust was founded by Monro and Keith Madders, young, liberal Rhodesians, who, like Metcalfe, lived in self-exile in England during the war, and returned after independence to help in their country's development. After establishing the trust, they came up with a creative way to raise an endowment. During the war for independence, when the international community imposed sanctions against the white Rhodesian government, one of the government's responses was to freeze the bank accounts of the foreign companies operating in Rhodesia. After independence, the new government offered these companies, most of which were British, bonds in the amount of their Zimbabwe accounts. Monro and Madders made them another offer: donate the money to this new trust, and take a tax deduction in Britain. They raised about $5 million, a considerable amount for a new charity, and Lady Soames, Winston Churchill's youngest daughter, became the trust's first president, a post she still holds.

The trust's approach to development differs from that of most humanitarian agencies and of institutionalized aid and development agencies such as the World Bank. "We establish right at the beginning the principle of business," says Monro. "This isn't aid." Aid has been ineffective at promoting development and alleviating poverty, he says—a criticism hard to dispute, looking at the billions of aid dollars that have been spent in Africa over the last quarter of a century and the plight of the people on the continent today. Most aid and development programs also tend to be "top-down"—planned by bureaucrats in Washington, London or from their offices in Third World capitals, too often without consulting the people the programs are intended to benefit. Finally, Monro noted, aid programs often create a dependency among the recipients; then, when the aid donors leave, as they invariably do, the people are worse off than they had been before.

The trust hopes to build institutions, such as the Nyaminyami Wildlife Management Trust, which will survive when the outside assistance is discontinued. In 1989, Zimbabwe Trust allocated $1.5 million over a five-year period to help Nyaminyami establish its wildlife management program; after that the trust expects the program to be self-sufficient. It almost certainly will be, because of CAMPFIRE.

Like many well-intentioned government projects in Africa, and throughout the developing world, CAMPFIRE languished for several years after the policy was announced in 1982, largely because the government did not allocate any money. Finally, in 1988, Zimbabwe Trust decided that CAMPFIRE fit with its own philosophy of development, and Monro approached his friend Metcalfe, offering him the equivalent of $25,000 a year (or less than half of what most of the Nairobi-based conservationists are paid).

Metcalfe is convinced that CAMPFIRE will make a radical difference in Nyaminyami. "From being one of the poorest areas in Zimbabwe, I predict that within a decade it could be one of the wealthiest," he said in 1990. He has calculated that by the mid-1990s, Nyaminyami will be earning $500,000 a year from wildlife, which is about $500,000 more than the district has now from all sources, except foreign aid.

Even before they recognize the full monetary value of their wildlife, however, the people of Nyaminyami have enjoyed a substantial nonmonetary benefit. Twice a year, beginning in 1989, the wildlife authorities have culled the impala herds and distributed the meat to the residents.

THE IMPALA is a graceful creature with a fawn coat, white stomach and black streaks on its white buttocks; the males have lyre-shaped horns. Shooting one, it seemed to me, would be as sickening as shooting Bambi. But the impala cull is integral to the success of CAMP-FIRE in Nyaminyami—to the human and conservation aspects of it—and during my second visit to Nyaminyami, in September 1990, I warily asked to observe a cull.

The headquarters for the operation was on the edge of Lake Kariba, where, just after dark, the professional hunters and their assistants moved out, in a roofless Land Rover. A man in the back danced the beam of a powerful spotlight through the mopane thicket and tall grass. When the sparkle of eyes answered back, the professional hunters, one in the front and one in the back, began to shoot. With the first crack of rifle fire, impala leaped into the air, arching their backs, searching for the danger and alerting others. In a moment, some froze; others ran. An impala that was hit would often sprint for ten or twenty yards before falling forward on its knees, then rolling over dead. After the herd had scattered beyond rifle range, the hunters' assistants moved through the grass locating the dead and wounded; their ability to find the animals in the tall grass on an almost moonless night was astonishing. If an impala was still twitching, a man would slit its throat. Every effort was made to limit the suffering and above all not to leave a wounded impala for the hyenas and other predators. One young impala, only slightly wounded with the first shot, proved particularly difficult for the hunters to capture, always just out of reach of the rifle range or hidden by grass as it tried to escape. The hunters pursued that one impala for at least ten minutes without success; finally one of the hunters left the vehicle and stalked it on foot, into a thicket of trees, where he delivered the final blow.

It required two men to heave a carcass into the open back of the vehicle and when all of the kills had been located and loaded, the vehicle and spotlight would begin moving through the night again, until the hunters saw more twinkles. Throughout the night, loaded vehicles returned to the Lake Kariba site, where the impala were hung by their hind legs from hooks on a long rail. Their heads were severed—they were sold to a nearby crocodile farm—and then the heart, lungs, gut and other organs were removed. Then they were skinned. About four in the morning, a seven-ton truck full of impala carcasses began moving out to the first of thirteen distribution sites throughout Nyaminyami.

In Mola, one of the four Nyaminyami chieftaincies, men and women arrived early and waited patiently in order to buy some meat, which was distributed from the community center, a whitewashed circular building with a thatched roof. Black plastic sheets were spread on the floor and a scale hung from the rafters. Rangers from the Nyaminyami Wildlife Management Trust hacked up the carcasses, weighed the pieces and collected the money. The impala meat was sold for Z$1 a kilogram—well below the market price of Z$4. (Two Zimbabwe dollars equaled one United States dollar, roughly.) The bargain price was not charity, however; it covered the cost of each cull. One woman bought an entire carcass, another half of one. Outside, a woman with a baby swaddled on her back chopped carcasses into smaller pieces with an ax; the meat was then stuffed into bags and pails of all sizes, shapes, colors and materials, and carried away. In Negande, another of the Nyaminyami chieftaincies, a girl of about ten, barefoot and wearing a patterned dress, walked down the dirt road, two impala legs hanging out of the shallow wicker basket balanced on her head. Scenes like this were repeated throughout Nyaminyami.

At the lakeside culling center, Russell Taylor, a short, balding man with a clipboard, paced around like a football coach on the sidelines during a close game. An ecologist with WWF in Harare, he had previously spent eighteen years with Zimbabwe's wildlife department. He monitors every cull, requiring the hunters to fill out detailed forms: what time they started, how many kilometers they drove, how many impala they killed, how many rounds of ammunition they used. The data he collects will allow him to determine what impact the culls have on the impala population. Do they affect their breeding? Their migration patterns?

During a wide-ranging conversation, Taylor stressed that the hunters used 1.1 bullets per each impala killed. "If a Green says anything to me, I can show him it's humane," he said. He and others working with CAMPFIRE are sensitive to public reactions to the cull, and driving around with the hunters, it was easy to envision animal rights militants bringing their sleeping bags and lying in the grass to prevent the operation.

"The animal rights people want to save individual animals. As a biologist, I want to save populations," Taylor said. His comment summarizes the critical distinction between the animal rights activists and more traditional conservationists; conservationists want to ensure the survival of species and ecosystems, and to do that requires management, such as culling elephant herds. Or as Taylor puts it, "To save populations in this world today, and especially in *this* world, means managing the populations." The world he is emphasizing is Africa. The reality of Africa is the expanding human populations, with the attendant pressures on land. "These land-use pressures and population pressures—that's what the people in the United States and Europe don't understand," Taylor said. Asked what he meant by "manage," Taylor was more graphic: "Populations may be conserved, but we may have to send a few to the wall to do it." It is that grim reality that Westerners find so hard to accept, and understandably. Culling is a brutal activity, and it seems inhumane. But is it not also brutal and inhumane to allow human beings to suffer from malnutrition amidst plenty? Metcalfe figures that the culls have doubled and maybe tripled the amount of meat protein for a Nyaminyami villager; the only other source is goats, and a family of eight to ten cannot afford to slaughter more than ten goats a year.

Culling the impala herds in Nyaminyami is an example of utilizing a resource for the benefit of impoverished people without jeopardizing the resource—that is, an example of the principle of sustainable utilization. Five hundred impala are killed in each cull; out of a total impala population of 15,000, this is a sustainable off-take. It was exactly the kind of program Sir Julian Huxley had in mind as a measure to save the African wildlife. One of the three articles he wrote for *The Observer* in 1960, the ones that led to the founding of WWF, was entitled "Cropping the Wild Protein." It began, "The wild lands of Africa and the wild life that they carry are a major asset, a natural resource waiting for proper utilisation." Noting that most Africans ate too little protein, he wrote, "Game-cropping . . . could become a major means for overcoming this dietary deficiency and putting the Africans on a proper plane of nutritional health." It could also be an antidote to poaching, he thought. "If extensive game-cropping schemes can be set up, whether the cropping is done by licensed local tribesmen, or Game Department staff, or selected white hunters or their clients on safari, this will go far to satisfy the Africans' legitimate meat-hunger, and to remove the financial and psychological incentives to poaching."

Huxley had the right ideas, but they were never put into practice because there were too few Western conservationists who cared about people, too few David Westerns, Garth Owen-Smiths, Simon Metcalfes. The major conservation organizations, such as WWF and AWF, paid little attention to the needs of people until the two organizations finally began to realize, in the mid-1980s, that they were not going to save the wildlife unless they did something for the people. And today, while both organizations believe in sustainable utilization, they do not have the courage of their convictions, fearing attacks from the animal rights activists, who in their championing of the rights of animals neglect the rights of people.

At the time of Nyaminyami's fourth cull, in September 1990, WWF was under siege because of its support for sustainable utilization. The attacks began in July 1990 with a segment about WWF on "The Cook Report," a popular British weekly television program similar to "60 Minutes" in America. Considered hard-hitting investigative journalism by its admirers, "The Cook Report" is criticized as assault journalism by others, who note Roger Cook's aggressive style of confronting people who do not wish to be interviewed. WWF's president, Prince Philip, and director-general, Charles de Haes, tried to derail "The Cook Report" segment on WWF. Philip filed a complaint with the Independent Broadcasting Authority—which has a power to control the content of broadcasting that is unparalleled in the United States—charging that Cook had engaged in subterfuge to gain royal papers containing exchanges between Philip and de Haes, and that the report was biased and unfair. The complaint was rejected. Altogether WWF spent $350,000 to counter Cook's exposé, according to one WWF insider, but the efforts by WWF and Philip only succeeded in creating so much publicity that an estimated six million people watched the show, about a million more than the normal audience.

The program generated a barrage of stories in newspapers throughout the United Kingdom, and many carried sensational headlines: "WWF Accused of Aiding Slaughter in African Bush"—Dundee *Courier & Advertiser*; "Charity 'Encourages Wildlife Slaughter' "—*Western Daily Press*; "Philip's Fund Is Slammed"—*Sunday Mirror*.

Among the many charges Cook leveled against WWF, the one he seemed to consider the most serious was that the organization raised funds from the public to save animals while at the same time it was supporting utilization programs. He was right, of course, that WWF did this. But if conservation is the goal, WWF should have been praised, not damned. Cook, however, was displaying the same lack of understanding about, and emotional bias against, sustainable utilization that the general public has.

Inspired by "The Cook Report" and repeating many of the same criticisms, an article in *Newsweek International* said that WWF "makes no secret of its belief in the 'sustainable utilization' of wildlife," and added, "hunting, that is." In fact, hunting is only one form of sustainable utilization, but it is the one that arouses the most intense public emotion. Cook, too, equated sustainable utilization with hunting, and for the show he went on a hunting safari—with a hidden camera. He described it as "about the most distasteful assignment" he had ever undertaken. Standing before a kudu, an antelope with swept-back horns, he told viewers, "For five hundred dollars I could have killed this magnificent kudu. For a few dollars more, I could have shot an eland or a leopard. . . . I could even have killed an elephant." He went on, "The remarkable thing about this safari project here in Zimbabwe is that it's actively sponsored and supported by the very organization that you would think would be against it—the World Wide Fund for Nature."

He was right that WWF supported hunting and he was right that he would have been able to shoot an elephant. He was not interested, however, in probing further, in asking why WWF supported this activity and, more important, what it meant for conserving Zimbabwe's wildlife and particularly its elephants.

In a single sentence, he might have noted that Nyaminyami alone earned enough from hunting in 1989 to pay the costs of running its own conservation program. With the money, the district hired twelve game rangers, provided them with uniforms, rifles, shovels, tents and rations, and paid them the equivalent of $100 a month. It was one of the best-paid, best-equipped ranger units in Africa. On their daily patrols the rangers pick up snares that have been laid along the animal trails, and their presence deters would-be poachers of elephants and rhino.

For the people of Nyaminymai the most lucrative animal has been the elephant, because it is the animal that has attracted the hunters. The government-set trophy fee for an elephant was $3,750 in 1989. This amount didn't go into the central treasury, as hunting and park entrance fees generally do throughout Africa. Rather, under CAMPFIRE, nearly all of this amount went to Nyaminyami. In addition, Nyaminyami was paid a concession fee by the hunting company.

NYAMINYAMI'S ELEPHANT hunters come from around the world—France, Germany, Canada, Australia—but most are from the United States. American hunters feared, with good reason, that if the elephant were declared an endangered species and placed on CITES Appendix I, they would not be able to bring trophy tusks into the United States, from Zimbabwe or any other place. So hunting organizations began to lobby against an Appendix I listing. But then they cut a deal with the African Wildlife Foundation and the other groups that wanted a ban on ivory trading: the hunters would not work against the ban, in Washington or with other countries, if the pro-ban people would do nothing to jeopardize sport hunting of elephants. During a meeting in April 1989 with Secretary of State James Baker, to lobby the Bush administration to support an Appendix I listing, Craig Van Note of Monitor and Christine Stevens of the Animal Welfare Institute said that if the elephant was declared endangered, they would not oppose trophy hunting.

In her opening address to the CITES meeting in Lausanne in October 1989, the head of the United States delegation, Constance Harriman, assistant secretary of interior for fish and wildlife and parks, strongly urged that the elephant be declared endangered, but at the same time she said, "The United States encourages African nations to continue to allow sport hunting." Her statement astounded many of the delegates, who found it confusing that the United States would be so passionate about declaring the elephant endangered while at the same time advocating hunting. They were unaware of the machinations of American domestic politics—Secretary of State Baker and President Bush were both avid hunters, and the gun lobby is one of the most feared in Washington.

Once the elephant was placed on Appendix I, however, the Bush administration and the hunting organizations worried that the African Elephant Conservation Act, which had been enacted in 1988, might be invoked to prohibit the importation of trophy tusks. When they returned to the United States, the hunting groups began working vigorously to insure that their members could bring in trophies even though the elephant was on Appendix I. The groups and individuals that had supported the ban countered with their own campaign to keep trophies out, which meant that they had to renege on the compromise they had arranged with the hunters before Lausanne, as well as on the specific assurances they had made to the Bush administration. The Humane Society sent letters to members of Congress calling on them "to resist efforts . . . to allow the importation of trophy tusks from sport-hunted elephants," and it threatened to mount demonstrations against congressmen who did not support laws to prohibit trophy tusks from being brought into the United States, a threat that had to be taken seriously given the society's strength. When AWF learned what the Humane Society was up to, it was furious. AWF was founded and is financially supported by hunters, and besides, it had made the deal with the hunting organizations. AWF's vice-president McMeekin confronted some of the organizers of the anti-hunting campaign (which included Stevens and Van Note, in spite of their pledge to Baker) and they backed off. In effect, AWF's position was that it was acceptable to kill elephants for sport, but not for the purposes of selling their ivory, a distinction that is as morally untenable as it is hypocritical.

Hypocrisy has never been in short supply in Washington, and it certainly wasn't on this issue. The hunters found an ally in congressman Jack Fields, a conservative Texas Democrat. Fields had been a vigorous champion of putting the elephant on Appendix I and ending the ivory trade. In March 1989, after a trip with President Bush aboard *Air Force One*, Fields wrote, "As I indicated to you, Mr. President, I am convinced that unless the United States and other nations take immediate action the African elephant will cease to exist as a viable species." The African elephant was being "decimated at a staggering pace," Fields wrote, adding that there were only 400,000 remaining—the number the most radical animal rights groups were using, even though it was well below what any responsible conservationist believed. After the Bush administration banned ivory imports into the United States, in June 1989, Fields wrote the President, "I would like to compliment you for your outstanding leadership on behalf of our largest and one of our most beloved land mammals, the African elephant."

Evidently, they were not so beloved and their decimation was not so staggering that Fields didn't think a few more could be shot—by hunters. He wrote to the Secretary of the Interior, Manuel Lujan, and asked him to issue a legal opinion that would ensure that elephant tusks could be imported without violating the African Elephant Conservation Act. Sport hunting of elephants "produced financial revenues which were desperately needed for effective elephant conservation efforts," Fields wrote. (This was, of course, the same argument that was made by African proponents of the ivory trade, but from them, Fields didn't buy it.) He closed his letter with a handwritten scrawl: "Manny—This is extremely important to me, and more to the point, it is the *right* thing to do for the elephant and conservation in Africa!" The Interior Department agreed and enacted regulations that permitted the importation of trophy tusks from Zimbabwe and South Africa. In justifying the decision, the department found that these countries had healthy elephant populations and a strong management program. That was precisely what the countries had been arguing all along, to no avail.

Though obviously pleased that sport hunting of elephants could continue in Zimbabwe, Rowan Martin, the somewhat acerbic senior ecologist in the country's wildlife department, pithily summed up the American position this way: "It's OK for elitist white hunters to come out and kill elephants, but it's not OK for local people to make money from them."

· · ·

TO DETERMINE how much Nyaminyami had lost because of the ivory ban, Elliot Nobula, the warden, looked at a ledger that listed the elephants that had been shot because they were damaging people's fields and could not be chased away. Taking the total weight of the tusks of these elephants and the price of raw ivory during the preceding few years, he calculated that Nyaminyami lost Z$40,000 (roughly $20,000) during the first eight months of 1990. And that was just ivory from elephants that had to be shot. In addition, had it not been for the ban, Nyaminyami would have culled a few elephants and sold the ivory and skins. With advice from the professional conservationists at WWF in Harare, the Nyaminyami Wildlife Management Trust had determined that a sustainable off-take of elephants was sixty-nine, or 3 percent of the elephant population. The sale of the ivory and skins from that off-take would have brought Z$250,000 to the poor community.

The advocates of a ban on ivory trading argued that the income from ivory sales was a small fraction of any African country's total exports— not more than 1 or 2 percent (1 percent of United States exports in 1989 amounted to $2.5 *billion*). While that may be so, the lost income looms much larger in an African village. The yearly earnings of a Nyaminyami household, which averages eight people, were less than Z$200 a year, according to Hove, the executive officer. He said that most of the families were so poor that they could not afford to send their children to secondary school, where the fee was only Z$40 and the total cost for a year, including books, clothes and shoes, was about Z$250. Nor could they buy the few goods that were for sale, unless they saved for many months. In the general store in Siakobvu, a blanket sold for Z$45.75; a small metal cooking pot, Z$13.75; a five-hundred-gram box of Cold Power Blue Strength ("Washes Out the Worst Dirt in Cold Water"), Z$4.75; men's shorts, Z$17.80. If Nyaminyami could have sold just the ivory from the problem elephants, and had then divided the proceeds among the households in Nyaminyami, it would have meant an increase of at least 25 percent in every family's income.

There is another way to look at the money that Nyaminyami lost because of the ban. In 1990 alone, it virtually equaled the amount of foreign aid the district received for development projects such as primary schools and nutrition programs. Not long after the ivory ban was imposed,

I had a conversation with a senior World Bank official in Nairobi. He was a passionate advocate of the ban. I pointed out the economic impact of the ban on a place like Nyaminyami. He dismissed the argument, claiming it was always possible to find some small community that would be hurt by an international action; he went on to say that it was up to international organizations like the World Bank to make up those losses. Given all the needy development projects in the world, one would think the World Bank should be pleased to find a community that could raise its own funds instead of looking for handouts from the international community.

IN SEPTEMBER 1990, the Nyaminyami Wildlife Management Trust held one of its bimonthly board meetings. It took place in Siakobvu, in a room with a concrete floor and yellow walls; there was a green chalkboard in one corner, listing various committees and the members. The meeting began at 10:30 in the morning; by 2:30, it was so stifling hot it was a wonder anyone was still awake, and there had not been any breaks, nor would there be before the meeting ended at 5:00. Seated around the long tables, arranged in an open-ended rectangle, were four-teen people, including two chiefs, four councillors, Elliot Nobula, Simon Metcalfe and Simbarashe Hove, the executive officer. A variety of items was discussed, including hiring four senior game guards, and a proposed joint venture between the Wildlife Trust and a private company for fishing the Lake Kariba kapenta, a freshwater sardine. The company was offering to provide some of its catch to the local people and to share the profits from what it sold with the district; it was another illustration of the principles of CAMPFIRE at work. Toward the end of the meeting, Chief Msampakaruma said the traditional village chiefs would like some recognition, and he suggested that at each cull they be given the meat from one impala. The suggestion startled some board members, and Metcalfe reminded the board that this issue had come up before the first cull and that the board had decided the chiefs should be given no privileges—everything should be democratic. Hove pointed out that whenever an elephant was killed, whether because it was destroying crops or for ceremonial purposes, the chief was traditionally presented with the trunk and the meat from the side it fell on. After more discussion, it was decided that the four chiefs would each be given an impala, the first four shot. With a slight grin, Nobula noted that it would be impossible to determine which were the first impala shot. Chief Msampakaruma said any one would be satisfactory.

Most of the session was taken up by one issue: what to pay villagers for losses suffered because of the wildlife. Paying compensation is another example of the boldness of Nyaminyami's approach to wildlife management; like Kenya and Tanzania, and most other African governments, Zimbabwe does not compensate people for such damage. Everyone at the board meeting spoke on the subject—in Shona, Tonga or English— and most more than once. The compensation schedule Nyaminyami had adopted provided payment of Z$20 for the loss of a goat and Z$20 for a 90-kilogram bag of maize or sorghum. When elephants and buffalo trample through fields before the crops are harvested, it is impossible to know exactly how many bags are lost, however, so the Wildlife Trust had settled on an average yield as the basis for compensation.

"We've told people compensation is provided for, but they're not satisfied," Councillor Wilson Nebiri told the board. Many farmers argued that they were better farmers and their yields were above the average, and so the compensation schedule was not fair to them. Others complained that they were compensated for only three goats, when in fact the lions had killed five. "The people are saying it's no better than it was when National Parks was in charge, so let us go back to hunting."

Because of dissatisfaction with the compensation they were receiving, many people were losing faith in CAMPFIRE, Hove said sharply.

Nobula told the board about a man who was asking for Z$200 because elephants had knocked over his granary and eaten all the maize. He claimed to have lost the equivalent of ten bags of it. Nobula said he had spent two days investigating the claim but that he was simply unable to determine how much maize had, in fact, been in the granary. Some members of the board expressed concern that the chief game warden had to devote so much of his time to such a matter.

Another issue on the agenda was much more pleasant. The board had before it proposals from several companies to establish tourist facilities, and all were offering the district a share in the profits. Buffalo Safari and Zambezi Canoeing Lake Wilderness Safaris wanted to put up a game-viewing and fishing camp on Lake Kariba's Bumi Bay. The camp would have ten tents or thatched huts, flush toilets, hot and cold water, and a swimming pool. The company said it would invest Z$200,000, and it was asking for no capital investment by Nyaminyami. What Buffalo Safari wanted in exchange was a lease on the land, and the company offered to give Nyaminyami 10 percent of its after-tax profits. Another safari company, Kushanya Africa Safaris and Wilderness Trails, wanted to establish a luxury tented camp for a maximum of twenty-four guests, also on the edge of Lake Kariba. It would give Nyaminyami Wildlife Management Trust 5 percent of its gross, which it projected would reach Z$100,000 within a few years.

These proposals for tourist joint ventures were received and discussed at the board meeting with what might be described as giddiness, as if this wildlife cup just kept running over. And they were, of course, far beyond anything Leakey has promoted in Kenya as part of what he calls "bold" programs to bring tourist benefits to rural people. In Kenya, Leakey was giving villages a fraction of gate revenues. In Nyaminyami, the people were negotiating their own benefits and relationships with the tourist industry, and coming out a lot richer.

In the past, before CAMPFIRE came along, only a small portion of the income generated by wildlife in Zimbabwe was returned to the districts where the wildlife was found; and even then the return was indirect—in the form of, say, a school or a health clinic or the grading of a road. This is the pattern throughout Africa: wildlife proceeds generally go into the national treasury and are then more likely to be used for paving a road in a wealthy section of the capital than for extending electricity to a rural area.

In Zimbabwe, now that the district controls wildlife revenues, it is facing a new problem: how to distribute them. One of the principles of CAMPFIRE is that the benefits from wildlife ought to correlate as closely as possible with where the wildlife is. "He who bears the costs gets the benefits," Metcalfe puts the theory. But it is not as simple as it sounds. Do the profits go to the district, the ward (which is a subdivision of the district), the village, or, getting down to the smallest unit, the family or household? The Nyaminyami Wildlife Management Trust decided to divide the 1989 profits among the district's twelve wards. With that, ward councils began thinking about what to do with the money. One considered building public latrines, another housing for teachers and nurses, and a lakeside ward talked about putting up a beer hall for thirsty, hard-drinking fishermen. The residents of Ward B in Negande held a public meeting to decide how to spend their share of the 1989 wildlife profits, which came to Z$16,500. Almost all of the ward's nine hundred adults showed up and the meeting lasted three hours.

The ward's councillor, Patrick Ngenya, a beefy man with muttonchop sideburns and a mustache, said nobody had suggested that the wildlife profits be divided among the families. One proposal was to build a general shop and warehouse, which would be stocked with grain, fertilizers, seeds, basic foodstuffs and agricultural implements, making all of these items more readily available and at lower prices than when they are hauled in by truck from Karoi, the nearest major commercial center, 120 miles distant. It would have been run like a cooperative.

But the cooperative wasn't built, because the women of Ward B said they wanted a grinding mill. The Zimbabwe government, which has done more to improve life for rural people than most African governments— CAMPFIRE is an example—has put up grinding mills around the country, where the women can take their corn and for a few cents have it ground by a machine, usually diesel-powered, since there is rarely electricity in rural areas. Most of the women of Negande Ward B, however, still had to walk a mile or more to the nearest mill. Their desire to build one closer to their village prevailed, and within a few months, the people had made four thousand bricks to house the mill. With future wildlife revenues, the villagers planned to build a footbridge across a stream that their children have to cross on their way to school.

I learned all this about Negande while sitting on the edge of a small field of bright green, knee-high maize stalks; it clashed with the dusty and parched brown surroundings and the mopane trees without leaves in September, the end of the dry winter months. What accounted for the vegetation was a small irrigation system put in by the government a few years ago. A shallow concrete culvert needed repair, and several women hauled plastic buckets filled with sand for mixing with cement. Other women, wearing patterned skirts and bright blouses, their hair tucked into bandannas, were bent over between the corn rows weeding with short-handled hoes. Thirty-nine families had plots in this twenty-two-acre field, and the women said that during the previous growing season, the average yield had been twelve bags of maize per family. Not all families had been so fortunate, however; some got only a bag or two, and a few got nothing. It was not because they were second-class farmers. It was because elephants had raided the field.

Asked if they would like to see all the elephants shot, the women answered with a quiet but unanimous "no." People from outside the country want the skins and tusks, one woman said. Elephants bring food and money, added another. They understood that the district will get the money from the elephants and then will use it to build schools and clinics. (It was clear that Elliot Nobula's efforts to educate the people about the benefits of wildlife have not been in vain.) Still, elephants in general are one matter, but specific elephants are another. The women were insistent that they wanted some elephants shot—any elephants that entered their fields. To guard against that happening, the Nyaminyami Wildlife Trust erected a fence around the field—ten strands of wire from ground level to about six feet, electrified by solar power. The women were clearly pleased about this.

ABOUT the same time that a CAMPFIRE program was launched in Nyaminyami, one was also begun in the district of Guruve, in northern Zimbabwe, along the border with Mozambique. Like Nyaminyami, Guruve is poor and undeveloped; there is too little rain and the soil is sandy. But there is an abundance of wildlife, and it is potentially quite lucrative. Although there is no national park in Guruve and no international-quality facilities to attract tourists, sport hunters like the area, and Guruve is capitalizing on that. Indeed, rather than sell concessions to private safari operators, as Nyaminyami does, Guruve runs its own hunting safaris, which means, of course, that all the profits from hunting, not just a percentage of them, belong to the district. The Guruve council decided to distribute the hunting profits to the wards and in proportion to where the animals had been killed. Most of the hunting was in Masoka—five elephant bulls were shot there—and so it received Z$47,000 from the 1989 revenues.

This unexpected bonanza has had dramatic consequences. For one thing, the Masoka villagers were once intent on using most of their land for cattle, but now they say they can earn more from wildlife, so they plan to set aside the majority of their grazing land for the impala, zebra, buffalo and so on. But the effect of receiving money from wildlife has been more far-reaching.

As part of CAMPFIRE, the residents of Masoka elected a wildlife committee, and it was for this committee to determine how to spend the wildlife revenues. There were no objections when it decided that half of the first year's revenue should be invested in community projects—a school and a health clinic, fences around people's fields to keep the animals out, and salaries for more game guards. The remaining amount, the committee decided, should be divided among the households in the ward, probably the first time that money from wildlife has ever been paid directly to individuals anywhere in Africa. Here is where a controversy erupted and something remarkable occurred.

To distribute the money, the ward's politicians drew up a list containing the names of eighty-six men who were heads of households. At a community meeting, as each man's name was called, he came forward and was handed a paper bag containing the money. Each man received Z$200, which more than doubled most families' income. That was all good. But then several women stood up and complained. Some of the young men who had received money had only very recently married, they said, and they had not really established a household. On the other hand, many of the women had been abandoned by their husbands and were running households with several children. Therefore, they were entitled to receive money, they said. They did not prevail—that time. But the process "let loose a new dynamic of female assertiveness," said Marshall Murphree, an advisor to the CAMPFIRE program in Guruve.

Murphree, who is CAMPFIRE's intellectual father, frequently recounts what happened at that meeting, and with great relish and enthusiasm. Born in Rhodesia of American missionaries, he received a Ph.D. in rural development from the London School of Economics in the early 1950s, and for many years he has been a professor of social sciences at the University of Zimbabwe in Harare and the director of the university's Centre for Applied Social Sciences. The Centre, along with WWF in Harare and Zimbabwe Trust, was critical to getting CAMPFIRE operational. But Murphree's association with wildlife conservation is not solely an academic one. Alone or with his youngest son, Michael, who is an ecologist in Zimbabwe's wildlife department, Murphree spends almost as much time in the bush as in his red-brick office. During a four-month sabbatical in 1990, Murphree traveled in Kenya, and one of the places he visited was Laikipia, where the elephants are wreaking havoc on the shambas and fences have failed. "The whole Kenyan policy against consumptive utilization dooms those elephants," he says.

But for Murphree, as for Metcalfe, the ramifications of CAMPFIRE extend beyond conservation. In addition to giving a new awareness and assertiveness to women, Murphree says, CAMPFIRE is teaching the people something about involvement in decision-making. He explains that while the politicians in Masoka had drawn up a list of eighty-six households to receive money, in fact, there were only sixty-nine households in Masoka; the politicians, desirous of helping a few friends, had padded the list. Many people in the community were angry when they realized what had been done. In the future, Murphree said, "they are going to make bloody sure that they are involved in drawing up that list." In other words, CAMPFIRE is developing grass-roots democracy. An individual who acquires the right to decide about the wildlife in his area and about how the money from that wildlife is spent might start asking how politicians in the capital spend public money; he might even want a say in electing the country's president. In Africa, these are radical concepts.

IF AFRICA'S WILDLIFE is to be saved, it will not be with celebrity appeals, or more firearms for anti-poaching units, or ivory bans. It will require radical policies and changes in attitudes. Westerners who contribute to conservation organizations will have to understand and accept sustainable utilization. Conservation organizations will have to stand up for their conservation principles and not be intimidated by the fund-raisers. Tour operators, hotel owners and governments will have to be sure that local people get the lion's share of benefits from wildlife, and not the carcasses after they have been picked over by the vultures.

David Western says that if Kenya had adopted the Zimbabwe approach to wildlife utilization and allowed landowners, private and communal, to reap the benefits, the Kenya Wildlife Service "would have become financially self-sufficient fairly quickly." Because it has proceeded with such caution, the Kenyan government "is locked into dependence on aid," he says. Kenya, which is receiving more than $150 million from the international community for conservation, would need only a fraction of that, according to Western, if Kenyan landowners had an incentive to protect the wildlife.

If villagers living around a park make money from wildlife, they will protect not only the animals on their own land, but those inside the park as well, for when the animals wander from the park, landowners can utilize them. In effect, the park becomes the villagers' bank and the wild animals in the park their assets. This will provide a powerful incentive against poaching: people are not likely to rob their own bank, and will report those who do.

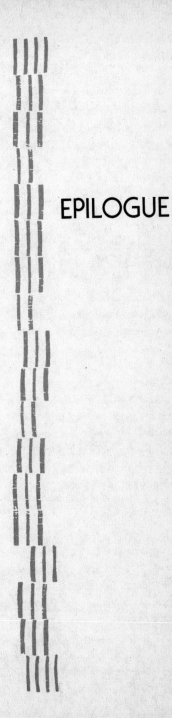

EPILOGUE

||||| IN FEBRUARY 1992, the governments that are members of CITES gathered in Kyoto, their first meeting since the one in Lausanne in 1989 when the elephant had been declared an endangered species and ivory trading banned. There was no serious movement at Kyoto to have the African elephant taken off Appendix I, but the southern African nations wanted to have their elephant populations "down-listed" to Appendix II, which meant they would be allowed to trade in ivory; knowing the strength of the opposition to ivory trading, however, they were willing to agree to a moratorium for two years. At Lausanne, it had been agreed that if a country could demonstrate that it was managing its elephant populations well it would be entitled to down-listing. At least four countries—Zimbabwe, Botswana, South Africa and Namibia—satisfied the criteria. But they didn't stand a chance. "No decision at Kyoto was made on the basis of science," a senior officer of WWF-US said after the meeting. "It was all politics." The politics, the lobbying, began well before the meeting, and though it was hard to believe, the pro-ban advocates were more shrill than they had been three years earlier.

In Britain, Allan Thornton, director of the Environmental Investigation Agency (EIA), revved up his operation. In the weeks before Kyoto, EIA ran ads in the British newspapers, including the front page of *The Independent*. Next to the picture of an elephant family, the bold print said, "WE DIDNT SAVE THEM FROM POACHERS JUST TO HAVE THEM CARVED UP BY POLITICIANS." The text of the ad read, "In 1992, 8,000 elephants will be shot by Zimbabwe, Botswana and South Africa for their skins and ivory." The British government, the ad noted, supported allowing these countries to sell skins. Not ivory, just skins, but even that was intolerable for EIA. The ad concluded, "If you think live elephants are priceless, help us to ensure that dead elephants are worthless." And, of course, EIA asked for a donation.

This time, EIA expanded its reach, taking its crusade to the United States, with its operations still financed primarily by Christine Stevens of the Animal Welfare Institute. One week before the CITES meeting, EIA held a press conference in Washington, D.C. "SOUTH AFRICA AND ZIMBABWE MILITARY EXPOSED IN IVORY SMUGGLING COVER-UP" was the headline on their press release. EIA released a fifty-six-page report which the organization said provided "shocking evidence of official involvement in the illegal trade." And EIA asserted that no southern African country met the criteria for down-listing.

It was true that corrupt officials in Zimbabwe and South Africa were involved in the ivory (and rhino horn) trade, but corrupt officials were hampering effective conservation in every country, including Kenya, about which EIA remained silent. EIA aimed at South Africa because even though Nelson Mandela had been released and the South African government was in negotiations with the African National Congress, South Africa was still a villain. And EIA attacked Zimbabwe because the country had the strongest case for being allowed to trade in ivory.

EIA's intemperance and tendentiousness were predictable. But it wasn't alone. Reflecting the abyss into which the entire controversy had now fallen, the African Wildlife Foundation matched EIA. A few weeks before the Kyoto meeting, AWF sent out more than 100,000 letters to its members and others whose names were on its mailing list. The yellow envelope had PRIORITY ALERT blazoned across it. Inside, the letter, signed by AWF president Schindler, began, "I need your help, today, as fast as possible." At Kyoto, the letter said, the members of CITES would consider "a heavily promoted scheme to *repeal* the ban on international ivory trade." This was blatantly misleading, arguably deceitful—no one was seriously asking for a repeal of the ban; a few countries were asking for a limited exemption.

A few paragraphs later, Schindler wrote: "Several nations in southern Africa (Botswana, Malawi, Namibia, Zimbabwe and Zambia—all quietly supported by South Africa) say that *their* ivory should receive a special exemption from the ban." That was at least true, but rather than explaining why, AWF condemned the idea. Not on the merits, but by attacking South Africa, of course. If the idea was "quietly supported" by South Africa, there was surely something sinister afoot, AWF implied. More seriously, the *African* Wildlife Foundation was opposing something that five black African countries thought was best for them and the elephants, and these countries had close to half of the continent's elephants.

Now Schindler was warming up. "Just imagine what will happen if the ivory ban *really is* overturned!" he warned (repeating the falsehood that this is what the southern Africans were seeking). "As soon as word gets out, elephant poachers will resume their butchery across Africa, trying to 'make up for lost time' since the ban went into effect in 1990. *And they'll get away with it!* Because Africa is vast, illegal ivory will burst out through every border."

"Ivory traders" were engaged in an "orchestrated press campaign," Schindler said, and they were getting "*big play*" in the world's media.

Ivory traders, in this instance, was synonymous with greed. But it wasn't greedy ivory traders who most desperately wanted an exemption from the ban. It was poor Africans in places like Nyaminyami, people and places that Schindler and the executives and wealthy, upper-class trustees at AWF knew little about, if they had visited them at all. Schindler's complaint about "orchestrated campaigns" and "big play" was a caricature of reality: It was AWF that was spending tens of thousands of dollars to orchestrate campaigns, and they invariably got "big play," as there were few journalists who weren't sympathetic.

Schindler wrote: "They [the ivory traders] say the ivory trade is necessary to maintain elephants' commercial value. In other words, we must kill elephants in order to save them—an irony elephants can't live with!"

It sounds contradictory to say that we must kill elephants to save them. Yet, this is what AWF has believed, and acted upon—in the cullings in Murchison Falls and Rwanda, for example. And, of course, AWF had no problems with big-game hunters killing elephants and putting their ivory tusks on display.

As Schindler approached the end of his letter, he wound up with his pitch for money:

> Needless to say, all this is taking a lot out of us. But there is no alternative. Because if the ivory ban *is* lifted . . . well, I shudder at the thought of the consequences!
>
> Lift that ban and I guarantee you that *a new kind of butchery will descend on Africa's elephants*. The slaughter will start anew; the elephant herds will once again be ravaged; courageous park rangers will once again have to put their lives on the line.
>
> WE JUST CAN'T LET THIS HAPPEN!

Please, sign and mail the enclosed postcard *today*. And then *send us as generous a gift as possible*. It *really is* up to you.

Back in February 1989, when several animal rights organizations had petitioned the Bush administration to have the elephant declared an endangered species under American law, AWF had not joined in the legal action. It wasn't because AWF objected to the action's purpose. Rather, it was because AWF didn't like the company. "We're not in those circles," McMeekin said dismissively, a wave of her braceleted wrist leaving no doubt that AWF considered itself superior to those groups. If it was, it is no longer. The African Wildlife Foundation has sacrificed the pride that it could once claim in being a leader in African conservation. It has become a follower, of public emotion.

THROUGHOUT the elephant controversy, the advocates of a ban on ivory trading said there had been more than a million elephants on the continent a decade ago, and today there are only 750,000; some organizations said 600,000, and the real alarmists shouted there were only 400,000. The figures were notoriously unreliable; nobody really knows how many elephants there are. On a continent where most governments can't even count their human populations, how can they accurately count their elephants, especially those in the forest? (Conservation organizations probably spend more money per elephant on counting elephants than African governments can afford to spend per human being on their human censuses.) Whatever the numbers, the fact is that elephant populations have been declining. But what is most astonishing is not that there are 750,000 or 600,000 elephants left on the continent. What's extraordinary is that there are still that many, even if only 400,000. After all, how many grizzly bears are there in California? How many wolves in England or France?

The advocates of the ban can rightfully claim that poaching has declined and the price of ivory has fallen. But that doesn't mean it was the right remedy. It is an extreme measure—just as AWF believed when it first asked people not to buy ivory but consciously stopped short of asking for a ban. Maybe the ban has acted as a deterrent, but so might cutting off the hand of a thief act as a deterrent to robbery.

Still, I could accept an ivory ban. Elephants are sentient animals: they form family relationships, grieve over the death of relatives, communicate over long distances with sounds we cannot hear. I have felt the thrill of going for a morning walk and coming upon a long line of elephants ambling across the grasslands, or an infant waddling alongside its mother, or a bull putting its tusks on each side of an acacia tree, then with its huge forehead shaking the tree until the pods fall and picking them up with its trunk. It is painful, the thought of killing one of these creatures just to make a profit from its ivory. But the poverty of Africans is just as painful, so I could accept an ivory ban if the world community compensated African countries for what they lost in ivory revenues, and if the developed world came up with money for conservation.

That doesn't mean giving Kenya or Tanzania or Zambia more firearms, helicopters and sophisticated equipment, and training paramilitary units. Some of this may be needed, but it is the easy way to deal with poaching—it is aimed at the little guy, just as the politically expedient way to go after the drug problem is to arrest the user or street pusher. If the West were really serious about stopping poaching, it would put money and resources—the FBI, Interpol—into catching the traders and the middlemen, the men who are paying the poachers, buying the ivory and making the huge profits. There has never been an arrest of one of these guys. It is less cumbersome and less expensive to kill some illiterate poacher.

GARTH OWEN-SMITH said during one of our conversations in the Namib Desert: "Africa's wildlife does not belong to the world. It belongs to Africa. It is an African resource to be used by Africans. Decisions about African wildlife will not be made in Washington or Geneva. They will be made in Africa." What he meant, of course, was that the decisions *should* not be made in the West, but in Africa. That aside, his comment raises a troubling but fundamental question: Whose wildlife is it?

Underlying the CAMPFIRE program is the premise that the wildlife belongs to the person on whose land it is found. This is an uncomfortable proposition, because taken to its fullest extension it means private ownership of parks and wildlife. Already in Kenya a few wealthy individuals have their own rhino and elephants in their own game parks. I don't like it. Surely there is a public right to the wildlife, just as there is to open spaces—the right to enjoy them without somebody making a profit.

If private ownership is one extreme, however, the other is the assumption in the West that the wild animals of Africa, like many other wonders of the world, belong to the world. I tend to believe that. But then I wonder. Elephants and rhino, lions and leopards, are not like whales living in international waters. For the most part, these land animals live within the borders of a specific country. Why don't these natural resources therefore belong to that country, just as copper, coal and oil belong to a country? Do we have more right to tell the Zimbabweans what to do with their elephants than we do to tell Saudi Arabia what to do with its oil? It is surely more noble to argue for saving elephants than for conserving oil. But I wouldn't want to put that proposition to a vote (except at a meeting of Luddites). Nor are the wild animals of Africa like the rain forests in Brazil. The destruction of the forests will have tangible adverse consequences for the entire planet—the greenhouse effect, for example. The same cannot be said about the elephants in Africa. But we will be poorer in spirit if they disappear; we will have lost a rich heritage.

If the wildlife of Africa is a priceless world heritage, if it belongs to all of us, and not just to the present generations, but to our children's children, then the world has an obligation to pay for its preservation. It is an obligation we haven't met; it's too easy to impose bans—and make the Africans pay. Someday the Africans are going to stand up to the rest of the world and do what they decide is best for themselves. If they decide to trade in ivory, what are we going to do? Send in the Marines? Africans will not always allow themselves to be dominated by Europe and the United States. They threw off colonialism; one day they will throw off eco-colonialism.

The confrontation need not come. It can be avoided with far less expenditure for conservation than is currently thought. The two most successful conservation programs in Africa—the community game guard project in the Kaokoveld and CAMPFIRE in Nyaminyami—are two of the least expensive. What makes them successful is that they are premised on the needs of people. All we have to do to preserve Africa's wildlife heritage is care about the people as much as we care about the wildlife. Both are in the hands of man.

ACKNOWLEDGMENTS
NOTES
SELECTED BIBLIOGRAPHY
INDEX

ACKNOWLEDGMENTS

Many of the individuals I have talked about in these pages deserve further recognition for their help. Among them are Garth Owen-Smith and Margaret Jacobsohn, in Namibia; Simon Metcalfe, in Zimbabwe; and in Tanzania, Costa Mlay and John Bennett, a superb guide, to politics and culture as well as wildlife. I don't think these people had any idea how pestering a journalist can be, but no matter how many times I visited or wrote or called, they were gracious and helpful. My thanks also to Sue Armstrong, who shared notes and interviews during the Botswana conference; Eleanor Patterson, of the Kalahari Conservation Society; and Laing Foster, who helped me in Makao.

In Kenya, I was the beneficiary of the professional generosity of Perez Olindo, and David Western became my professor of the history of conservation in Africa. I owe special thanks to WWF's Holly Dublin—spirited, intellectual and committed to bringing more Africans into conservation— and to Bob Munro, a humanitarian and environmentalist who recognizes that the two must be linked if man and the environment are to survive; he read drafts of the manuscript and constantly challenged me (and beat me too often in tennis). Still in Kenya, I enjoyed the friendship and benefitted from the knowledge of Petal and David Allen, and Jens and Tuti Hessel, who have been attending to safari clients for years. Gitashvar Shah at the Antiquity Shop in Nairobi found old books and tutored me in the history of East African tourism. Dan Shiyukah kept my computer going. Hanson Otundo did just about everything—spending hours at the copying machine, locating old Kenyan newspapers, and dealing with diplomatic bureaucracies to get me visas. Hannah Wakiru, Stanley Njaungiri and Grace Okeyo were always helpful and cheerful. It is almost impossible for me to express my gratitude and affection for Alphonce Odoyo. And Waithaka kept my spirits high, his life putting everything in perspective.

Abroad, first in Britain, I had the invaluable assistance of Maryann Bird. Scouring through libraries and archives, she found the London newspapers with the accounts of the 1900 and 1933 Conventions, Huxley's articles in *The Observer*, the *Strand Magazine* with Churchill's articles, and much more. My thanks also to Gina Douglas at the Linnean Society of London; Amanda Hillier at the Fauna Preservation Society; Fred Pearce, for his book *Green Warriors* and for leading me to Max Nicholson and others; and Sarah Glasby. In the United States, Jim Sugarman, Khalid Khalid and Julie Gozan at the Multinationals and Development Clearinghouse in Washington, D.C., became available at a critical moment and got me more materials, and faster, than I could have imagined possible. As on my earlier books, Craig Nelson also did research. I am grateful for the extraordinary fact-checking labors of Schellie Hagan and Patti Hagan, who worked over key parts of the text under extreme pressure.

As is evident from these pages, I had the cooperation of many current and former employees at WWF. It should be equally clear why they cannot be thanked by name. As one of them said, "I don't want to be around when the witch-hunt starts." The galleys were read by one person with WWF, one with AWF and one with IUCN. They saved me from embarrassing factual errors and made many suggestions, not all of which I accepted. Without question, the book is better because of their contributions. Unfortunately, each asked to remain anonymous.

Every writer needs the assistance of colleagues, and I received it. Alan Riding, one of the finest journalists in the profession today, volunteered to read a draft at a time when I was struggling. Ben Cheever, Johanna McGeary and Fiammetta Rocco read drafts and provided needed advice; Chris Dickey sketched ideas for organization, which I taped on the wall above my computer.

I was extremely fortunate in being able to write for Bob Gottlieb at *The New Yorker*. He gave me assignments like "Go to Peru," and "Why don't you go to Kurdistan." No long discussions, no memos—those were the parameters. He trusted journalists to find the story. When a piece was submitted, Bob got back to the writer twenty-four hours later—when he was slow. And there aren't many editors like *The New Yorker*'s "Chip" McGrath, for many years the magazine's "number two"—a person of remarkable decency and grace, who is constantly encouraging writers, bringing out the best in them. My editor at the magazine was Pat Crow. He is the best in the business. And with extraordinary pleasantness, Martha Kaplan, Chris Knutsen and Nancy Boensch at the magazine made my work away from "home" possible.

My editor on this book, as on my previous ones, was Jonathan Segal. The author-editor relationship is not an easy one, and in response to one of my grumblings, Jonathan said, "I'm pushing you." He certainly did. I'm grateful—now. One hears over and over again that there are few editors left in publishing who actually sit down with a manuscript and edit it. Jonathan did. At one point, Gloria Loomis, my agent, said about Jonathan, "He's one of the best there is." Now, I know why. At Knopf, my thanks also to Ida Giragossian, who was patient with my requests and hardworking in fulfilling them, and to Karen Mugler, who under tremendous pressure gave the manuscript extra effort and attention.

Nonwriters (and even some fledgling writers) often ask, Why does a writer need an agent? One answer, of course, is that she spares you from having to deal directly with the publisher and gets you as much money as possible. Gloria Loomis does that and much more. When I'm down and struggling, she says nice things and encourages me. When I need to be kicked, she kicks me. On this book she would never let me quit, though many times I wanted to. As I've said often, Gloria is much more than an agent: she is a friend.

As everyone who knows me will understand, this book would not have been possible without one person, Jane Perlez. It is not easy to live with a writer—at least not this one, on this book—and at times when she was off dealing with Africa's dictators, wars and famine, I wondered if she didn't find that more pleasant than being at home. But she was always here when I needed her, as she has always been.

R.T.B.
Nairobi, Kenya

NOTES

Most of this book is based on my own experiences and interviews, which I have not noted, except for a few instances that I think might be of value to other journalists and historians. The notes below are also, for the most part, limited to material not in the general public domain.

ONE LISTENING TO AFRICA

13 Most of the material about Owen-Smith came from him when I was in Kaokoveld; I filled in gaps from Reardon, *The Besieged Desert*; and *Kaokoveld: The Last Wilderness*, by Hall-Martin.

Sadly, very little has been written about the Himba and Herero. *Himba: Nomads of Namibia* is a photograph book with enlightening text by Margaret Jacobsohn.

18 AWF's praise for Moi: AWF's *Wildlife News*, Spring 1989.

"faint of heart": Trip Report, Visit to Zimbabwe and Botswana, August 5–20, 1990. The American delegation was headed by Constance Harriman, assistant secretary for fish, wildlife and parks, U.S. Department of Interior.

Leakey's comments about the number of poachers was reported by the American embassy in Nairobi to Washington, cable number 15500, dated May 22, 1989. (Hereafter cables will be cited by their place of origin, number and date.)

19 *The Guardian* editorial: September 4, 1990.

26 Martin, "It doesn't matter": Interview.

TWO THE WHITE MAN'S GAME

There is no one single history of conservation in Africa; it needs to be written. The most comprehensive account I found is a Ph.D. thesis written in 1978 by Nora Kelly, at Simon Fraser University: "In Wildest Africa: The Preservation of Game in Kenya 1895–1933." Thoroughly researched and well written, it examines everything from settler and African attitudes toward wildlife to the ivory trade. I also relied on *The Empire of Nature: Hunting, Conservation and British Imperialism*, by John M. MacKenzie, a history lecturer at the University of Lancaster; it has an intended academic tone to it—it is heavy with footnotes—but it will be of interest and value to the general reader.

There are volumes of books and academic papers and generously funded studies about the behavior of elephants, lions, cheetah, wild dogs and other wild animals, about everything from their mating habits to their social relationships, but by contrast virtually nothing has been written about the relationships between the African people and the wildlife. The early colonialists did not care what Africans thought; and the current generation of conservationists working in Africa has not understood that a knowledge of African traditions and values can determine the success of their programs.

For the history of conservation generally and particularly in the United States, there are two very good books, both by Roderick Nash: *Wilderness and the American Mind* and *The Rights of Nature*. I also found helpful *Righteous Pilgrim*, by T. H. Watkins, a biography of Harold Ickes, who as Secretary of the Interior advanced the conservation agenda in the United States as much as any Washington official ever has. See also Oelschlaeger, *The Idea of Wilderness*.

Many books have been written about the European colonization of Africa, but I relied mostly on a recent one, *The Scramble for Africa*, by Thomas Pakenham.

39 *Times* of London, May 30, 1900.

40 Locating a copy of the 1900 Convention was more difficult than I thought it would be. I eventually found one in vol. 1 (1904) of the *Journal of the Society for the Preservation of the Wild Fauna of the Empire* (hereafter, JSPFE). It is also in the *Times* of London, May 30, 1900.

41 Pease, "Most settlers": Pease, Sir Alfred E., "The Southern Game Reserve, British East Africa," JSPFE 6 (1913): 24.

    "Among our enemies": "Kenya's Game," JSPFE, New Series 52 (December 1945): 33–34.

42 Caldwell: Caldwell, Capt. Keith, "Game Wardens of Kenya," JSPFE, New Series 35 (December 1938): 23–25. Caldwell, "Game Preservation: Its Aims and Objects," JSPFE, New Series 4 (July 1924): 45.

43 Selous: quoted in Simon, *Between the Sunlight and the Thunder*, 41.

45 Eliot: "Extract from Sir Charles Eliot's Reports of the British East Africa Protectorate for the Years 1902 and 1903," JSPFE 1 (1904): 49–54.

47 Stanley and Tippu-Tib: vol. 2 of *Through the Dark Continent*, 95; vol. 1 of *In Darkest Africa*, 63–64.

48 Southworth: Southworth, *Four Thousand Miles of African Travel*, 178.
    Thomson: quoted in MacKenzie, *The Empire of Nature*, 150.
    For a concise history of the Imperial British East Africa Company, see Kelly, "In Wildest Africa," 88–98.

49 Sadler: "Extract from the Report of Col. Hayes Sadler for the Uganda Protectorate for the Years 1902 and 1903," JSPFE 1 (1904): 55–57.

50 Caldwell: Caldwell, "Game Preservation: Its Aims and Objects," JSPFE, New Series 4 (July 1924): 45.
    sale of ivory financed the Kenyan game department: Many of the Kenyan Colony Game Department reports were published in the *Journal of the Society for the Preservation of the Wild Fauna of the Empire*. E.g.: "Kenya Colony Game Department, Annual Report for 1932, 1933, and 1934," JSPFE, New Series 27 (January 1936). With some luck and diligence they can also be found in Nairobi, in the basement of the MacMillan Library.

51 AWF's warning: African Wildlife Leadership Foundation *News*, Winter 1973: 1.
    Jarman: "Confidential Report to the Chief Game Warden Concerning Elephants and the Ivory Trade in Kenya," October 25, 1973. Copy in author's files.
    Parker's 27-page report, dated October 18, 1973, has no title. Copy in author's files.
    Sunday Times: Three-part series about corruption in Kenya appeared August 10, 17 and 24, 1975.

54 The account of AWF's founding and Train's role in it comes primarily from author's interview with Train in May 1991. (He did not, however, tell me that he was related to the Erroll family.)

56 Markham's account of Guest's hunting safari: *West With the Night*, 210, 220.
Biographical sketches of AWF's first trustees and the editorial appeared in the organization's first newsletter, *African Wildlife News*, January 1963.

60 Huxley's articles: *The Observer*, November 13, 20 and 27, 1960.

61 Stolan letter. Copy in author's files.

62 Author's interview with Nicholson, April 1991. For more biographical matter about
Nicholson and the founding of WWF, see Pearce's *Green Warriors*, 1–9. Nicholson
has contributed two valuable books to the history of conservation, *The Environmental
Revolution* (1970) and *The New Environmental Age* (1987).

63 Minutes of meetings of founding group are in boxes of documents that Nicholson has
donated to the Linnean Society in London. Hereafter referred to as Nicholson,
Linnean Society.

64 Scott, "I hope this was all right": handwritten note from Scott to Nicholson, July 14,
1961; Nicholson, Linnean Society.
"State of Emergency," Nyerere's and Scott's reactions: Nicholson, Linnean Society.

65 "beacon in the history": Kinloch, *The Shamba Raiders*, 342–43.
There is a dispute about who wrote the Arusha Manifesto. In an interview with the
author in 1991, Ian MacPhail asserted that he did—a claim that has found some
acceptance (see, for example, *Wildfight: A History of Conservation*, p. 45). Nicholson,
however, told me that it was he who wrote it, and he dismissed any contribution by
MacPhail. WWF documents seen by the author show that Nicholson, MacPhail and
others all had a hand in drafting it.
Daily Mirror: October 9, 1961.

66 "unctuous," "too wordy" and "great bore": Philip memorandum to Scott, and Scott
to Nicholson, July 20, 1961. Nicholson, Linnean Society.
Scott to Bernhard: August 9, 1961. Nicholson, Linnean Society.

68 1001 Club: Lists of members in 1987 and 1989 in author's files. *Private Eye* carried
the names of some members in articles on August 1, August 15 and September 27,
1980.

70 SanGeorge, de Haes not seconded. Interview, April 1991.
"period of secondment": Letter from WWF's executive vice-president, Luc Hoff-
mann, to "WWF Honorary Officers," dated August 14, 1975. Copy in author's files.
SanGeorge, "an anonymous donor": Interview, April 1991.
"scandal": Interview, April 1991.

71 efforts of British, Netherlands and Swiss and Norman's role: Interviews.

73 criticism of WWF-US and Train response: "Confidential. Agenda and Supporting
Documentation for the Meeting of the WWF International Board of Trustees," Buckingham Palace, London, July 3, 1990.

74 "Its financial accounts are not": Interview.
fight between U.S. and International: Interviews with officials at WWF-US and
WWF-International.
Train's proposal for one-year contract: Confidential minutes of the meeting of board
of trustees, Buckingham Palace, July 3, 1990.

76 Phillipson Report: A copy of Phillipson's "Executive Summary," dated September
1989 and marked "Confidential," is in author's files; as are portions of the full report,
marked STRICTLY CONFIDENTIAL and NOT FOR FURTHER CIRCULATION.
Geer: Confidential Memorandum, September 22, 1989. Copy in author's files.

77 Philip's reaction, "not altogether enthusiastic": Memorandum to de Haes, October
2, 1989. Copy in author's files.

78 "enormous difference to staff morale": WWF document II 3792 Zimbabwe—Black
Rhino Conservation. Copy in author's files. Brown's article, September 4, 1990.
Brown, *The Guardian*: September 4, 1990.

78 guns for Tanzania: WWF document II 3173 Tanzania—General Support for the Selous Game Reserve, November 11, 1987.

79 Powell's article was datelined Nairobi, July 6, 1989. Ellis, *Africa Confidential*, July 28, 1989. Ellis, *The Independent*, January 8, 1991. Stirling, Crooke and KAS Limited sued Reuters and *Africa Confidential* for libel, and both defendants settled. (It is far easier for a plaintiff to prevail under British libel laws than under American laws. To begin with, under British law the plaintiff does not have the burden of proving that a statement is false. Moreover, under American law, a plaintiff who is a public figure must show that a false statement was made with malice or a reckless disregard of the truth. Under British law it is almost enough for the plaintiff to show that his reputation has been harmed by the published statements.) The settlements did not dispute the fact that the undercover operation had been set up to catch dealers in rhino horn and ivory. In a note to subscribers, Reuters said, "Reuters regrets any implication in its story that KAS was set up to destabilize black African countries, under cover of wildlife conservation. Any suggestion to this effect was unintentional and erroneous." *Africa Confidential* issued an apology to Stirling and others it had named in the original article and said they were "happy to emphasize their commitment to wildlife preservation" (*Africa Confidential*, November 17, 1989).
SanGeorge's transcript of Ellis interview: Copy in author's files.
WWF statement, "It is, and always has been": January 5, 1991. Copy in author's files. Interestingly, WWF's January 5 statement seems to have "disappeared" from WWF's files. When I interviewed SanGeorge, in April 1991, he went through his files and pulled out what he said were all of WWF's statements pertaining to Operation Lock. The January 5 release was not among the material he gave me. Perhaps this was because after the statement was released, Stroebel, in a letter that went to de Haes and SanGeorge, said, "Until now I have kept quiet on this whole matter. . . . I intend doing this in the future, unless of course WWF-International releases statements deploring the conduct of Dr. Hanks. . . ." It was following this communication from Stroebel that WWF-International sent out its memorandum to the national organizations, which, while not so directly blaming Hanks, nevertheless fell far short of the truth.

80 Stroebel's explanations of what happened: Letter to "HRH The Duke of Edinburgh," January 6, 1991; memorandum to Lord Benson (whom WWF-International brought in to investigate), January 8, 1991. Copies in author's files.
Bernhard asking for funds to Juliana's account: Memorandum from Tatiana Gortcha-cow to Charles de Haes, January 12, 1989. Copy in author's files.
"agreed to the use": Stroebel memo to Benson, January 8, 1991.

87 Western, "would not solve": *New York Times*, May 15, 1988. At the time of AWF's press conference, Philip Shabecoff, a veteran reporter, decided to go beyond what AWF was saying and called around for other views, Western being one of those he called.

89 Minutes of WWF's meeting in Lusaka and the post-meeting report: in author's files.

90 Schindler's letter, June 10, 1988. Copy in author's files.

94 "is not yet endangered": Memorandum from Jorgen Thomsen and Tom McShane, re: WWF Elephant Action Plan, May 24, 1988.
The best history and explanation of CITES is in *International Wildlife Law*, by Simon Lyster; an analysis of all international conservation treaties, the book is a valuable resource. CITES has published its own history, *The Evolution of CITES*.

95 "the single most important conservation measure": Nash, *The Rights of Nature*, 175.

97 "no action," "should not sit on the fence," "no choice": from the minutes of the meeting.

100 "trying to bring our members along": Interview, May 1991.

102 Parker, *Ivory Crisis*, 68. This book, which explores the history of ivory and European conservation policies in Africa, deserves to be considered among the most important conservation books about Africa; that it has not had a wider audience and recognition is not only because of the author's iconoclastic views, but also because it was published as a coffee table photographic book. Parker's partner in iconoclasm has long been Alistair Graham, an ecologist who worked as a warden in Kenya for a time; his *The Gardeners of Eden*, about conservation history and practices, is essential reading, the first half seriously, the second half with some skepticism as Graham invokes Freud to explain man's infatuation with the giraffe.

Rwanda cull: Interview and Parker, "An Elephant Extermination," *Environmental Conservation* 6 (Winter 1979): 305–9. (*Environmental Conservation* is published by The Foundation for Environmental Conservation in Switzerland.) AWF's role: Parker's interview and cable from American embassy in Kigali to embassy in Nairobi: Kigali 27, January 14, 1975.

Schaaf: "The Reason Why Elephants and Hippos Are Shot in Murchison Falls Park," Ref: AWLF IV–1. Copy in author's files.

104 Much has been written about the Tsavo cull, in scientific and conservation journals and in books. See, e.g., Rensberger, *The Cult of the Wild*, a book that challenges many of the romantic notions that Westerners have about wildlife and ought to be on the top of any reading list about African wildlife; published in 1977, it is still timely and should be brought out again in paperback. Also Parker, *Ivory Crisis*, 68–72.

105 Thornton: *The Guardian*, June 26, 1989.

106 Cumming and Craig: Interviews.

107 Moss's views on culling: Interview.

108 Copies of the memoranda and comments from national organizations are in the author's files, as is Reilly's letter to Lyster, November 11, 1988.

112 "obstreperous": Opinion of Federal Magistrate Thomas P. Smith, Federal District Court, Norwalk, Conn., April 24, 1992.

113 "concepts are not understood": Memorandum from Jorgen Thomsen and Tom McShane, re: WWF Elephant Action Plan, May 24, 1988.

115 Jones's views: "CITES African Elephant Working Group. Summary of 1988 Meeting in Nairobi, Kenya," by Marshall P. Jones.

116 Caughley: "A Projection of Ivory Production and Its Implications for the Conservation of African Elephants," December 1988.

"A proposition for an all-embracing moratorium": "Submission to the CITES African Elephant Working Group," by I. Douglas-Hamilton, consultant to EEC/WWF African Elephant Population Study.

117 Oria, "hole in the head": *The Independent*, February 13, 1992.

119 Feral's and McMeekin's claims about why Sotheby's canceled the auction: Interviews.

120 The amount of money the ads raised was provided to the author by the organizations.

121 "You cannot believe," "everyone agitating": Stout memorandum February 20, 1988. Copies in author's files.

122 "Prima bwanas" is from the Washington *Post*, March 15, 1988, a lengthy and well-written article by Mary Battiata, which appeared in the paper's vaunted Style section, about the conservation community in Nairobi in the context of the elephant controversy.

123 Stanley Price and Bradley Martin meetings with U.S. diplomat: reported to Washington in Nairobi 09770, March 30, 1989.

127 The amount of money the Animal Welfare Institute gave to the Environmental Investigation Agency was reported by the former in its Form 990, which all American charitable organizations are required to file with the IRS, and which are available to the public through the Freedom of Information Act.

127 Thornton's account of how he got into meetings, how he recruited Thomsen, and his
     work in Tanzania is in his *To Save an Elephant*. It says a lot about this book that the
     authors spell Thomsen's name "Thompson," and he is one of the heroes of their
     account.

129 Philip, " 'knee-jerk' reaction": Memorandum from Philip to de Haes, August 11,
     1989. Copy in author's files.
     "quick turnabout": Nairobi cable number 14471, May 11, 1989.

130 Bradley Martin's opposition to ivory ban: Interview, January 1989.
     "alarmed by the GOK's inaction": Nairobi 09770, March 30, 1989.

134 Leakey's report: "A Policy Framework and Five-Year Investment Program," Kenya
     Wildlife Service, revised edition, June 1990. This report was circulated publicly. The
     final report was issued in November 1990: "A Policy Framework and Development
     Programme, 1991–1996."

136 Douglas-Hamilton report on the Mara: "Identification Study for the Conservation
     and Sustainable Use of the Natural Resources in the Kenyan Portion of the Mara-
     Serengeti Ecosystem," Final Report, December 1988.

137 Rating of environmental groups: "Inside the Environmental Groups," *Outside*, Sep-
     tember 1990. Schindler's letter, August 14, 1990.

138 How widespread African support: Memorandum from Simon Lyster, ref: SL/JA/
     May389/7, May 18, 1989. Copy in author's files.

142 Pearce memo to Cobb: May 27, 1989. Copy in author's files. For a fuller exposition
     of the economists' argument against the ban, see Barbier et al., *Elephants, Economics
     and Ivory*, by the economists who were members of the Review Group.
     Cumming's response: "Review of the Ivory Trade and the Future of the African
     Elephant: Main Report," September 2, 1989.

149 I was present at the burn. The observations of the eighteen-year-old and the social
     worker about the ban were made to the author.
     "unacceptable waste of resources": Nairobi 20820, July 15, 1989.

152 "too sympathetic": Interview.
     "undermines" and "to hold his fire": State Department cable number 281686, Sep-
     tember 1, 1989.

154 "big lie," "double counting," "fanatic": Interviews.

THREE WHOSE HERITAGE IS IT?

     I was in Ngorongoro and the Serengeti several times from 1989 to 1992, and most of
     this chapter comes from those experiences. Surprisingly, very little has been written
     about the crater and the dispute that led to the Maasai being evicted first from the
     Serengeti then from Ngorongoro Crater. *Ngorongoro: The Eighth Wonder*, by Henry
     Fosbrooke, is the only book about the crater I found, and it is an account of everything
     from the crater's geological history to the lives of the tribes who have lived there;
     published in 1972, it is another of those books which I believe should be reissued,
     surely of interest to anyone visiting the crater. *The Last Place on Earth*, by the late
     Harold T. P. Hayes, contains the only account of the 1950s fight over the Serengeti
     I was able to find. Hayes was an acclaimed writer, and this book captures the majesty
     of the Serengeti better than any; it is also an insightful account of the conservationists
     who populated East Africa in the 1960s; the book suffers only from the absence of an
     index. There are many books about the Maasai. In addition to Thomson's classic
     Through Masai Land, I relied on *Maasai*, by Saitoti and Beckwith; *Maasai Days*, by
     Cheryl Bentsen; *Kenya*, by Norman Leys; and Sankan, *The Maasai*.

167 Hingston: "Report on a Mission to East Africa for the Purpose of Investigating the
     Most Suitable Methods of Ensuring the Protection of Its Indigenous Fauna," by

Major R. W. G. Hingston, JSPFE, New Series 12 (1930): 21–57. See also MacKenzie, *The Empire of Nature*, 269–70.

168 The 1933 conference was reported in the *Times* of London, November 1–7 and 9, 1933.

172 Sessional Paper: "The Serengeti National Park," Sessional Paper no. 1–1956, Legislative Council of Tanganyika, 1956, printed by the government printer, Dar es Salaam. "appalled": Turner, *My Serengeti Years*, 43.

I found Talbot's report, dated April 30, 1956, and Coolidge letter, November 21, 1956, among the papers of Louis Leakey at the Kenya Museum. It was in Leakey's papers that I found most of the documents that allowed me to put together the story of the fight over the Serengeti, a story told in bits and pieces and incompletely in other books. Sadly, Leakey's papers—and there are more than just about the Serengeti—are not well kept, and anyone concerned about the preservation of these historically valuable documents should provide funding quickly.

173 Pearsall: "Report on an Ecological Survey of the Serengeti National Park, Tanganyika, November and December 1956," prepared for the Fauna Preservation Society by W. H. Pearsall. Published by the Fauna Preservation Society.

176 Collett: "Pastoralists and Wildlife: Image and Reality in Kenya Maasailand," in Anderson and Grove's *Conservation in Africa: People, Policies and Practice*. This book contains many other valuable papers about conservation.
Western: Interview.

177 Maasai agreement: A copy of the agreement was shown to me by the Maasai in Ngorongoro. It has been printed in Fosbrooke, *Ngorongoro: The Eighth Wonder*, 199–201.

178 guidebook: *Serengeti National Park*, published by Tanzania National Parks and the African Wildlife Foundation (AWF).
Turner and celebrities: Kay Turner, *Serengeti Home*, 194–200.

179 Owen: Interview.

195 The percentages of protected land are calculated from the figures in the 1990 *United Nations List of National Parks and Protected Areas*, published by IUCN.

196 The account of the objections to the lodges by the board of the Ngorongoro Conservation Area Authority is based on confidential minutes of several meetings, which were provided to the author. I visited the site of Ngorongoro Sopa on two occasions.

197 Stephenson: Interview.
water supply "inadequate": "A Conservation and Development Strategy for the Ngorongoro Conservation Area," Report of the Ad Hoc Ministerial Commission on Ngorongoro, August 10, 1990.

199 "Serengeti National Park Management Plan: 1990–1995," edited by A. R. Kajuni, K. L. I. Campbell and S. A. Huish. Final Draft, June 1990.

FOUR SPACE FOR LARGE SPECIES

207 Sclater: P. L. Sclater, "On the Best Mode of Preserving the Existence of the Larger Mammals of Africa for Future Ages," JSPFE 2 (1905): 46–50.

African Game Trails has been recently reprinted by Peter Capstick, one of a series under the Peter Capstick Library imprint, which includes several notable books written earlier this century by big-game hunters in Africa. Many of these books are classics of the genre and offer early insights into animal behavior, including *The Book of the Lion*, by Sir Alfred Pease; *The Man-Eaters of Tsavo*, Lt. Col. J. H. Patterson; *Big Game Hunting in Central Africa*, William Buckley; *Hunting the Elephant in Africa*, Captain C. H. Stigand. The Capstick series is not widely sold, but I found it in the United States (where it is published by St. Martin's

Press) at Travel Books and Language Center in Bethesda, and in London at Holland and Holland.

208 Churchill's accounts in *Strand* appeared monthly from March through November 1908.

209 Bror von Blixen-Finecke's account of hunting with the Prince of Wales: *African Hunter*, Chapter 13. This is another book in the Peter Capstick series.

210 Princess Elizabeth's visit: from Kenyan newspapers at the time, primarily the *East African Standard*, February 1–6, 1952. I found these papers in the basement of the MacMillan Library in Nairobi, but like the Leakey papers, they are not well preserved and will undoubtedly be lost to historians within too few years. A slim, personal memoir of the visit was written by Jim Corbett, a British military officer and sportsman who had retired in Kenya and was with the Princess hours before she received the news about her father's death. It is called simply *Tree Tops*, the name of the lodge where the Princess stayed.

211 Lipscomb: March 28, 1960. I found this among the Leakey papers at the museum. David Allen: Interview.

212 Dublin: One of the most energetic and intelligent of the Nairobi conservationists; her 1988 report for USAID, "Tourism and Wildlife in Kenya," is comprehensive and essential material for any discussion about conservation policies in Kenya and Africa.

213 Moss: *Elephant Memories*, 54.
Western: "A Review of the Ivory Trade and Policy Options," by David Western and Stephen Cobb, June 1, 1988. Copy in author's files.

215 Kuki Gallmann's book, *I Dreamed of Africa* (Viking, 1991), is a gripping memoir of a tragic life: an auto accident when she was a lively teenager, which nearly crippled her for life; the death of her husband in another collision; the death of her son from a snakebite. The book is also revealing about Ms. Gallmann, and her friends—and, indeed, about white life in Kenya today—in a way not intended: with one or two exceptions, the only Africans one meets in its pages are servants.

216 "pressure for land": "A Policy Framework and Five-Year Investment Programme," Kenya Wildlife Service, June 1990. Throughout this chapter, what Leakey says about sharing revenues, the need to provide benefits to local people, the ecological viability of Amboseli and the Maasai Mara, etc., are from this report, unless otherwise noted.

219 "viewing value" of elephants: Brown, "The Viewing Value of Elephants" (unpublished ms.), August 30, 1989.
Huxley, "would prophesy": *The Observer*, November 27, 1960.
"Severe congestion" and revenues for the Mara and where they go: Douglas-Hamilton, "Identification Study for the Conservation and Sustainable Use of the Natural Resources in the Kenyan Portion of the Mara-Serengeti Ecosystem," Final Report, December 1988.

223 The Royal National Park reports—or at least some of them—are also in the basement of MacMillan Library and also not well cared for.

224 I was with David Western in Amboseli in March 1991.

226 Leakey on culling in Amboseli: Interview, August 1992.
birth control: "Elephantine Contraception," *The Lancet*, September 5, 1992, 583–84; see also "Elephants and Birth Control," Roger Short, *The New Scientist*, August 1, 1992, 21–23.

227 Kadzo: Interview.

FIVE HUNTED AND HUNTERS

239 Churchill's letter to his mother: *Companion Volume II, Part 2, 1907–1911*, edited by Randolph S. Churchill, Boston, 1967, 692–93.

239 "They shoot everything": Correspondence with author.
    Markham, "It is absurd": *West With the Night*, 205.
241 Train's views on hunting: Interview.
    hunting licenses in Zambia: N. Leader-Williams, "Black Rhinos and African Elephants: Lessons for Conservation Funding," *Oryx* 24 (January 1990).
    Jackson: Interview.
    Siberian tiger: "Perestroika for Siberian Tigers," in *Cat News* 12 (January 1990): 18.
    Cat News is published by IUCN's Species Survival Commission and is edited by Peter Jackson.
242 Wilson: "Cheetah in Zimbabwe," *Cat News* 8 (January 1988): 9–10.
243 "probably reopen": "Farewell to Africa," *Audubon*, September 1990, 75.
    Leakey request that elephant not be declared endangered under U.S. law: Nairobi cable number 15500, May 22, 1989.
244 "hide from tourist vehicles": Wesley R. Henry, "Tourist Impact on Amboseli National Park," African Wildlife Leadership Foundation *News* 12 (Fall 1977): 4–8. Far too little research has been done about the impact of tourism on wildlife. Henry's research eventually led to a doctoral thesis, "Relationships Between Visitor Use and Tourist Capacity for Kenya's Amboseli National Park," submitted to the Department of Recreation Resources, Colorado State University, Summer 1980.
    "Harassment": Norman Myers, "National Parks in Savannah Africa," *Science* 178 (December 22, 1972): 1255–63.
247 Schindler's views: letter of April 19, 1990. Copy in author's files, as is Hurt's response of April 24.
248 Weyerhaeuser: letter to Hurt, with copies to several people, January 17, 1991. Copy in author's files.

SIX HOPE

260 tsetse: See MacKenzie, *The Empire of Nature*, Chapter 9.
266 "The Cook Report" aired on July 30, 1990. Most of the newspaper articles appeared on July 30 and 31.
267 $350,000: Interview.
    Newsweek: September 24, 1990, p. 54. The article appeared in the magazine's International edition.
269 Van Note and Stevens meeting with Baker: Memorandum of Conservation. Subject: SENV: Conservation of Whales and Elephants. April 28, 1989.
    deal between conservation organizations and hunting organizations and AWF's intervention after CITES: Author's interviews with McMeekin.
270 Fields to Bush and Lujan: March 20, 1989, June 7, 1989, and November 16, 1989. Copies in author's files.
    "elitist white hunters": Interview.

EPILOGUE

282 The EIA report was prepared by two Americans, Kathi Austin and Steve Galster. I had met them briefly before they took up the ivory trade issue. When Austin came to Africa to pursue her objectives, she told people she was working for me. She was not; nor was Galster.

SELECTED
BIBLIOGRAPHY

Adams, Jonathan S., and Thomas O. McShane. *The Myth of Wild Africa: Conservation Without Illusion*. New York and London: W. W. Norton, 1992.

Anderson, David, and Richard Grove, eds. *Conservation in Africa: People, Policies and Practice*. London and New York: Cambridge University Press, 1987.

Barbier, Edward B., Joanne C. Burgess, Timothy Swanson and David W. Pearce. *Elephants, Economics and Ivory*. London: Earthscan Publications, 1990.

Beard, Peter. *The End of the Game*. New York: Viking Press, 1965.

Bechky, Allen. *Adventuring in East Africa*. San Francisco: Sierra Club Books, 1990.

Bennet, E. *Shots and Snapshots in British East Africa*. London and New York: Longmans, Green and Co., 1914.

Bentsen, Cheryl. *Maasai Days*. New York: Summit Books, 1989.

Bull, Bartle. *Safari: A Chronicle of Adventure*. New York: Viking, 1988.

Churchill, Winston S. *My African Journey*. London: Hodder & Stoughton, 1908. Reprint. New York: Mandarin Paperbacks, 1990.

Corbett, Jim. *Tree Tops*. London and New York: Oxford University Press, 1955.

Dinesen, Isak. *Letters from Africa 1914–1931*. Chicago: University of Chicago Press, 1981.

Douglas-Hamilton, Iain, and Oria Douglas-Hamilton. *Among the Elephants*. New York: Viking Press, 1975.

———. *Battle for the Elephants*. London and New York: Penguin, 1992.

Dugmore, A. Radclyffe. *Camera Adventures in the African Wilds*. London: William Heinemann, 1910.

Fitter, Richard, and Sir Peter Scott. *The Penitent Butchers*. London: Fauna Preservation Society, 1978.

Fosbrooke, Henry. *Ngorongoro: The Eighth Wonder*. London: André Deutsch, 1972.

Gallmann, Kuki. *I Dreamed of Africa*. London and New York: Viking, 1991.

Graham, Alistair. *The Gardeners of Eden*. London: George Allen & Unwin, 1973.

Grzimek, Bernhard. *No Room for Wild Animals*. London: Thames and Hudson, 1956.

Grzimek, Bernhard, and Michael Grzimek. *Serengeti Shall Not Die*. Reprint. London: Collins, 1978.

Hall-Martin, Anthony, Clive Walker and Jdu P. Bothma. *Kaokoveld: The Last Wilderness*. Johannesburg: Southern Book Publishers, 1988.

Hayes, Harold T. P. *The Last Place on Earth*. New York: Stein and Day, 1977.

Hemingway, Ernest. *Green Hills of Africa*. London: Jonathan Cape, 1936.

IUCN. *1990 United Nations List of National Parks and Protected Areas*. Gland, Switzerland, and Cambridge, U.K.: IUCN, 1990.

Jacobsohn, Margaret, with photographs by Peter and Beverly Pickford. *Himba: Nomads of Namibia*. London: New Holland, 1990.

Kinloch, Bruce. *The Shamba Raiders. Memories of a Game Warden*. London: Collins and Harvill Press, 1972.

Leys, Norman. *Kenya*, 2d ed. London: Hogarth Press, 1925.

Lyell, Denis D. *The African Elephant and Its Hunters*. London: Heath Cranton, 1924.

Lyster, Simon. *International Wildlife Law*. Cambridge: Grotius Publications, 1985.

MacKenzie, John M. *The Empire of Nature: Hunting, Conservation and British Imperialism*. Manchester and New York: Manchester University Press, 1988.

Markham, Beryl. *West With the Night*. San Francisco: North Point Press, 1983.

Matthiessen, Peter. *The Tree Where Man Was Born*. New York: Dutton, 1983.

Moorehead, Alan. *No Room in the Ark*. (First published in Great Britain in 1959; there have been several reprints.)

Moss, Cynthia. *Portraits in the Wild: Animal Behavior in East Africa*. Chicago: University of Chicago Press, 1975; 2d ed., 1982.

————. *Elephant Memories: Thirteen Years in the Life of an Elephant Family*. London: Elm Tree Books; New York: William Morrow & Co., 1988.

Myers, Norman. *The Sinking Ark*. Oxford and New York: Pergamon Press, 1979.

————. *A Wealth of Wild Species*. Boulder, Colo.: Westview Press, 1983.

Neumann, Arthur H. *Elephant Hunting in East Equatorial Africa*. London: Rowland Ward, 1898.

Nicholson, Max. *The Environmental Revolution*. New York: McGraw-Hill, 1970.

————. *The New Environmental Age*. Cambridge: Cambridge University Press, 1987.

Oelschlaeger, Max. *The Idea of Wilderness*. New Haven and London: Yale University Press, 1991.

Olivier, Willie, and Sandra Olivier. *Visitor's Guide to Namibia*. Johannesburg: Southern Book Publishers, 1989.

Pakenham, Thomas. *The Scramble for Africa*. London: Weidenfeld and Nicolson; New York: Random House, 1991.

Parker, Ian, and Mohamed Amin. *Ivory Crisis*. London: Chatto & Windus, 1983.

Pearce, Fred. *Green Warriors: The People and the Politics Behind the Environmental Revolution*. London: The Bodley Head, 1991.

Percival, A. Blayney. *A Game Ranger's Note Book*. London: Nisbet & Co., 1924.

Pickering, R. *Ngorongoro's Geological History*. Nairobi, Kampala, and Dar es Salaam: East African Literature Bureau, 1968.

Reardon, Mitch. *The Besieged Desert: War, Drought, Poaching in the Namib Desert*. London: William Collins Sons and Co., 1986.

Rensberger, Boyce. *The Cult of the Wild*. Garden City, N.Y.: Anchor Press/Doubleday, 1977.

Roosevelt, Theodore. *African Game Trails*. New York: Scribner, 1910. Reprint. New York: St. Martin's Press, Peter Capstick Library ed., 1988.

Rosenblum, Mort, and Doug Williamson. *Squandering Eden: Africa at the Edge*. New York: Harcourt Brace Jovanovich, 1987.

Saitoti, Tepilit Ole. *The Worlds of a Maasai Warrior: An Autobiography*. New York: Random House, 1986.

————, with photographs by Carol Beckwith. *Maasai*. New York: Henry Abrams, 1980.

Sankan, S. S. *The Maasai*. Nairobi, Dar es Salaam, Kampala: East African Literature Bureau, 1971.

Sheriff, Abdul. *Slaves, Spices & Ivory in Zanzibar*. London: James Curry; Athens, Ohio: Ohio University Press, 1987.

Simon, Noel. *Between the Sunlight and the Thunder: The Wild Life of Kenya*. London: Collins, 1962.

Singer, Peter. *Animal Liberation*. New York: New York Review, 1975; 2d ed. 1990.

Southworth, Alvan S. *Four Thousand Miles of African Travel*. New York: Baker, Pratt & Co. London: Sampson, Low & Co., 1875.

Stanley, Henry M. *Through the Dark Continent*. Vol. 2. New York: Harper & Brothers, 1879.

————. *In Darkest Africa*. Vol 1. London: Sampson Low, Marston, Searle and Rivington, 1890.

Stevenson-Hamilton, Major J. *Animal Life in Africa*. London: William Heinemann, 1912.

Stigand, Captain C. H. *Hunting the Elephant in Africa*. New York: Macmillan, 1913. Reprint. New York: St. Martin's Press, Peter Capstick Library ed., 1986.

Stone, Roger D. *The Nature of Development*. New York: Alfred A. Knopf, 1992.

Teede, Jan, and Fiona Teede. *The Zambezi, River of the Gods*. London: André Deutsch, 1990.

Thomson, Joseph. *Through Masai Land: A Journey of Exploration Among the Snowclad Volcanic Mountains and Strange Tribes*. London: Sampson, Low & Co., 1885.

Thornton, Allan, and Dave Curry. *To Save an Elephant: The Undercover Investigation into the Illegal Ivory Trade*. London: Doubleday, 1991.

Tober, James A. *Who Owns the Wildlife? The Political Economy of Conservation in Nineteenth Century America*. Westport, Conn., and London: Greenwood Press, 1981.

Turner, Kay. *Serengeti Home*. New York: Dial Press/James Wade, 1977. Reprint. Nairobi: Kay Turner, 1985.

Turner, Myles. *My Serengeti Years*. London: Elm Tree Books/Hamish Hamilton, 1987.

Von Blixen-Finecke, Baron Bror. *African Hunter*. New York: St. Martin's Press, 1986.

Watkins, T. H. *Righteous Pilgrim: The Life and Times of Harold L. Ickes, 1874–1952*. New York: Henry Holt, 1990.

Wijnstekers, Willem. *The Evolution of CITES*. Lausanne, Switzerland: CITES Secretariat, 1988.

Williams, J. G. *A Field Guide to the National Parks of East Africa*. 1967. London: Collins, New ed., 1981.

Willock, Colin. *Wildfight: A History of Conservation*. London: Jonathan Cape, 1991.

INDEX